GCSE 9-1 geography AQA

Exam Practice

Grades 7-9

SECOND EDITION

SERIES EDITORS
Bob Digby
Simon Ross **Nicholas Rowles**

OXFORD
UNIVERSITY PRESS

Great Clarendon Street, Oxford, OX2 6DP, United Kingdom

Oxford University Press is a department of the University of Oxford. It furthers the University's objective of excellence in research, scholarship, and education by publishing worldwide. Oxford is a registered trade mark of Oxford University Press in the UK and in certain other countries

© Oxford University Press 2023

Series Editors: Bob Digby, Simon Ross

Author: Nicholas Rowles

The moral rights of the authors have been asserted

First published in 2020

Second edition 2023

All rights reserved. No part of this publication may be reproduced, stored in a retrieval system, or transmitted, in any form or by any means, without the prior permission in writing of Oxford University Press, or as expressly permitted by law, by licence or under terms agreed with the appropriate reprographics rights organization. Enquiries concerning reproduction outside the scope of the above should be sent to the Rights Department, Oxford University Press, at the address above.

You must not circulate this work in any other form and you must impose this same condition on any acquirer

British Library Cataloguing in Publication Data
Data available

978-138-202907-0

978-138-202908-7 (ebook)

10 9 8 7 6 5 4 3 2 1

Paper used in the production of this book is a natural, recyclable product made from wood grown in sustainable forests.

The manufacturing process conforms to the environmental regulations of the country of origin.

Printed in India by Manipal Technologies Limited

Acknowledgements

The publisher and authors would like to thank the following for permission to use photographs and other copyright material:

Cover: watchara/Shutterstock; Billion Photos/Shutterstock.
Photos: p9: Washington Imaging / Alamy Stock Photo; **p11:** Jason Knott / Alamy Stock Photo; **p14 (l):** Jemastock/Shutterstock; **p14 (m):** Quarta/Shutterstock; **p14 (r):** Man As Thep/Shutterstock; **p15:** Geoffrey Robinson / Alamy Stock Photo; **p16:** BlueRingMedia/Shutterstock; **p17:** ZUMA Press, Inc. / Alamy Stock Photo; **p18:** Designervn/Shutterstock; **p19:** Blaine Harrington III / Alamy Stock Photo; **p27:** Kevin Foy / Alamy Stock Photo; **p40:** robertharding / Alamy Stock Photo; **p42:** RomeoFox / Alamy Stock Photo; **p43:** omnitsky/Shutterstock; **p44:** RomeoFox / Alamy Stock Photo; **p47:** domnitsky/Shutterstock; **p55:** Stuart Kelly / Alamy Stock Photo; **p56:** cgwp.co.uk / Alamy Stock Photo; **p57:** domnitsky/Shutterstock; **p58:** cgwp.co.uk / Alamy Stock Photo; **p60:** cgwp.co.uk / Alamy Stock Photo; **p61:** Minden Pictures / Alamy Stock Photo; **p62:** domnitsky/Shutterstock; **p64:** Minden Pictures / Alamy Stock Photo; **p71:** Adrian B. / Alamy Stock Photo; **p72:** © Ordnance Survey; **p76:** domnitsky/Shutterstock; **p81:** domnitsky/Shutterstock; **p94:** Anya Douglas/Shutterstock; **p100:** Kevin Eaves/Shutterstock; **p105 (b):** NOAA / Alamy Stock Photo; **p105 (t):** Anya Douglas/Shutterstock; **p108:** Kekyalyaynen/Shutterstock; **p118:** Nick Rowles; **p120 (t,l):** Valerijs Novickis/Shutterstock; **p120 (t,r):** Dirk Ercken/Shutterstock; **p120 (b,l):** buddhawut/Shutterstock; **p120 (b,r):** seubsai/Shutterstock; **p124:** Dorset Media Service / Alamy Stock Photo; **p127:** wonganan/Getty Images; **p130:** Dave Ellison / Alamy Stock Photo; **p139(l):** rvimages/Getty Images; **p139 (r):** alexsl/Getty Images; **p157:** robertharding / Alamy Stock Photo; **p158:** Jo-Anne Albertsen / Alamy Stock Photo; **p164:** agefotostock / Alamy Stock Photo; **p165 (a):** sydeen/Shutterstock; **p165 (b):** SUWIT NGAOKAEW/Shutterstock; **p165 (c):** adirekjob/Shutterstock; **p165 (d):** Peter Dazeley/Getty Images.

Artwork by Barking Dog Art, Kamae, Q2A Media, Aptara Inc, Mike Phillips and Oxford University Press.

Every effort has been made to contact copyright holders of material reproduced in this book. Any omissions will be rectified in subsequent printings if notice is given to the publisher.

Links to third party websites are provided by Oxford in good faith and for information only. Oxford disclaims any responsibility for the materials contained in any third party website referenced in this work.

The publisher would like to thank Katy Patchwood for reviewing this book and providing thoughtful and constructive feedback.

Contents

Introduction	4
Top tips for exam success	6
Extending your understanding	14
Social, economic and environmental factors	14
Geographical scale	16
Sustainability and sustainable development	18
Development	20
Synopticity	22
Master the topic	24
1 The challenge of natural hazards	24
2 The living world	27
3 Physical landscapes in the UK	28
4 Urban issues and challenges	30
5 The changing economic world	32
6 The challenge of resource management	34
Max your marks	36
Mopping up the 1–3-mark questions	36
Multiple choice, Other short answer questions	
Excelling at 4-mark questions	42
'Suggest', 'Explain'	
Stepping up to 6-mark questions	56
'Explain', 'Suggest', 'Discuss'	
Hitting the heights on 9-mark questions	74
'Evaluate', 'Do you agree?', 'Assess'	
Focus on Paper 3: Geographical applications	92
Section A: Issue evaluation	92
Section B: Fieldwork	99
Issue evaluation resources booklet	103
Specification checklist	109
Skills and case studies checklists	111
Exam practice papers	113
Paper 1 Living with the physical environment	113
Paper 2 Challenges in the human environment	132
Paper 3 Geographical applications	150
Resources booklet	161
Answer guidance	167

Guided answers and mark schemes for the exam practice papers are available on the Oxford Secondary Geography website: **www.oxfordsecondary.com/geog-aqa-answers**

Please note: the exam-style questions and mark schemes have not been written or approved by AQA. The answer guidance and commentaries provided represent one interpretation only and other solutions may be appropriate.

Introduction

About this book

What are the aims of *Exam Practice: Grades 7–9*?

GCSE 9-1 Geography AQA Exam Practice: Grades 7–9 is a practical workbook for you to complete. It is full of useful advice and practice that will help you to achieve or better your target grade.

The book can be used to support your learning at any point in your course, including when revising for exams. There are plenty of activities and exam-style questions to help you practise and develop the skills needed for exam success.

How is the book organised?

There are five main sections:

1 Top tips for exam success (pages 6–13)

This focuses on key aspects of exam technique to help you gain the top grades, such as interpreting command words, maximising resources such as photos and graphs and understanding the system of marking.

2 Extending your understanding (pages 14–23)
Master the topic (pages 24–35)

The specification includes some tricky high-level concepts, such as development, sustainability and scale, as well as key topics such as ecosystems, natural hazards and resource management. Mastering these topics and concepts helps to improve the academic quality of your answers in order to attain the highest grades.

3 Max your marks (pages 36–91)

This section shows you how to maximise your marks for each type of question, including multiple-choice, short-answer and extended-writing questions. Here you will have many opportunities to attempt practice questions and also see how an examiner will mark your answer.

4 Focus on Paper 3: Geographical applications (pages 92–108)

This section focuses on the two parts of Paper 3 – issue evaluation (Section A) and fieldwork (Section B). It includes a resources booklet for you to practise with.

5 Exam practice papers (pages 113–166)

This final section contains a complete set of exam papers for you to practise all that you have learned.

In these sections, quick **Activities** test your knowledge, while **Worked examples** break down how to approach exam questions. You can apply what you've learned to answer exam-style questions in **Now try this!**

Answer guidance for all the Activities and 'Now try this!' questions can be found in the back of this book. **Mark schemes** for the exam papers can be found at **www.oxfordsecondary.com/geog-aqa-answers**.

How to be successful in your exams

It's not what you know...

... but what you do with it! Your success depends on your ability to adapt your extensive geographical knowledge to the demands of the exam questions. You will need to:

- identify what the question is asking you to do
- answer it precisely and concisely
- demonstrate your geographical knowledge (including your examples and case studies)
- interpret resources, such as photos and graphs, that you have never seen before.

Some student traits... do you recognise yourself?

To improve, you first have to recognise your weaknesses. For example, **admitting to yourself** that you have a fear of flying is the first step towards solving the problem and getting on a plane.

Introduction

Activity 1

(a) Take a look at the cartoon and descriptions below.
- Be honest, and highlight any characteristics that you recognise in yourself.
- Can you think of **two** more characteristics that apply to you? Complete the blank boxes.
- In the Action Plan below, identify **three** key aspects to address to maximise your full potential.

I am a bit lazy and don't revise enough.

I often run out of time and have to leave some questions unanswered.

I tend to rush and make silly mistakes.

I tend to write too much and my teacher says I waffle!

I am not very precise when using resources such as photos and graphs.

There are some Geography topics or geographical terms that I don't fully understand.

I have difficulty interpreting some questions.

My answers sometimes lack depth and detail.

Action Plan

To maximise my potential, I need to focus on making the following three improvements:

- _____
- _____
- _____

Organisation is the key to success

Students who do well in exams are usually well organised. They know the specification inside out, they have correctly sequenced and detailed notes, and they know the requirements of each exam.

Here's what you can do:

- Make sure your notes are clearly structured to reflect the exam papers and topics. ☐
- Consider highlighting key geographical terms in your notes and revising their definitions. Good use of geographical vocabulary will help boost your mark and contribute towards SPaG (Spelling, Punctuation and Grammar) marks. ☐
- Make sure you know where the examples, case studies and geographical skills are within your notes. ☐
- Plan your revision well in advance, working backwards from the date of your exams. ☐
- Complete the specification and skills confidence checklists on pages 109–112 of this book as you go. ☐

Introduction 5

Top tips for exam success

1. Understand the specification and assessment objectives

Look at the specification outline below. There are three exam papers with roughly the same number of marks available for each. Organise your notes carefully to reflect the structure and content of the specification. (A more detailed version of the specification is available on pages 109–110 and on the AQA website.)

Paper 1	Paper 2	Paper 3
Living with the physical environment: 88 marks (35%), 1 hr 30 min	Challenges in the human environment: 88 marks (35%), 1 hr 30 min	Geographical applications: 76 marks (30%), 1 hr 15 min
Date:	Date:	Date:
Challenge of natural hazards: tectonic hazards, tropical storms, extreme weather in the UK, climate change	**Urban challenges:** global patterns, two contrasting cities, sustainable urban futures	**Issue evaluation:** critical thinking and problem solving based on pre-release resources booklet, including a decision-making exercise
The living world: local ecosystems, tropical rainforests, **one** from *hot deserts, cold environments*	**The changing economic world:** global patterns, closing the development gap, contrasting studies of economic development (*UK and one city in LIC/NEE*)	**Fieldwork:** general questions based on enquiry process together with questions on the two (physical and human) individual student investigations
Physical landscapes in the UK: two from *coastal, river, glacial landscapes*	**Challenge of resource management:** global resource security, resources in the UK, **one** from *food, water, energy*	

Activity 2

(a) In this table, write the date and time that you will be sitting each exam.

(b) Use a highlighter to identify the optional topics that you are taking.

Assessment objectives

There are four assessment objectives for GCSE Geography. When writing the exam papers, examiners must set questions that meet these assessment objectives. Note that **AO2 (understanding)** and **AO3 (application)** are worth far more marks than **AO1 (knowledge)**. Also note that a high proportion of marks are available for **geographical skills (AO4)**.

Assessment objective (AO)	Component weightings (approx. %)			Overall weighting (approx. %)
	Paper 1	Paper 2	Paper 3	
AO1 Demonstrate knowledge of locations, places, processes	7.5	7.5		15
AO2 Demonstrate geographical understanding of concepts, interrelationships (explain)		11	3	25
AO3 Apply knowledge and understanding (interpret, analyse, evaluate)	8.5	8.5		35
AO4 Geographical skills	8	8	9	
Overall weighting of components	35	35	30	100

Activity 3

(a) Complete the missing boxes in this table.

(b) How are the AOs different for Paper 3 compared with Papers 1 and 2?

_____

_____

_____

_____

Top tips for exam success

2. Understand command words

A 'command' is an order to do something. In an exam question, the 'command word' directs your focus when answering a question (e.g. it tells you whether to 'describe' or 'explain' something). You need to understand the command words and make sure you stick to them rigidly; failure to do so will probably restrict your marks.

Command word	Typical marks	Meaning	Student advice
Identify/state/give	1	Name, find or give a simple word or statement. E.g. 'Identify the glacial landform at grid reference 653532.'	Usually a simple and direct question requiring a precise and accurate answer.
Calculate	1 or 2	Work out the value of something. E.g. 'Using Figure 7, calculate the increase in the retail sales value of Fairtrade bananas between 2000 and 2012.'	Be precise. Double-check your calculation. Give the correct units, e.g. kilometres or metres.
Complete	1 or 2	Finish the task by adding information. E.g. 'Complete the following sentences.'	Should be simple – just double-check you have understood the question.
Compare	2, 3 or 4	Identify similarities and differences. E.g. 'Using Figure 4, compare HDI values in Africa and South America.'	Look for both similarities and differences. Use words like 'whereas' or 'as opposed to' when talking about differences.
Outline	2 or 4	Set out main characteristics and give an overview. E.g. 'Outline one way that Fairtrade helps to deal with the problems of unequal development.'	A relatively brief overview of the key points or characteristics.
Describe	2 or 4	Set out more detailed characteristics. E.g. 'Using Figure 9, describe the distribution of areas with existing licences for fracking in the UK.'	Write what you can see. This might include shape, size, movement. With data, include highest and lowest values, rate of increase or decrease.
Explain	2, 4, 6 or 9	Give reasons why something happens. E.g. 'Using Figure 12 and your own knowledge, explain how different landforms may be created by the transport and deposition of sediment along the coast.'	Give reasons why something has formed or occurred. This requires you to show your understanding. Use the word 'because'.
Suggest	2, 4, 6 or 9	Give a possible reason. E.g. 'Suggest how the sea defences shown in Figure 11 help to protect the coastline.'	Put forward an idea/outcome/judgement/point of view. Usually requires evidence in support.
To what extent	6 or 9	Judge the importance or success of a strategy/scheme/project. E.g. 'To what extent do urban areas in lower income countries (LICs) or newly emerging economies (NEEs) provide social and economic opportunities for people?'	Imagine a line that extends from 0–100%, or yes–no or good–bad. Where is your opinion on that imaginary line and why? Words like 'mostly' or 'strongly' might work well.
Assess (may be 'Assess the extent to which…')	6 or 9	Make an informed judgement by weighing up most/least important factors. E.g. 'Assess how effective your presentation technique(s) were in representing the data collected in this enquiry.'	Use evidence to judge the level of success or importance, for example. Use words like 'very', 'not very', 'extremely well', 'poorly', etc.
Evaluate	9	Judge from available evidence, often giving both sides of an argument or referring to +/– points. E.g. 'Evaluate the effectiveness of an urban transport scheme(s) you have studied.'	Use evidence to weigh up and make judgements. Often to do with levels of success or effectiveness. Make comparisons and use words like 'whereas' or 'on the other hand'.
Discuss	6 or 9	Present key points about different ideas or strengths and weaknesses of an idea. E.g. 'Discuss the effects of urban sprawl on people and the environment.'	Give both sides of an argument – pros and cons, advantages and disadvantages. Try to be balanced. Words like 'whereas' are good.
Justify	9	Support a case or decision using evidence. E.g. 'Transnational corporations (TNCs) only bring advantages to the host country. Do you agree with this statement? Justify your decision.'	Back-up your views or a decision. Refer to evidence to support your answer.

Top tips for exam success

3. Understand the question types

The exam papers are made up of several different types of question. This is to enable the examiners to satisfy the assessment objectives (AOs) and to cover as much of the specification as possible. (The 'Max your marks' chapter has extensive advice on how to maximise your marks from different types of question.)

Question type	Common command words	Example	Student advice
Multiple choice (1 mark): involves making a choice of one from four options.	State, what, calculate	Calculate the area of the reservoir on the OS map extract. Is it…? (1 mark)	Multiple choice does not necessarily mean 'easy', so take time making your decision. Use a process of elimination to identify the correct answer.
Short-answer questions (1–3 marks): may involve factual recall or using a resource.	State, give, calculate (and show your working), outline, describe, suggest	Outline the role of decomposers in an ecosystem. (2 marks)	Try to answer precisely and concisely. Use correct geographical terminology. Refer to facts and figures (including measurement units).
Resource-focused questions (4/6 marks): often require detailed use of a resource together with your own understanding.	Describe, suggest, explain	Using Figure X and your own understanding, explain the effects of deindustrialisation on the UK's economy. (6 marks)	These questions often have multiple strands. In the example, you need to refer to Figure X, demonstrate your own understanding (refer to an example or outline a process), and make clear links between deindustrialisation and the UK's economy.
Extended-writing questions (6/9 marks): usually require engaging in a discussion or evaluation.	Assess, to what extent, discuss, justify	Using a case study of an LIC/NEE, evaluate the role of transnational corporations (TNCs) in promoting industrial development. (9 marks)	Again, this is likely to be a question with multiple strands, so make sure that you address all parts of the question. You should try to engage in a discussion considering both sides of an argument. Write a conclusion.

Deconstructing questions

Before starting to write an answer, you should take time to **deconstruct** the question. This will help you to focus and apply your knowledge and understanding to the precise requirements of the question.

To deconstruct a question, consider using '**BUG**':

- **B**ox the command word.
- **U**nderline words to pick out the geography content and focus, any evidence required (e.g. linked to a resource or case study), and any links or connections required. Consider using colours, circling key words, or linking the connections required.
- **G**lance back to the question to make sure you include everything in your answer.

The 'Max your marks' chapter in this book has many **BUG** examples and activities.

> **Worked example**
>
> 'Use an example to explain how urban regeneration can help to solve urban problems.'
>
> [4 marks]

Top tips for exam success

4. Understand the marking

There are two types of marking: '**point marking**' and '**levels marking**'. It is important that you recognise this and write your answer accordingly.

	Point marking	**Levels marking**
Marks	1–3-mark questions	4-, 6- and 9-mark questions
Advice	Examiners are looking for precise, accurate points. For 2/3 mark questions, try to develop your answer to achieve maximum marks.	Examiners decide if answers belong to Level 1, 2 or 3: • **Level 1:** basic answer; limited application/knowledge or use of stimulus material • **Level 2:** clear understanding/application; good use of stimulus material; accurate use of locational information • **Level 3:** thorough/detailed knowledge, understanding and application; coherent argument; extensive use of examples/case studies

Activity 4

Read the exam question and sample answer below.

Figure 1

> Study **Figure 1**, a photo of High Force waterfall in County Durham. Using **Figure 1** and your own understanding, explain the processes involved in the formation of river erosion landforms. **[6 marks]**

Firstly, waterfalls are formed by the falling water, which will erode the river bed and start to make a plunge pool. Rocks and other debris will be thrown around by the water and further erode out the plunge pool with the process of abrasion. The plunge pool will continue to grow and will form an undercut below the cliff that the water is falling from. Eventually, the cliff will be undercut so much that it will help to further the erosion of the plunge pool and the process will repeat.

Now complete the grid below.

Does the student...	Tick/cross and explanation
Make use of and refer to the photo?	
Refer to their 'own understanding'?	✗ Limited evidence of understanding of processes. No reference made to geography knowledge beyond the photo.
Write about more than one process?	✔ Direct reference made to abrasion; also to 'undercutting' though this is not really a specific process. There is reference to erosion.
Write about more than one landform?	
Make links between processes and landforms?	✔ The student does show a clear understanding but it could be more detailed.
Show an understanding of the sequence of landform formation?	

> **Tip**
> It is very important to address **all** aspects of the question, particularly when you are required to use a figure, example or a case study. Consider using the sentence starter 'Figure 6 shows...'.

Top tips for exam success

5. Make full use of the resources

Many exam questions will expect you to make use of a geographical resource, such as a photo, map, graph, table of data or extract of text. These questions usually begin 'Using Figure…'. When answering these questions you **must** refer to the resource, quoting precise and accurate information to support your answer. Failure to refer to the resource will prevent you reaching the top level.

Interpreting maps

There are several different types of map, including Ordnance Survey (OS) maps, maps showing global patterns (e.g. urbanisation) and maps showing locational details (e.g. the location of a science park). Among other special types of map, there are dot maps, choropleth maps and isoline maps.

> **Worked example**
>
> Study **Figure 2**, a map of the global distribution of volcanoes. Using **Figure 2** and your own understanding, describe the global distribution of volcanoes.
>
> [4 marks]
>
> **Figure 2**
>
> Key
> ▲ Volcano
> ▮ Volcano belts
>
> Figure 2 shows that volcanoes are widely distributed across the world. The map shows that most volcanoes form linear concentrations, for example around the edge of the Pacific Ocean (the so-called 'Ring of Fire'). Here, there is a line of volcanoes stretching through Japan, the Philippines and along the west coast of North and South America. Elsewhere, there are concentrations of volcanoes in East Africa, central Europe and in Iceland. While most volcanoes occur in these linear belts, there are some anomalies with isolated volcanoes in parts of Asia and Africa.
>
> The examiner made the following comments in awarding the candidate Level 2, 4 marks:
>
> - Good use of the map ('Figure 2 shows…').
> - Detailed description with frequent references to specific locations.
> - Clear understanding of 'distribution', observing patterns (e.g. linear concentrations) and anomalies.
> - No explanation is offered; for example, there is no reference to plate tectonics, which is not required by the command word 'describe' and would be a waste of time.
> - The answer is well written.

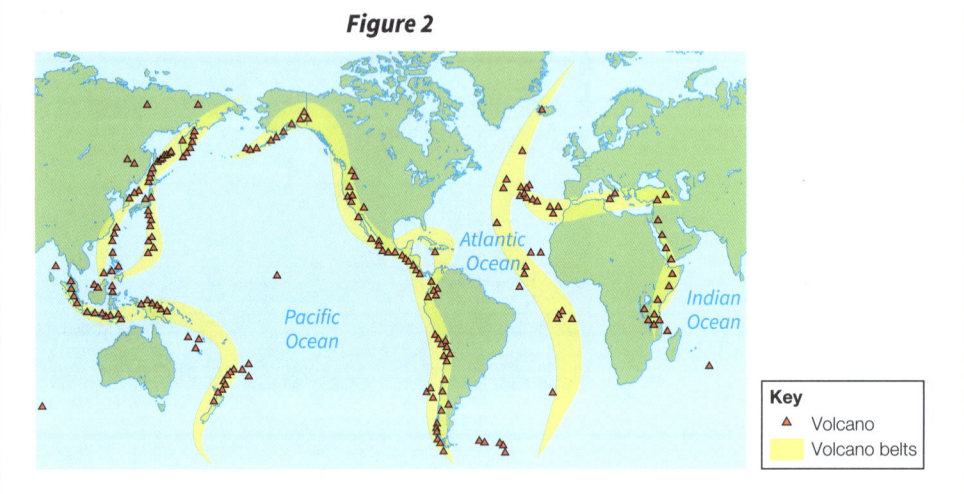

Tip Make full use of information in the key (the key is the key to success!). The examiner has deliberately selected information to appear in the key and it will be relevant to the question asked. Most maps should have a scale and a north arrow; try to use them when answering a question.

Tip When describing patterns on a map or a graph, consider using '**GCSE**':
- **GC** – **g**eneral **c**omment (describe the overall pattern)
- **S** – **s**pecific (refer to names of places, locations or data)
- **E** – **e**xceptions (are there any anomalies to the general trend?)

Activity 5

Annotate the answer of this worked example (using circles, highlighting or underlining) to pick out evidence to support the examiner's feedback.

Tip There is a subtle difference between '**distribution**' and '**pattern**'. Distribution refers to 'where things are'. Pattern implies a degree of regularity or repetition, for example a radial or linear pattern.

Top tips for exam success

Interpreting graphs

There are many different types of graph – bar graphs, scattergraphs, pie charts, line graphs. You may be asked to complete a graph by plotting a value and shading an area. Every year, many students throw away easy marks by failing to complete graphs.

Activity 6

Look at the exam question below.

> Study **Figure 3**, a graph of tourist arrivals in Nepal in 2019. Using **Figure 3**, describe the pattern of tourism in Nepal. **[4 marks]**

Use the following steps to annotate **Figure 3** to help you plan an answer.

(a) Draw circles around the two peaks (March and October) and the trough (July).

(b) Use a ruler to draw vertical and horizontal lines to enable you to read accurate values for the two peaks and the trough. (The peak in March has already been done for you.)

(c) Locate the anomaly where, having risen from July, there is a slight dip in September.

Tip Rather than simply quoting values from the graph, try to **manipulate** the data to enable you to make comparisons in terms of percentages or fractions. For example, 'almost twice as many tourists visited Nepal in October compared to July.'

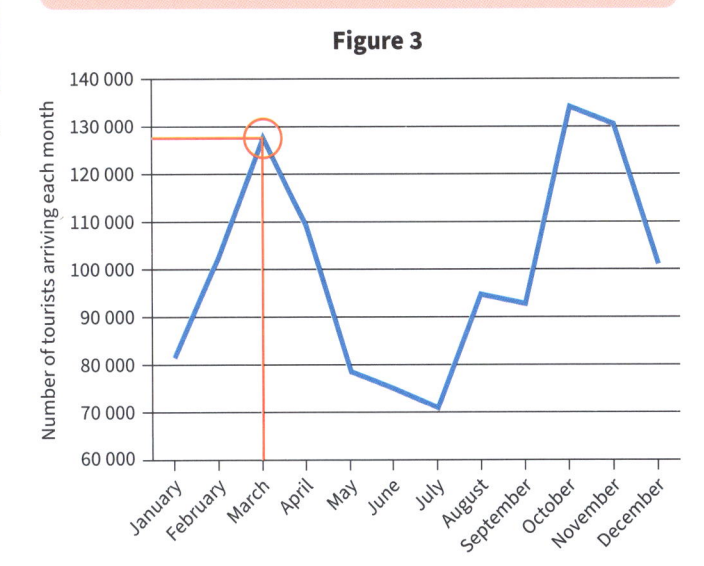

Figure 3

Interpreting photos

Photos are widely used in all three Geography exam papers. Examiners often report that they are poorly used by students. When examining a photo you need to:

- examine the photo, making detailed observations. Use locational language such as 'foreground', 'background', 'in the top right', 'behind', etc.
- infer processes and potential actions from what you can see, for example, economic and social consequences of traffic congestion in a city or the impacts of flooding on an environment.

Tip Consider annotating or drawing circles directly onto a photo to identify the main features and suggest appropriate inferences.

Activity 7

Study **Figure 4**, a photo showing urban greening in Singapore.

(a) Use arrows or circles to add the following labels to **Figure 4**:
- Crops grown on a rooftop
- Trees planted on pavements and open spaces

Figure 4

(b) Describe the urban greening in **Figure 4**.

_____

_____

Top tips for exam success **11**

Top tips for exam success

6. Learn and use your examples and case studies

What are 'examples', 'case studies' and 'exemplars'?

- **Examples**: in-depth studies used to support themes in the specification. For example, in Paper 1 you are required to study an **example** of a tectonic hazard and a tropical storm. In Paper 2, you are required to study an **example** of an urban regeneration project and tourism in an LIC/NEE. These are places that an examiner can reasonably ask you to include in an answer.

- **Case studies**: these provide a more extensive real-world focus, involving the study over several weeks of a number of themes, for example within a city such as Rio de Janeiro or a country such as Nigeria. An examiner can expect you to know about particular projects in that city, such as housing or water projects, and the names of districts.

- **Exemplars**: these are brief references used to support a statement. For example, 'such as the M25' or 'e.g. Mount Etna'. You should try to use exemplars whenever you can.

It is really important to learn and refer to your examples and case studies when asked to do so in the exams. This level of supportive detail will affect the level you achieve. A revision checklist for you to complete and refer to is provided on page 112.

> **Tip**
> Try to learn four to six specific facts or figures for each topic example/case study. However, remember too that marks for 'knowledge' (AO1) are limited, so simply regurgitating a string of facts and figures will probably only achieve a Level 1 mark. It is the 'application' (AO3) of your knowledge (i.e. using the facts and figures to support an argument or discussion) that will take you to Levels 2 and 3. Examples and case studies are most likely to be required in 6- or 9-mark questions.

7. Write to the space and time available

Space

- Exam papers are structured to provide you with **2 lines per mark**. So, for a 2-mark question, you will have 4 lines to write your answer, and for a 6-mark question, you will have 12 lines.

- You will be given extra lines for 4-, 6- and 9-mark questions. Beyond this, you can use supplementary sheets provided in the exam room.

- Try to stick to the lines available. Be precise and concise in your answers to avoid the need to use extra space.

Time

You have roughly **1 minute per mark**. Monitor your timing very carefully to avoid running out of time and losing precious marks.

Activity 8

Look at the answer to the following exam question. It is too long and the student has wasted time waffling.

Highlight or underline parts of the answer that could have been left out, saving space and time.

> Study **Figure 5**, a map showing the predicted locations of megacities in 2030. Using **Figure 5** and your own understanding, describe the distribution of megacities in 2030. **[4 marks]**

Figure 5

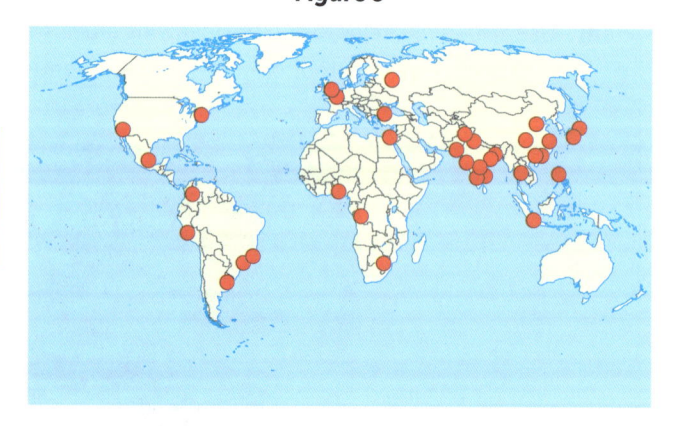

Figure 5 shows the location of megacities in the world in 2030. Megacities are located all over the world. They are concentrated particularly in Asia, for example in India and China. There are lots of megacities in China. There are few megacities in Africa – only three. Elsewhere, there are some megacities in Europe and in North and South America. A lot of megacities are located on the coast. This is because they are ports and have developed as trading centres. So, as the map shows, there are lots of megacities all over the world.

8. Think (plan) before you write

The time allocated to each question takes account of your need to **observe, interpret, think** and **plan**. So, for a 4-mark question, you should use up to 1 minute for thinking and planning and about 3 minutes for writing.

9. Check your answers

Ideally, you should have a few minutes left at the end of the exam. However well you think you have done, it is extremely unlikely that you have scored 100%! If you have time, methodically check your answers, especially the shorter, more factual answers:

- Double-check answers to multiple-choice questions.
- Make sure all diagrams are complete.
- Check calculations and that measurement units are included.

Then look at the higher-mark questions and make sure you have followed all the instructions precisely.

> **Tip** Make a simple plan (in the margin) before starting to answer 6- and 9-mark questions. This will enable you to write effectively and with clarity, expressing your opinions and writing balanced arguments.

Activity 9

Look at the following student answer. It contains careless mistakes that could cost marks. Identify and correct the mistakes.

> Study **Figure 6**, a graph showing economic sectors in selected countries. Using **Figure 6** and your own understanding, compare the economic sectors between Malaysia and Ethiopia.
> **[3 marks]**

Figure 6

(Bar chart showing Primary, Secondary, Tertiary sectors for UK, Brazil, Malaysia, Kenya, Ethiopia)

Key: Primary, Secondary, Tertiary

Malaysia has a much smaller primary sector than Ethiopia (about 7% compared to about 85%). However, Malaysia has much larger secondary and primary sectors than Ethiopia. Malaysia's secondary sector (about 40%) is larger than Ethiopia's (about 7%) and its tertiary sector (64%) is larger than Ethiopia's (about 6%).

10. Look after yourself!

You need to be at your best when you sit your exams. You will need to do a great deal of thinking 'on your feet'.

- Structure and plan your revision well in advance. Revise in intensive 40-minute sessions and take a complete break between each one.
- Try to take exercise regularly. It's good for the body and the mind!
- Eat well and drink water regularly. Don't skip breakfast on exam day: food is mind fuel!
- Get plenty of sleep and put social media 'on hold'.

Extending your understanding
Social, economic and environmental factors

AQA Specification links

Paper 1	Paper 2	Paper 3
• Extreme weather in the UK • River landforms – flood management scheme • Glacial landforms – impacts of tourism	• Urban – case study of LIC/NEE city • Urban – case study of UK city • Economic – case study of LIC/NEE • Economic futures in the UK • Resources in the UK	• Section A – issue evaluation (especially the decision-making question)

Understanding social, economic and environmental factors

When studying Geography, it often makes sense to categorise different aspects, whether these are 'factors' affecting an outcome or 'effects' and 'impacts' resulting from events, actions or processes.

The terms '**social**', '**economic**' and '**environmental**' are used widely across the specification and in the exams. You need to have a clear understanding of their meaning.

Tip If you are instructed to write about only one factor in an exam question, such as 'economic factors', you will gain no credit if you write about other factors.

Social – this applies to people and people's behaviour, so might include aspects of population, health, employment, education, communications and recreation.

Economic – this applies to financial aspects, such as farming, fishing and industry. It can also include retailing and the provision of services where the focus is financial. Essentially, it's anything to do with money!

Environmental – this applies to the environment and includes aspects such as pollution, biodiversity and climate change. While the focus is most often on the natural environment, such as rivers and forests, you should also consider the built environment, such as towns and cities.

There are two other similar terms that appear in the specification:

- **Political** – this commonly refers to the role of the government in decision-making. For example, the UK government makes decisions about national transport developments or the location of industry.
- **Cultural** – this can refer to aspects of ethnicity and its impacts on culture, such as literature, music, theatre, fashion and food.

Tip When writing about **causes** and **effects**, consider using 'social', 'economic' and 'environment' to provide a framework for your answer. Be confident in using these terms even if the question does not explicitly require you to do so. This particularly applies to levels-marked questions (4-, 6- and 9-mark questions).

Activity 1

Widespread flooding from Typhoon Haiyan (2013) caused landslides and blocked roads. Suggest how this might have had secondary social, economic and environmental effects.

Social	Economic	Environmental

Social, economic and environmental factors

Activity 2

Look at **Figure 1**, an aerial photo of Cambridge Science Park. The science park is the triangular area of land in the centre of the photo bounded by three main roads.

Figure 1

(a) Write annotations to suggest social, economic and environmental factors that explain why this is a good location for a science park.

(b) Can you suggest how political factors may have also been important?

Now try this!

Using **Figure 1** and your own understanding, suggest the economic and environmental advantages of the location of Cambridge Science Park. **[6 marks]**

Extending your understanding 15

Geographical scale

AQA Specification links

Paper 1	Paper 2	Paper 3
• Tectonic hazards • Weather hazards • Climate change • Living world	• Urban issues and challenges • Changing economic world • Resources	• Section A – issue evaluation

Understanding scale

Spatial scale	Temporal scale
Spatial scale refers to 'space'. There is a hierarchy of spatial scales, with **local** scale as the smallest and **global** scale as the largest. • *Local* scale: the smallest spatial area. Good examples include a freshwater pond, an area of forest and a few streets in a town. • *Regional* scale: this may be a political region (e.g. the south-west in the UK). A region can also apply to an area with distinctive characteristics (e.g. relief, vegetation or proximity to a large body of water). Examples include the European Alps, the Mediterranean or the Sahara Desert. • *National* scale: this refers to a country, such as the UK, Brazil or Nigeria. • *Global* scale: this is the largest spatial scale, involving vast areas of the world. For example, it includes global ecosystems, such as tropical rainforests or tundra. It also includes the water cycle and climate change.	Temporal scale refers to 'time'. For example, it is possible to consider **short-term** and **long-term** effects of an earthquake or the effects of deindustrialisation. Some actions can have negative short-term consequences yet can bring long-term benefits, such as building a new airport runway or a new motorway.

> **Tip** When writing about the consequences of natural or human actions, consider the importance of scale as this demonstrates your awareness of different perspectives (which is very important in answering 6- and 9-mark questions).

Scale warnings!

Be careful when using scale. Potential 'banana skin' topics include:

Tectonics

Simple diagrams of plate margins can be misleading. For example, a constructive margin is not simply a single crack in the ground but a highly complex landscape of ridges and rift valleys extending for hundreds of kilometres.

Landscapes

• The formation of landscapes (e.g. rivers and coastlines) is generally extremely slow, involving hundreds or thousands of years.
• Landscape change can be sudden. For example, river landscapes may show little change for decades until a serious flood event causes dramatic change in just a few hours.

Climate change

• Graphs may show trends over hundreds or thousands of years, so read the axes carefully.
• Remember that a **short-term** individual weather event does not on its own provide evidence for **longer-term** climate change.

UK city and LIC/NEE country

In an exam, focus only on the spatial scale identified in the question.

Development

Development indicators (such as GNI) can be very misleading because within a single country there could be huge extremes of wealth. For example, Nigeria has quite a high level of development but at the local scale (e.g. in squatter settlements) there is a lot of poverty.

> **Tip** Be careful when reading graph axes. The time units can vary (single years, decades or centuries?) on the horizontal (x) axis. Use a ruler to accurately read data off the x- and y-axes when describing trends.

Geographical scale

Activity

A new road development is proposed in the Peruvian Amazon tropical rainforest. It will open up the forest, connecting indigenous tribal communities with large towns and cities in the area. It will provide opportunities for trade and tourism.

Complete the table below by suggesting advantages (A) and disadvantages (D) of the road development at various scales.

	Local	National (Peru)	Regional (Amazon)	Global
Short term				
Long term				

Now try this!

Study **Figure 1**, a photo showing earthquake and tsunami damage in Pau, Indonesia in 2018. Using **Figure 1** and your own understanding, suggest the immediate and long-term responses to the natural hazard. **[6 marks]**

Figure 1

Tip

In referring to 'your own understanding', you can draw on other examples that you may have studied. Your answer must refer to both immediate and long-term responses to be awarded top marks.

Extending your understanding

Sustainability and sustainable development

Specification links (AQA)

Paper 1	Paper 2	Paper 3
• Tropical rainforest management	• Urban sustainability • UK economic futures (modern industrial developments) • Resources	• Section A – issue evaluation

What is sustainability?

The concept of sustainability underpins much of modern-day geography. It is a term that you should use widely both within physical and human geography.

'Sustain' means to keep going or to be long-lasting. In geography, 'sustainable' means that an action or strategy (e.g. river management to prevent flooding) is designed to be long-lasting and have a minimal negative impact on people and the environment.

Sustainable development

Sustainable development is about long-term improvements in people's quality of life, and it is ideally able to maintain itself. It should have minimal (if any) harmful impacts on the environment. For example, a small-scale hydro scheme can provide long-term benefits to the local community with few, if any, harmful impacts on the environment.

Figure 1 shows that sustainability is not just about the environment. It is also about sustaining communities (social benefits) and the economy. For example, Fairtrade's sustainable development projects are embedded within local communities, helping to increase food production, increase incomes and improve people's quality of life (education, health centres, etc.).

Figure 1 Concept of sustainable development

Activity

Look at **Figure 2**, which shows some features of sustainable urban living.

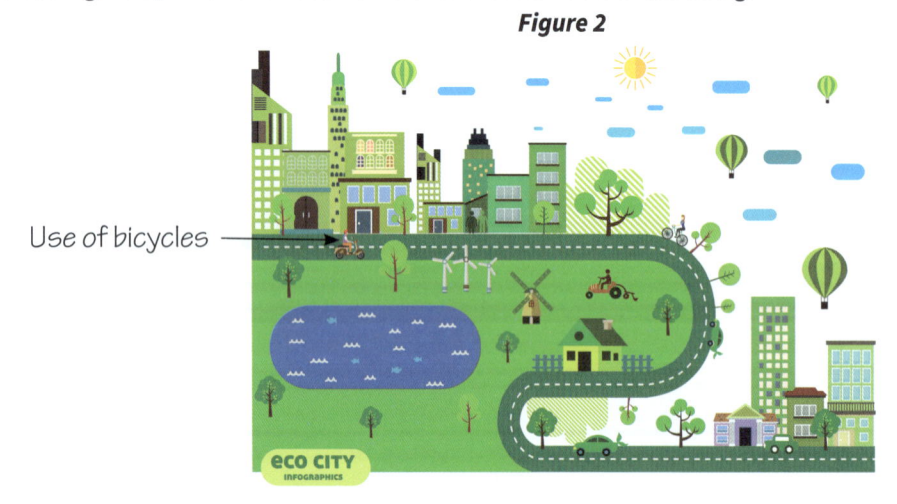

Figure 2

Use of bicycles

(a) Use labels to identify features of sustainable urban living. One has been done for you.

(b) Can you suggest some other features of sustainable urban living not shown in **Figure 2**?

_____

_____

Sustainability and sustainable development

Worked example

Study **Figure 3**, a photo showing ecotourism in Kibale National Park in Uganda. Using **Figure 3**, suggest how ecotourism can support the sustainable management of tropical rainforests. **[4 marks]**

Figure 3

> Focuses on ecotourism and makes good links with sustainable management

> Direct reference to the figure at the start

> Considers sustainability in a broad sense (environmental and economic)

Figure 3 shows a small group of tourists in a rainforest. Small-group tourism is a good example of sustainable management because it has minimal effects on the natural environment. In the photo, the tourists walk on a raised boardwalk to avoid trampling the forest floor. The boardwalk takes a narrow route between the trees, avoiding the need to cut down trees. This is a good example of sustainable management as it preserves wildlife habitats. The boardwalk is probably made from local wood, providing jobs for local people. Local people may benefit financially from ecotourism by acting as guides, building accommodation and selling food and crafts.

Now try this!

For **one** of food, water or energy, explain how different strategies can be used to make supplies more sustainable. **[6 marks]**

_____
_____
_____
_____
_____
_____
_____
_____
_____
_____
_____

Extending your understanding

Development

AQA Specification links

Paper 1	Paper 2	Paper 3
• Tectonic hazards (contrasting levels of wealth)	• Urban issues and challenges (urbanisation, LIC/NEE case study) • Changing economic world (measuring development, demographic transition model, tourism, LIC/NEE case study) • Resources	• Section A – issue evaluation

What is global development?

The term '**development**' applies to social and economic progress within countries. It is possible to divide the world into three broad development categories:

- **HICs:** high-income countries, which have a high and stable level of social and economic development, where people enjoy a high quality of life (e.g. high life expectancy, good healthcare and education, high levels of income). Examples include the UK, the USA, Japan, Australia and much of Europe.
- **NEEs:** newly emerging economies, which are developing rapidly with improvements in social and economic wellbeing. Examples include India, China, Nigeria and Brazil.
- **LICs:** low-income countries with low levels of development (e.g. low life expectancy, poor services, shortages of food). They tend to rely on agriculture and have limited industrial development. Some LICs experience conflict. Examples include Sudan, Ethiopia and Afghanistan.

The development gap

The term '**development gap**' is used in the specification to describe the gap between the rich and the poor. This can apply at several different scales: globally (for example, there may be uneven global development), regionally (say within Africa) and within individual countries (such as Nigeria) and cities (such as Lagos).

Activity 1

The table below shows strategies used to reduce the development gap. Use your textbook or revision notes to help you complete the table. Try to refer to examples of projects and/or countries.

Strategy	How it reduces the development gap
Investment	
Industrial development and tourism	
Aid	
Using intermediate technology	
Fair trade	
Debt relief	
Microfinance loans	

Extending your understanding

Development

Activity 2

Figure 1 shows the Demographic Transition Model (DTM).

(a) Label the following lines on the diagram:
- Birth rate
- Death rate

(b) Shade and label the part of the graph that shows natural increase.

(c) The population pyramids (and their labels) below the graph are in the wrong order. Number them from 1 to 5 to match them up with stages 1 to 5 of the model.

(d) Draw and label an arrow to show the 'increase in levels of development'.

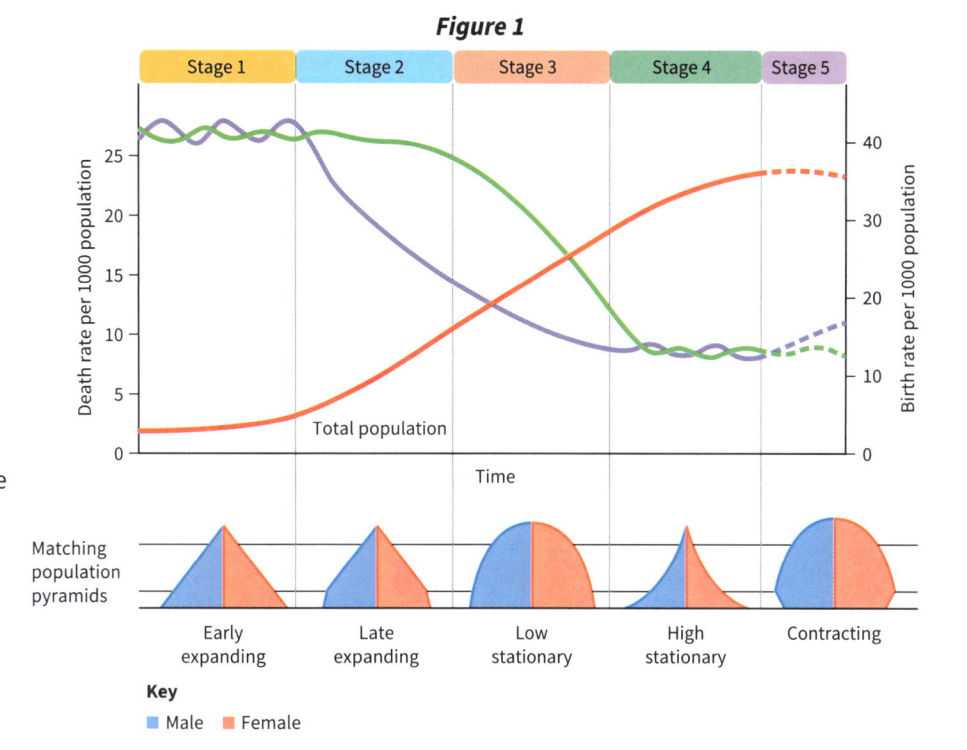

Figure 1

Stage 1 | Stage 2 | Stage 3 | Stage 4 | Stage 5

Matching population pyramids: Early expanding | Late expanding | Low stationary | High stationary | Contracting

Key: Male Female

(e) Outline the links between the Demographic Transition Model and levels of development.

_____
_____
_____
_____

Worked example

Explain how **one** physical factor can lead to uneven development. **[3 marks]**

Extreme weather events can lead to uneven development. For example, parts of Africa (e.g. the Sahel) suffer from extended periods of unreliable rainfall and drought causing crop failures, loss of earnings and food shortages. People living in these areas are often poorer than people living in areas that do not experience such extreme weather events. Tropical cyclones bring costly devastation to countries such as the Philippines, Bangladesh and the countries of the Caribbean, reducing their levels of development.

Examiner feedback

This is a good answer earning top marks:
- The answer focuses on climate (extreme weather), one of several possible **physical** factors.
- There is a good use of examples in outlining the causal links between climate and uneven development.
- The final sentence nails the top mark. If you have time, it's always worth adding a supplementary sentence just to be certain of maximum marks.

Extending your understanding

Synopticity

What does synopticity mean?

The term '**synopticity**' involves bringing together information from across the subject. It is one of the highest level concepts at GCSE. There are several parts of the specification where a synoptic approach is encouraged and rewarded, especially at Level 3 in the 6- and 9-mark questions.

Geography is rather like a multifaceted diamond in that it has many 'faces'. In showing an understanding of synopticity, you need to bring together the many 'faces' of the subject when explaining a pattern or justifying an outcome.

> **AQA Specification links**
>
> Synoptic links can be made across and within the topics of the specification.
>
> A synoptic practice question can be found on page 62.

Activity 1

The Venn diagram in **Figure 1** identifies a number of synoptic concepts that are common to both physical and human geography, such as place and space. They will help you to make geographical connections (synoptic links) between different aspects of the subject.

Figure 1

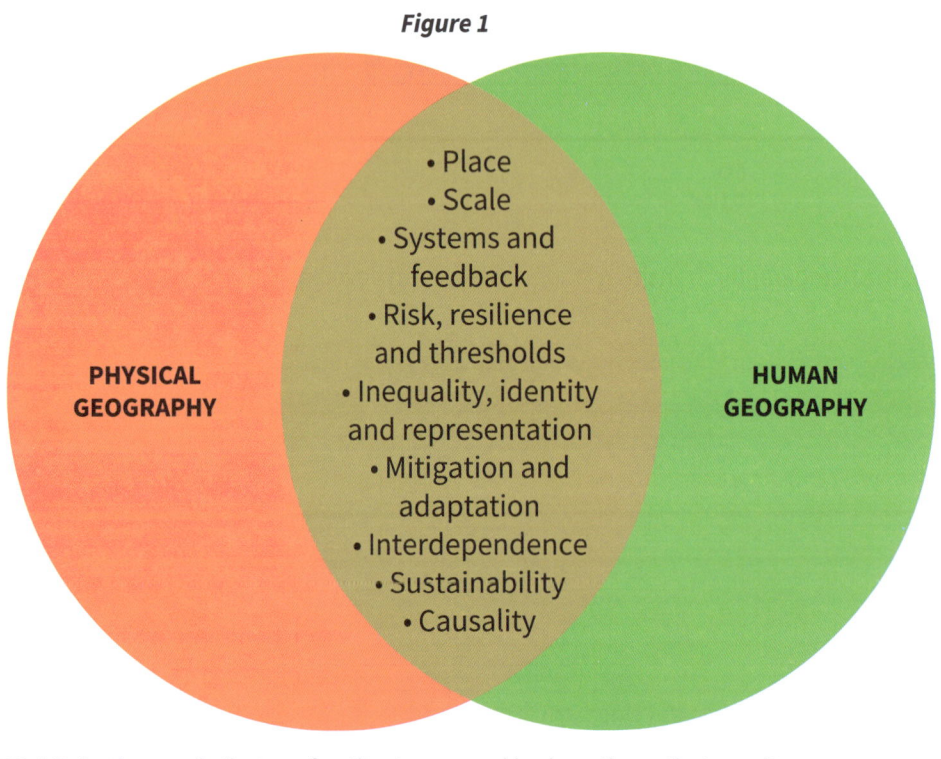

PHYSICAL GEOGRAPHY | **HUMAN GEOGRAPHY**

- Place
- Scale
- Systems and feedback
- Risk, resilience and thresholds
- Inequality, identity and representation
- Mitigation and adaptation
- Interdependence
- Sustainability
- Causality

> **Tip** When answering a question that requires a **discussion**, a **debate** or an **evaluation**, look at the bigger picture. Consider the range of factors, both physical and human, that contribute towards a particular outcome or decision. You could use a writing/planning frame similar to Figures 2 or 3, or a spider diagram.

Highlight the words that are familiar to you and look up those that aren't.

Activity 2

Figure 2 provides a simple 'petal' writing frame for considering synoptic links. Use this framework to suggest the causes of uneven global development. Try to make them as wide-ranging as possible.

One has been done for you.

Figure 2

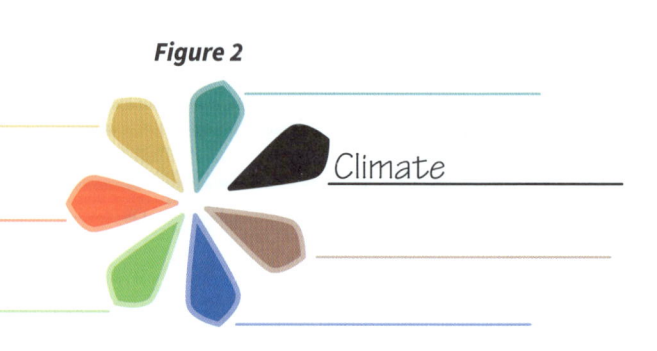

Climate

---

22 Extending your understanding

Synopticity

Activity 3

(a) Suggest how the following factors can affect undernutrition.

- Land use

  _____

  _____

- Climate change

  _____

  _____

(b) Suggest what is meant by the term 'natural systems'.

  _____

  _____

Worked example

Discuss the economic and environmental issues associated with the exploitation of energy sources in the UK. **[6 marks]**

There are both advantages and disadvantages of exploiting energy sources in the UK. For example, fracking (extracting natural gas using high pressure liquids) brings economic benefits in providing energy and creating jobs. However, it also brings significant environmental problems including earthquakes and water pollution. Economically, fracking is very expensive.

Wind farms are becoming increasingly efficient in converting wind energy to electricity, but they remain controversial in the UK. Economically, they are expensive to construct and have a negative visual impact on the landscape. While they can attract tourists, on balance I think that most local people are against their development. In the Lake District, there are concerns about falling visitor numbers. Environmentally, while wind farms do not emit greenhouse gases, damage to habitats may occur during the construction phase.

Examiner feedback

This answer achieves Level 3 and the full 6 marks:
- There is a good balance between economic and environmental issues.
- Advantages and disadvantages are discussed throughout the answer.
- There is reference to a range of issues (e.g. tourism, ecosystems, tectonics, climate change), demonstrating synopticity (these are highlighted in red).
- It is well written and focused, with good use of geographical terminology.

Extending your understanding 23

Master the topic
1 The challenge of natural hazards

Tectonic hazards: plate tectonic theory

The mechanisms responsible for plate movement are highly complex. The simple model involving interconnecting circular **convection cells** (currents of heat) is still valid. However, scientists now consider **ridge-push** and **slab-pull** to be important mechanisms as shown in **Figure 1**.

- **Ridge-push:** At a constructive plate margin, magma forces its way to the surface, forming a linear ridge (such as the Mid-Atlantic Ridge). The two plates either side of the *ridge* are forced or *pushed* apart by the upwelling magma.
- **Slab-pull:** At the other end of an oceanic plate there is a destructive plate margin, where one plate dives (subducts) below another. Here, the force of gravity acts on the dense oceanic plate, effectively *pulling* the *slab* downwards.

Figure 1

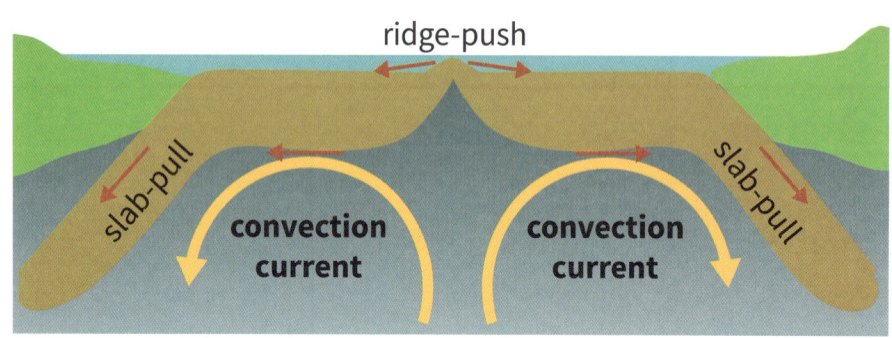

Activity 1

Figure 2 is a simplified outline diagram showing a destructive plate margin.

(a) Label the following on **Figure 2**:
- Convection current
- Subducting plate
- Slab-pull
- Ocean trench
- Magma
- Erupting volcano
- Earthquake foci

Figure 2

(b) Use **Figure 2** to explain why earthquakes at a destructive plate margin form a broad zone on a map.

_____

_____

24 Master the topic

1 The challenge of natural hazards

Weather hazards: global atmospheric circulation

Look at **Figure 3**, the global atmospheric circulation. Notice the following key features:

- There are three interlocking circulation 'cells' in each hemisphere – the Hadley cell, the Ferrel cell and the Polar cell.
- On the surface, there are distinctive alternating belts of high and low atmospheric pressure. Notice that air is sinking towards the ground to create the high pressure belts and rising from the surface to form the low pressure belts.
- Surface winds move from high to low pressure, curving due to the effect of the Earth's rotation (this is called the Coriolis effect).

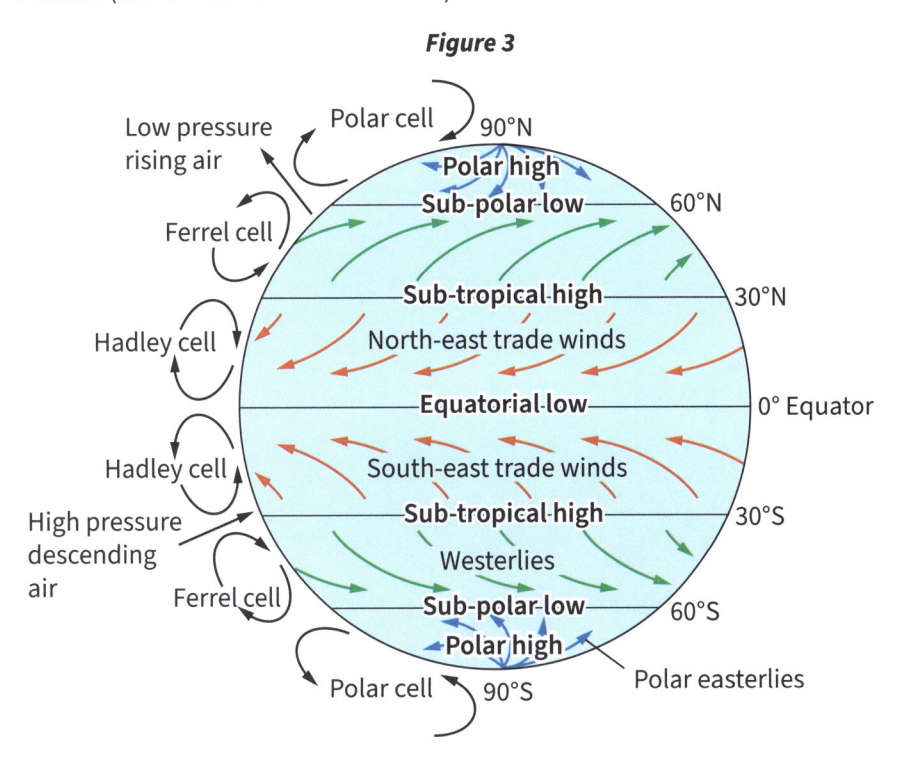

Figure 3

Activity 2

Look at **Figure 4**, a cross-section through the atmosphere in the northern hemisphere.

(a) Label the Hadley cell and the Polar cell.
(b) Draw arrows to show the circulation of the Ferrel cell.
(c) Use labelled arrows to show the location of tropical rainforests and deserts.

Figure 4

Tip

In an exam, you are most likely to refer to the global atmospheric circulation in the context of tropical storms. Notice that in the tropics, tropical storms are carried from east to west by the trade winds.

Master the topic 25

1 The challenge of natural hazards

Climate change: the enhanced greenhouse effect

The **greenhouse effect** is a natural blanket of atmospheric warmth. Without it, it would be too cold for life to exist on Earth.

In recent decades, farming, industrialisation and burning fossil fuels have led to the release of huge quantities of so-called **greenhouse gases** (e.g. carbon dioxide, nitrous oxide and methane) into the atmosphere. This has enabled the atmosphere to absorb an increasing amount of infrared radiation emitted from the Earth, enhancing (exaggerating) the greenhouse effect, hence the term '**enhanced greenhouse effect**', which is explained in **Figure 5**. It is this that has led to increasing global temperatures (global warming) associated with climate change.

> **Tip** When asked to link burning fossil fuels to increased global temperatures, make sure that you make clear links to the enhanced greenhouse effect – it is the critical link between cause and effect.

Figure 5

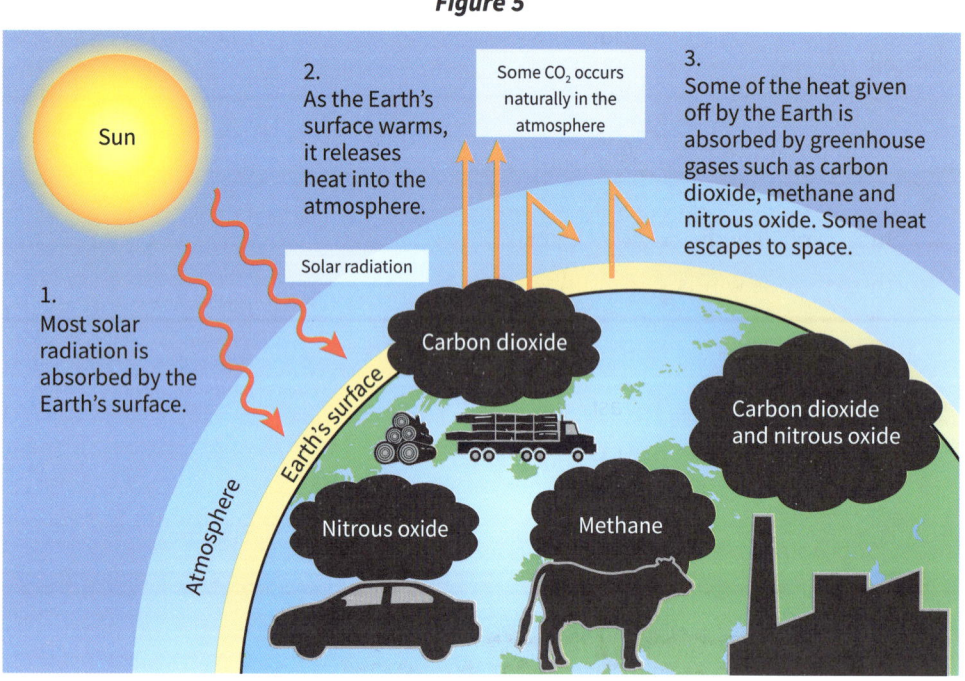

1. Most solar radiation is absorbed by the Earth's surface.

2. As the Earth's surface warms, it releases heat into the atmosphere.

Some CO₂ occurs naturally in the atmosphere

3. Some of the heat given off by the Earth is absorbed by greenhouse gases such as carbon dioxide, methane and nitrous oxide. Some heat escapes to space.

Now try this!

Using **Figure 5**, explain how alternative energy production can reduce the rate of climate change.

[4 marks]

_____

_____

_____

_____

_____

_____

_____

_____

> **Tip** You should refer to the enhanced greenhouse effect in your answer.

26 Master the topic

2 The living world

Ecosystems

An **ecosystem** is a natural system made up of living organisms (plants, animals, bacteria, etc.) and the natural environment. Ecosystems can be identified at the local scale (e.g. a freshwater pond) and at the global scale (e.g. tropical rainforest), where they are called global **biomes**.

Interrelationships

Ecosystems at all scales involve complex **interrelationships** (links) between biotic (living) and abiotic (non-living) components. Biotic interrelationships can be illustrated by food chains or food webs, which show who is eating whom!

Interdependence

Components of an ecosystem depend on one another for their survival, thereby demonstrating **interdependence**. This is nutrient cycling.

If an ecosystem is affected by change (e.g. a drought causes a freshwater pond to dry up) this can have significant knock-on effects. Some plants may thrive under drier conditions whereas others may die. Aquatic organisms, deprived of the water they depend on, may die or migrate elsewhere.

Biodiversity

Biodiversity describes the **variety of life** in an ecosystem or global biome. High biodiversity is a feature of a healthy, sustainable ecosystem.

In some ecosystems, biodiversity is being reduced by human actions – both direct (e.g. deforestation) and indirect (e.g. climate change). In tropical rainforests, deforestation to create plantations or cattle ranching has led to many plant and animal species becoming endangered or even extinct.

> **Tip** Try to use the high-level terms 'interrelationships' and 'interdependence' in your answers.

Activity

Look at **Figure 1**, which shows deforestation in Laos, South-East Asia.

Figure 1

(a) How is the man clearing the forest?
_____

(b) Describe the land in the foreground that has already been cleared.
_____

(c) Annotate the photo to identify **three** likely effects on biodiversity.

Now try this!

For **either** hot deserts **or** cold environments, outline two ways in which the ecosystem shows interdependence. **[2 marks]**

_____
_____
_____
_____

3 Physical landscapes in the UK

Physical processes

When describing the formation of landforms, you need to refer to the physical processes involved. It is really important that you use the correct terminology and that you show understanding of each process.

Weathering: the disintegration or decay of rocks. Chemical weathering involves a chemical change taking place, which is usually associated with water. Mechanical weathering involves rocks breaking apart physically, with no chemical change.

Mass movement: the downhill movement of weathered material under the force of gravity.

Erosion: the wearing away and removal of material by a moving force, such as a breaking wave.

Transportation: the movement of eroded material, carried by the sea, a river or a glacier.

Deposition: when transported material is dropped, usually when there is a fall in velocity (e.g. at the inside bend of a river meander).

Activity 1

For the two landscapes that you have studied, add a letter in each box in the 'Process' column to indicate the correct definition.

Coastal landscapes

Process	Definition
Mass movement: sliding	A Transport of sediment along a beach
Mass movement: slumping	B Rocks smash together making smaller, rounder particles
Mass movement: rock falls	C Slab of cliff slides rapidly downhill along a saturated shear-plane
Hydraulic power	D Individual rocks or slabs of rock collapse from a cliff onto the beach below
Abrasion	E Waves compress air in cracks in a cliff, widening cracks and causing rocks to break off
Attrition	F Loose, unstable material on a slope collapses downhill
Longshore drift	G Rocks carried by the sea wear away cliffs or wave cut platforms

River landscapes

Process	Definition
Hydraulic action	A Erosion: dissolving of rocks or minerals. Transportation: transport of dissolved chemicals in the water
Abrasion	B Material is carried in the flow of a river
Attrition	C Rocks carried by the river wear down the river bed and banks
Solution	D Material is rolled along a river bed
Traction	E Material bounces along a river bed, is picked up and dropped by water currents
Saltation	F The power of water erodes the bed and banks of a river
Suspension	G Rocks smash together making smaller, rounder particles

Glacial landscapes

Process	Definition
Freeze-thaw weathering	A Loose rocks are 'plucked' from solid bedrock as meltwater freezes them to the base of a glacier
Abrasion	B Repeated cycles of freezing and thawing, enlarging cracks, causing rocks to break away
Plucking	C Slippage of ice along a curved surface
Rotational slip	D The snout of an advancing glacier pushes deposited sediment
Bulldozing	E Rocks are carried beneath a glacier, grinding away the underlying bedrock

28 Master the topic

3 Physical landscapes in the UK

Sequence of landform formation

One common criterion for achieving a top-level mark is demonstrating accuracy in the **correct sequencing of landform formation**.

> **Tip**
> When describing landform formation, write a plan to ensure that you have a correct sequence of events (stages) in the landform's formation. When writing your answer, consider using simple annotated sketches or diagrams to describe the sequence of events.

Activity 2

Figure 1

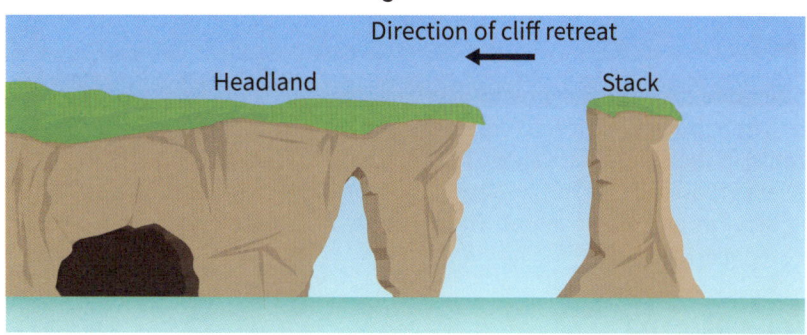

Figure 2

Study **Figure 1** which shows the formation of a coastal stack.

(a) Write annotations onto **Figure 1** to describe the formation of these landforms.

Study **Figure 2** which shows the formation of an ox-bow lake

(b) The four diagrams in **Figure 2** are not in the correct sequence. Write the numbers 1 to 4 above the diagrams to put them in the right order.

Now try this!

Explain how distinctive coastal/river/glacial* landforms are created by erosion. **[4 marks]**

*Choose only one type of landform to write about.

_____
_____
_____
_____
_____
_____
_____
_____

4 Urban issues and challenges

Describing global patterns of urban change

It is likely that you will be asked to describe distributions and patterns on maps at a variety of scales. In your descriptions, you need to be very precise, referring to geographical locations and making full use of the data provided.

- **Distribution** involves stating where things are located. Try to identify dense and sparse concentrations and refer to precise geographical locations.
- A **pattern** implies a degree of regularity in a distribution, for example by forming lines (linear pattern) or radiating out from a central point (radial pattern).

What is urbanisation?

The term '**urbanisation**' is used to describe the growth of urban areas. It results from a combination of in-migration from poverty-stricken rural areas and high rates of natural increase (births minus deaths) in the cities themselves. Today, urbanisation is almost static in HICs. However, in less urbanised LICs, urbanisation is occurring rapidly, putting a lot of pressure on housing, services and employment. The existence of extensive squatter settlements is the result of rapid urbanisation.

Spatial and temporal patterns

Urban change resulting from urbanisation can have a **spatial** element (the global spread of cities) and a **temporal** element (how they have grown over time). For example, look at **Figure 1**. It is a map showing both the spatial and temporal global pattern of urban change. It shows not only patterns of cities but also patterns of city growth (urbanisation).

> **Tip** An exam question could use either the term 'distribution' or 'pattern'. If the latter is used, then look for regularity. Consider the strength of the regularity. Is there a causal link with another factor (such as sea trading routes), or just a vague pattern?

Activity

Study **Figure 1**, which shows the global pattern of population change 1950–2030.

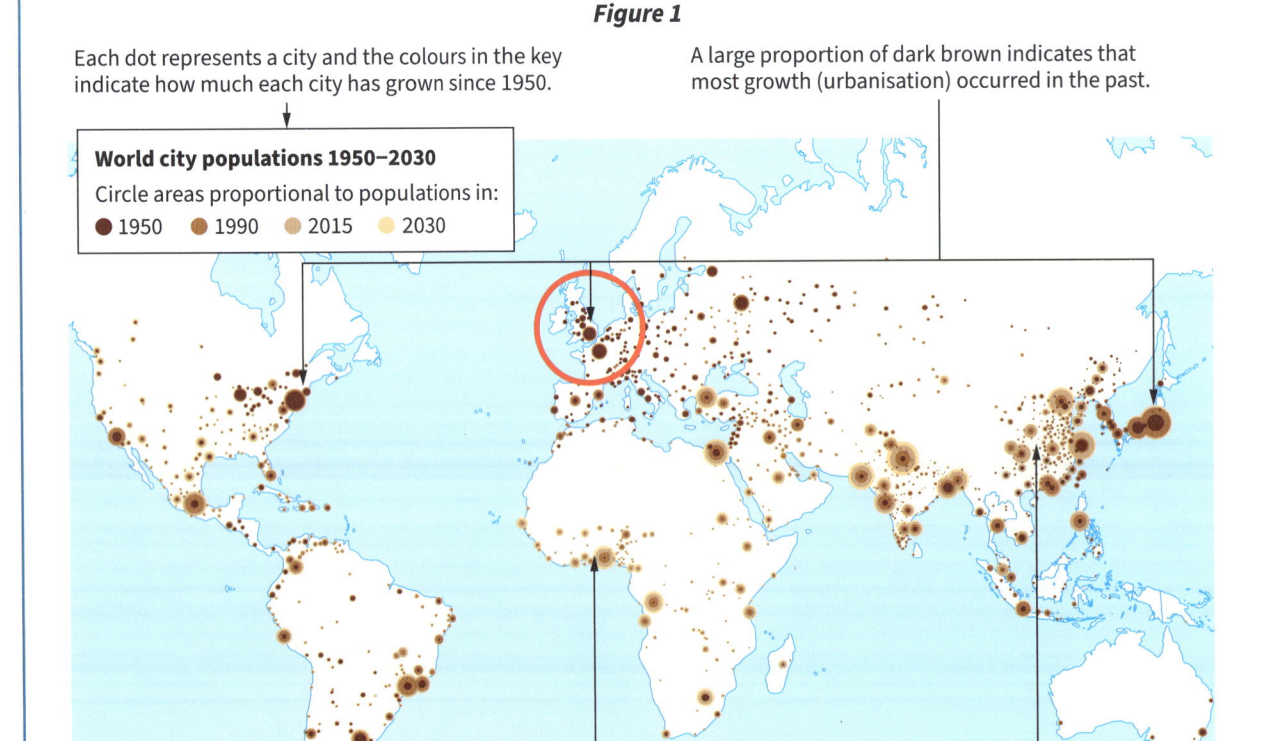

Figure 1

Each dot represents a city and the colours in the key indicate how much each city has grown since 1950.

A large proportion of dark brown indicates that most growth (urbanisation) occurred in the past.

World city populations 1950–2030
Circle areas proportional to populations in:
● 1950 ● 1990 ● 2015 ● 2030

The greater the proportion of light brown, the more a city is expected to grow in the future.

Master the topic

4 Urban issues and challenges

(a) What type of map is **Figure 1**?

Choropleth map ☐   Dot map ☐

Isoline map ☐   Flow line map ☐

(b) A circle has been drawn around cities in north-west Europe. They are mostly shaded dark brown, indicating that they have not grown much since 1950. For each of the following, circle **one** area of the world with:

- Large cities in 1950 that have not grown much since that date
- Cities that grew considerably between 1950 and 1980
- Cities that grew considerably between 1980 and 2015

Now try this!

Figure 2 is a line graph showing the growth of Guangzhou, a city in China.

1.1. Use the data in **Figure 2** to plot the projected population value for 2030 and complete the line graph. **[2 marks]**

Figure 2

Year	1950	1990	2015	2030
Population (millions)	1.0	3.1	12.5	17.6
Global rank	71	63	20	16
National rank	7	7	4	3

1.2 Describe the growth of Guangzhou from 1950 to 2030. **[2 marks]**

_____

_____

_____

_____

1.3. What is the evidence that Guangzhou is projected to grow faster than other cities in China and the rest of the world? **[2 marks]**

_____

_____

_____

_____

Master the topic 31

5 The changing economic world

What is economic development?

Economic development involves the growth of a region based on the creation of wealth. This might involve, for example, the development of farming, fishing or manufacturing industries. Wealth can be used to improve people's quality of life through education, public services and infrastructure. As a country's economy grows, so (in theory) does the quality of life of its people.

The multiplier effect

Look at **Figure 1**. It is a model of economic growth called the **multiplier effect**. Follow the flowchart to see how the introduction of a new industry (or the expansion of an existing industry) leads to a series of events that result in wealth creation and the growth of the economy.

> **Tip** Try to refer to the multiplier effect if it is appropriate to do so. It is a high-level concept and will help you to achieve a top mark.

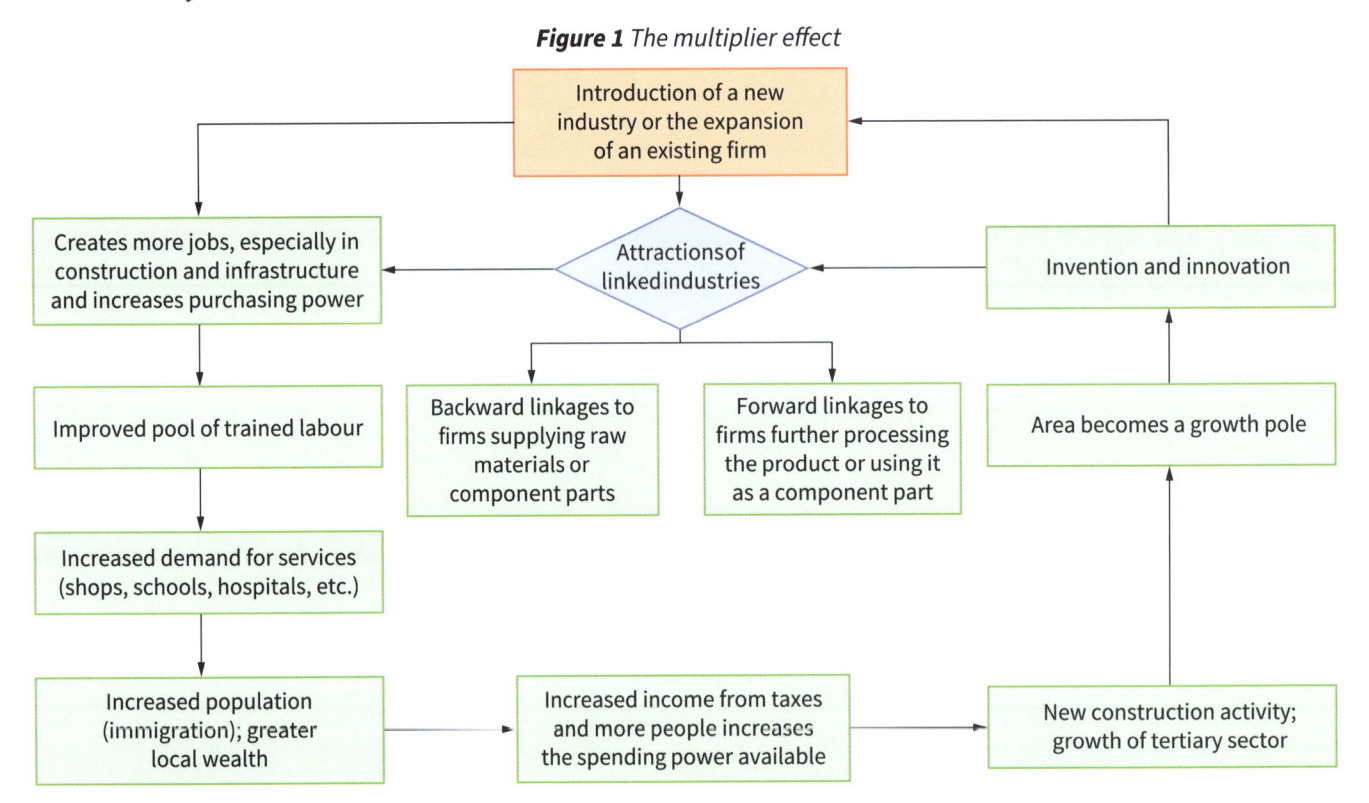

Figure 1 The multiplier effect

[Flowchart showing:
- Introduction of a new industry or the expansion of an existing firm
- Creates more jobs, especially in construction and infrastructure and increases purchasing power
- Attractions of linked industries
- Invention and innovation
- Improved pool of trained labour
- Backward linkages to firms supplying raw materials or component parts
- Forward linkages to firms further processing the product or using it as a component part
- Area becomes a growth pole
- Increased demand for services (shops, schools, hospitals, etc.)
- Increased population (immigration); greater local wealth
- Increased income from taxes and more people increases the spending power available
- New construction activity; growth of tertiary sector]

Activity

The table below lists economic developments in Nigeria associated with the development of the oil industry.

A	Oil workers need houses, shops, schools, etc. which create further job opportunities in construction, retailing and services.
B	The government spends money to improve people's quality of life (education, services, infrastructure).
C	Industries generate government wealth through taxes, and export earnings as oil products are exported.
D	Achieving the status of an NEE, Nigeria attracts further investment from abroad.
E	Oil extraction provides job opportunities to attract workers (over 65 000 now employed).

Complete the flowchart below by writing the letters A to E from the table in their correct places in the blank boxes.

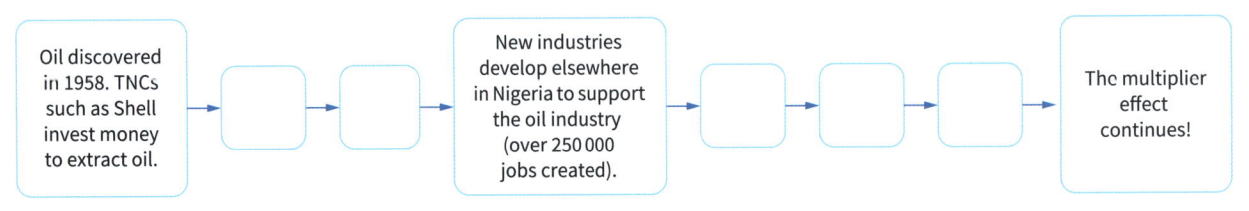

[Flowchart: Oil discovered in 1958. TNCs such as Shell invest money to extract oil. → ☐ → ☐ → New industries develop elsewhere in Nigeria to support the oil industry (over 250 000 jobs created). → ☐ → ☐ → The multiplier effect continues!]

5 The changing economic world

> **Worked example**
>
> Explain how economic development can lead to improvements in people's quality of life. **[4 marks]**
>
> Economic development can lead to improvements in people's quality of life through the ==multiplier effect==. When a resource is exploited (such as oil in Nigeria) or a new factory built, jobs are created in construction and in the factory. ==People have money to spend in shops, boosting the local economy and improving the quality of their lives.== Supply industries expand, creating more jobs. Taxes provide money for the government to spend on improving services such as healthcare, improving the quality of life.

- Multiplier effect is clearly understood
- References a case study, which, although not required, is good practice
- Clear link between economic development and quality of life
- Includes a range of economic developments at different scales

Deindustrialisation in the UK

The multiplier effect can also work in reverse. This happened in the UK during the 1970s and 1980s when many old industries closed, leading to industrial decline and unemployment. This is an example of **deindustrialisation**. It was the result of out-of-date working practices and increased competition from abroad, where goods were produced more efficiently and cheaper.

When an industry closes, it causes unemployment. Spending (and tax income) is reduced, which results in the closure of shops and other services. Supply industries lose a market, and may also be forced to close down. A spiral of decline sets in and a previously thriving region becomes run down and derelict.

The post-industrial economy in the UK

Following deindustrialisation, the UK has become a **post-industrial economy**. The manufacturing industry has been largely replaced by the service sector (about 80% of the UK's workforce). This sector includes finance, construction and public services (such as healthcare, waste management and education). Much of this growth has been driven by developments in information technology.

> **Now try this!**
>
> Explain how deindustrialisation can cause economic decline. **[4 marks]**

Master the topic

6 The challenge of resource management

Understanding resource security and insecurity

- **Resource security** applies to a country or region that has a plentiful supply of food, water and energy that matches demand (consumption), both now and in the future. Resources could be home-produced or imported from safe and reliable (secure) sources abroad.
- **Resource insecurity** applies to countries or regions experiencing shortages, where demand exceeds supply.

Resource security in the UK

As an HIC, the UK enjoys reasonably high levels of resource security. It has high levels of self-sufficiency and strong trading links with the rest of the world to make up shortfalls in food and energy.

Food	Water	Energy
The UK has a good level of food security. It is about 60% self-sufficient in food and has reliable access to sources of food from overseas.	The UK has a high level of water security. However, water security varies across the UK – demand exceeds supply in parts of the south and the east.	The UK has a reasonably high level of energy security with access to gas reserves in the North Sea and renewable options, such as wind turbines.

Activity 1

Figure 1 shows the threat to water security in the UK.

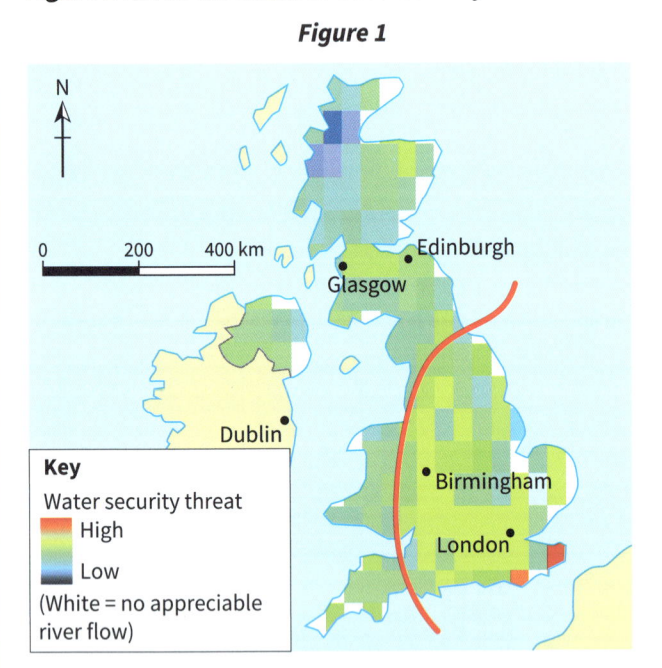

Figure 1

Map of the UK showing water security threat. Key: Water security threat — High to Low (White = no appreciable river flow). Cities labelled: Edinburgh, Glasgow, Dublin, Birmingham, London.

> **Tip**
> The terms 'security' and 'insecurity' are used throughout this part of the specification. Try to include these terms when answering exam questions. Other terms to use include 'supply', 'demand' and 'consumption'.

> **Tip**
> When describing, don't use the word 'because'! 'Because' leads into a reason for something, which is not required in 'describe' questions. Also, use 'GCSE' (see page 10) to provide a structure for your description.

(a) Circle the following areas on the map:
- Highest threat in South East England
- Relatively high level of threat in Scotland

(b) Describe the pattern of water security in the UK.

_____

_____

Resource security and development

Many LICs and some NEEs have low levels of resource security. They may have few natural resources and be limited in the imports they can afford to buy. Richer HICs, even if they are resource-poor, can afford to import resources from elsewhere (see table on page 35).

6 The challenge of resource management

Food	Water	Energy
LICs/NEEs are more vulnerable to food insecurity than HICs due to low levels of agricultural productivity and the lack of money to import food.	Water insecurity can affect all countries. Security in LICs/NEEs tends to be more regional, reflecting supply (rainfall) and demand (population centres).	HICs are able to source and secure energy supplies. Some LICs are resource-rich but have to depend on TNCs for their capital input, expertise, technology, etc. Electricity supply in many LICs is unreliable and this affects development.

Activity 2

For the resource you have studied, add another point as to how food/water/energy affects economic and social wellbeing.

	Food	Water	Energy
Economic wellbeing	• Commercial food production in HICs can generate high personal incomes and contribute money to the government through taxes. •	• Water is increasingly becoming a high-value resource, particularly in countries experiencing unreliable rainfall due to climate change. •	• Energy is required to power industry, fuel vehicles and generate electricity for domestic and commercial uses. •
Social wellbeing	• In HICs, obesity has become a significant problem, increasingly among children. •	• Water is essential for life. In semi-arid regions, people spend many hours collecting water. •	• Electricity supports education, improvements in healthcare, and energy for cooking and lighting. This leads to considerable improvements in people's quality of life. •

Worked example

Using **Figure 2**, a map of global water scarcity, describe the pattern of global water scarcity. **[4 marks]**

Figure 2

Key:
- Physical water scarcity
- Economic water scarcity
- Little or no water scarcity
- Not estimated

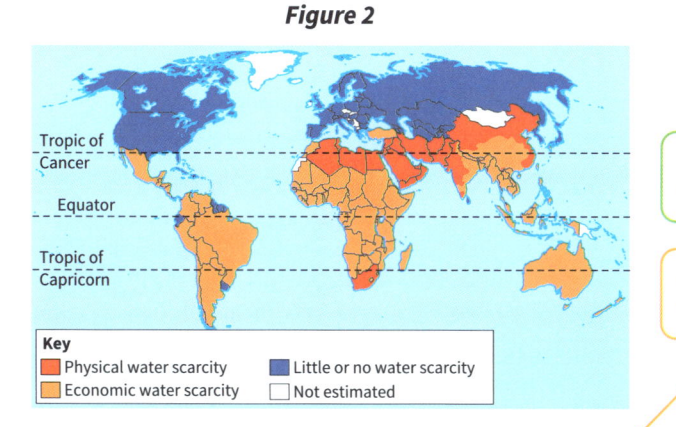

This answer gains the full 4 marks

Makes frequent references to the figure

Identifies patterns

Identifies some anomalies

Figure 2 shows that most of North America, Europe and northern Asia do not experience water scarcity – they have high levels of water security. Most regions experiencing physical water scarcity are located at the tropics and largely coincide with hot deserts, such as the Sahara. Within the tropics, most countries experience economic water scarcity (water insecurity). This includes much of Africa, South America and parts of southern Asia. There are one or two anomalies, for example Uruguay and Ecuador in South America do not experience water scarcity.

Master the topic 35

Max your marks
Mopping up the 1–3-mark questions

It may surprise you to learn that high-performing students frequently perform poorly on short-answer questions, throwing away important marks. This often happens because they rush through what can be seen as easy questions, but just because there are only a few marks available for a question, that doesn't mean it's an easy one!

How to succeed in multiple-choice questions

What are the common mistakes?

- Giving more than one answer in multiple-choice questions.
- Not writing the units of measurement (e.g. metres above sea level).
- Misreading key terms (e.g. constructive/conservative plate margin).

In your exam, you will be provided with (usually) four options of which one will be correct. The best approach is to eliminate the answers you know are wrong, leaving you with one or two plausible options. This prevents a knee-jerk reaction and is more likely to give you the correct answer.

> **Tip** You need to exercise care and caution. Read through the question more than once and then check your answers immediately and again at the end of the exam.

Worked example

Study **Figure 1**, a graph showing variations in average temperature in Australia (1910–2018).

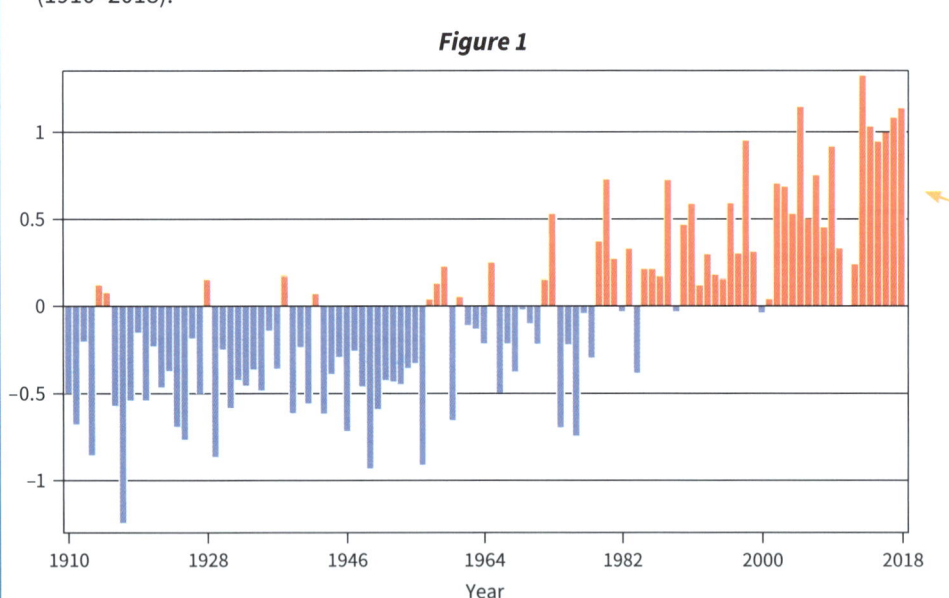

Figure 1

[Graph showing temperature variations from 1910 to 2018, with blue bars below 0 and red/orange bars above 0, y-axis from -1 to 1]

> This is the long-term average temperature. The blue bars show years where the average temperature was below the long-term average. The red bars show where the average temperature was above the long-term average.

> Take time to look closely at both axes to make sure you understand the scales. Think about what's happening over time – what's the story?

Using **Figure 1**, which **one** of the following statements is true?

Shade **one** circle only.

- A ~~Australia's temperatures were below average every year before 1946.~~ ◯
- B ~~Australia's temperatures showed a steady increase 1982–2018.~~ ◯
- C Australia's temperatures have been above the 1961–1990 average every year since 2001. ●
- D ~~Since 2000, Australia's temperatures have exceeded 0.5°C above the 1961–1990 average.~~ ◯

[1 mark]

> Carefully work your way through the four options, looking closely at the graph. Try to identify the options that are definitely incorrect and draw a line through them. Take your time to make the correct decision. By elimination, you should be left with the correct answer.

Multiple-choice questions

Now try this!

1. Study **Figure 1**, which shows the tectonic plates in Iceland.

   Figure 1

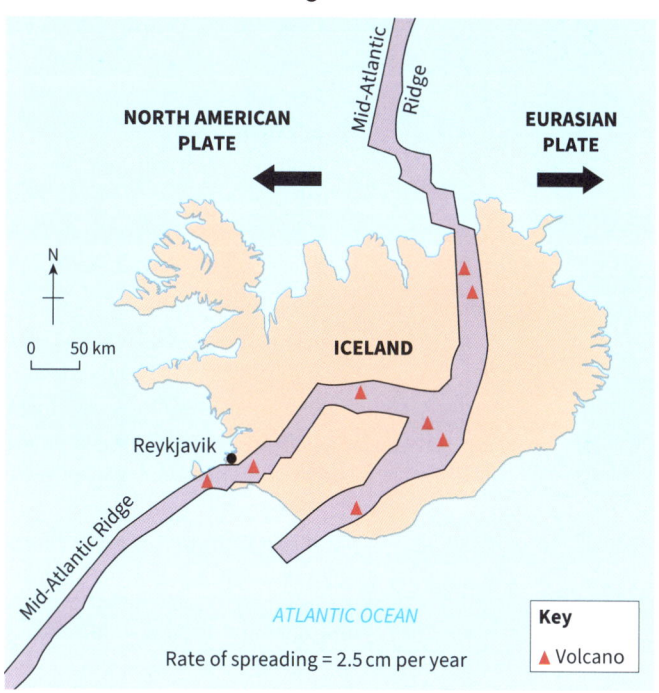

   NORTH AMERICAN PLATE ← Mid-Atlantic Ridge → EURASIAN PLATE

   ICELAND

   Reykjavik

   Mid-Atlantic Ridge

   ATLANTIC OCEAN

   Rate of spreading = 2.5 cm per year

   Key ▲ Volcano

   Using **Figure 1**, calculate how long it will take the plates to spread by 100 m.

   Shade **one** circle only.

   A   400 years ○
   B   4000 years ○
   C   2500 years ○
   D   40 years   ○

   [1 mark]

2. Which term is best defined by the phrase 'the unplanned growth of urban areas into the surrounding countryside'?

   Shade **one** circle only.

   A   Urbanisation   ○
   B   Urban regeneration ○
   C   Urban greening   ○
   D   Urban sprawl   ○

   [1 mark]

3. Which of the following best describes how sedimentary rocks are formed?

   Shade **one** circle only.

   A   Formed from molten rock beneath the Earth's surface   ○
   B   Formed from molten rock upon the Earth's surface   ○
   C   Formed when earth movements occur   ○
   D   Formed from material laid down by rivers, moving ice or the sea ○

   [1 mark]

Max your marks 37

Mopping up the 1–3-mark questions

Common command words for other short-answer questions

The table below identifies commonly used command words for short-answer questions. Look back to page 7 to check your understanding of these commands.

1-mark questions	2–3-mark questions
• Name • Calculate • Suggest **one** • State • Give • Identify (the landform) • Describe These tend to have single-word answers requiring identification, calculation or a requirement to consider a single aspect, such as a landform. Remember to give units of measurement. Do not write about more than **one** aspect – you'll be wasting time and will not get another mark.	• Describe • Outline • Calculate (showing your working) • State **two** • Using **Figure x** and your own understanding, suggest how • Give **two** • Draw a sketch and add labels/annotations • Suggest You are expected to do more here to earn 2 or 3 marks. You may be asked to show your working in a calculation or refer to a resource. You will often be instructed to write about **two** aspects – make sure you select two really clear and distinctly different aspects or observations.
Point marked: aim to make one point clearly and accurately.	**Point marked:** you will either be awarded marks for the points you make (e.g. 2 marks for two separate points), or marks for the **development** of an answer (e.g. 1 mark for one point and another mark for developing that point).

Many questions worth 1–3 marks will test your geographical skills (see pages 111–112). These could require you to complete graphs and diagrams, interpret OS maps or make calculations. You need to be very precise and ensure that you always express the units of measurement (e.g. m or km). When making calculations, you will often be asked to show your working.

Don't forget to take a calculator into your exams, or you may ask for one.

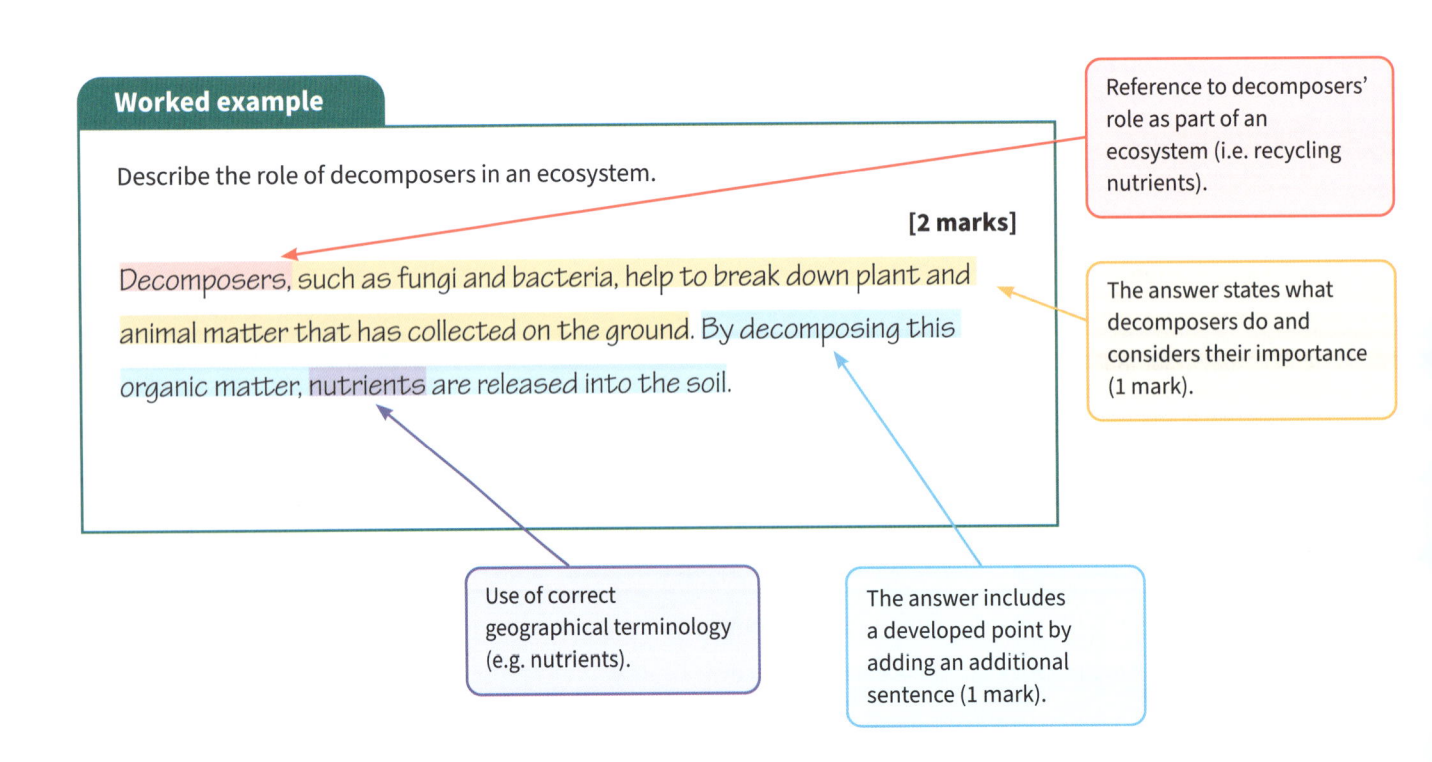

Worked example

Describe the role of decomposers in an ecosystem.

[2 marks]

Decomposers, such as fungi and bacteria, help to break down plant and animal matter that has collected on the ground. By decomposing this organic matter, nutrients are released into the soil.

- Reference to decomposers' role as part of an ecosystem (i.e. recycling nutrients).
- The answer states what decomposers do and considers their importance (1 mark).
- Use of correct geographical terminology (e.g. nutrients).
- The answer includes a developed point by adding an additional sentence (1 mark).

Max your marks

Other short answer questions

Now try this!

1. Study **Figure 1**, a map showing the track of Typhoon Haiyan, November 2013. Numbers 1–5 refer to the Saffir-Simpson hurricane categories.

Figure 1

Saffir-Simpson hurricane categories	
Category	Wind speed (km/h)
1	119–153
2	154–177
3	178–208
4	209–251
5	252 or higher

Tip Use circles on the map to identify the two distinct directions of tracking. This will help to focus your answer on two clear points to gain the 2 marks available for 1.1.

Tip Remember to refer to names of cities, countries and oceans and give directions (e.g. tracking north-westwards).

1.1. Using **Figure 1**, describe the track of Typhoon Haiyan.

[2 marks]

_____
_____
_____
_____

1.2. Using **Figure 1**, state the wind speed of Typhoon Haiyan as it passed through the Philippines.

[1 mark]

_____
_____

1.3. Give **one** reason why the wind speed of a tropical storm (typhoon) may change when it reaches land.

[1 mark]

_____
_____

2.1. Outline why life expectancy is a good measure of a country's level of development.

[2 marks]

_____
_____
_____
_____

Max your marks 39

Mopping up the 1–3-mark questions

Study **Figure 2**, a table showing life expectancy data for selected countries (2015).

Figure 2

Country	Life expectancy at birth, both sexes (years)
Afghanistan	60.5
Bangladesh	71.8
Japan	83.7
Mali	58.2
Norway	81.8
Pakistan	66.4
Peru	75.5
Sierra Leone	50.1
Sri Lanka	74.9
UK	81.2

2.2. Calculate the median value for the life expectancy data in **Figure 2**.

[2 marks]

Show your working.

Median =

2.3. Suggest **one** reason why life expectancy varies between the countries shown in **Figure 2**.

[1 mark]

_____

_____

3. Study **Figure 3**, which is a photo of Thornton Force waterfall in the Yorkshire Dales.

Figure 3

40 Max your marks

Other short answer questions

Using **Figure 3**, draw a simple sketch of the waterfall in the empty box below.
Add labels to identify **two** features of the waterfall.

[3 marks]

> 💡 **Tip**
> There is 1 mark available for your sketch. Draw the outline shape of the waterfall in **Figure 3** and keep it simple. Now add **two** distinct characteristics using arrowed labels. Make sure the tip of the arrow touches the characteristic you are labelling. These labels are worth 1 mark each, making 3 marks in total.

4. Study **Figure 4**, a table showing avocado imports into the UK, 2012–2017.

Figure 4

Year	Avocado imports (1000 tonnes)
2012	38
2013	41
2014	53
2015	77
2016	96
2017	105

4.1. Calculate the percentage increase in avocado imports into the UK between 2012 and 2017. Give your answer to the nearest whole percentage.

[2 marks]

Show your working.

Percentage increase =

4.2. Give **one** environmental effect of the increase shown in **Figure 4**.

[1 mark]

4.3. Describe **one** advantage of sourcing food locally.

[2 marks]

Max your marks 41

Max your marks

Excelling at 4-mark questions

4-mark questions using a resource

In this section you'll learn how to maximise marks on 4-mark questions that use a resource, such as a photo or table of data. 4-mark questions:

- involve writing short paragraphs. To succeed with questions worth 4 or more marks, you must write in full sentences.
- are marked using levels (see page 9). The examiner reads your whole answer first and then decides what mark to give it using specific criteria.

What are the common mistakes?

Like the question below, many 4-mark questions begin with the words 'Using **Figure 1** and your own understanding…'. Many candidates use one or the other – but not both! If you only use **either** Figure 1 **or** your own understanding, you can only gain Level 1 in the mark scheme. That means a maximum of 2 marks. To give you the best chance of receiving high marks, make sure you mention features from Figure 1 **as well as** your own knowledge. First, look at the question below.

Questions using 'suggest'

> Study **Figure 1**. It shows a house damaged by Typhoon Haiyan in 2013.
>
> **Figure 1**
>
> Using **Figure 1** and your own understanding, suggest **two** reasons why tropical storms have such a big impact in low-income countries (LICs).
>
> [4 marks]

For this 4-mark 'suggest' question, you will:

1. Plan your answer
2. Mark an answer
3. Mark a different answer

1. Plan your answer

Before attempting to answer the question, remember to **BUG** it. That means:

✓ **Box** the command word, as shown below.

✓ **Underline** the following:
- The focus of the question
- The evidence you need to answer the question
- The number of reasons you need to give for 4 marks.

✓ **Glance** back over the question to make sure you included everything in your answer.

42 Max your marks

Resource questions: 'suggest'

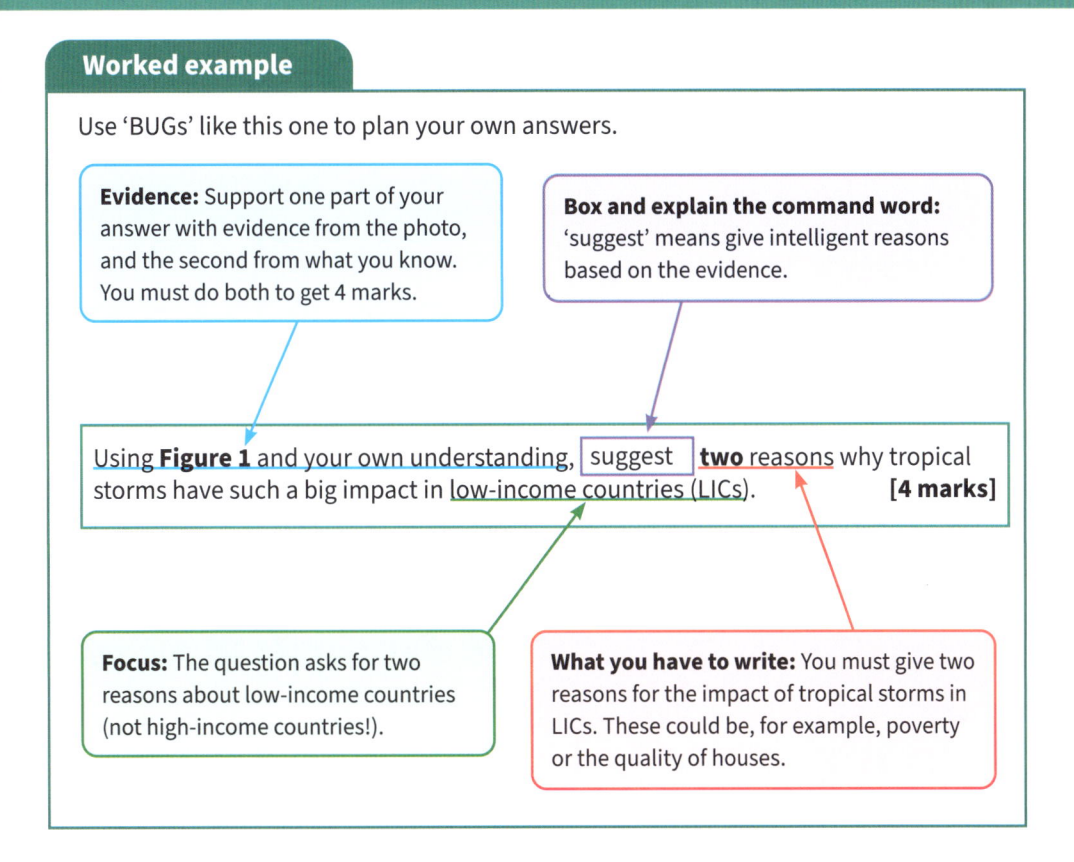

Worked example

Use 'BUGs' like this one to plan your own answers.

Evidence: Support one part of your answer with evidence from the photo, and the second from what you know. You must do both to get 4 marks.

Box and explain the command word: 'suggest' means give intelligent reasons based on the evidence.

Using **Figure 1** and your own understanding, suggest **two** reasons why tropical storms have such a big impact in low-income countries (LICs). **[4 marks]**

Focus: The question asks for two reasons about low-income countries (not high-income countries!).

What you have to write: You must give two reasons for the impact of tropical storms in LICs. These could be, for example, poverty or the quality of houses.

Use the **PEEL** technique (**P**oint, **E**vidence, **E**xplanation, **L**ink) to help you draft your answer. You will have many opportunities to practise PEEL throughout this chapter. PEEL will help you in your GCSE exam to write answers in the clearest way.

Activity 1

Answer the questions below (which are based on the exam question above). They demonstrate the first three stages of PEEL.

(a) **Point:** Make **two** points (i.e. two reasons) why tropical storms have such a big impact on developing countries.

- _____
- _____

(b) **Evidence:** Include **one** piece of evidence from the photo and **one** from your own knowledge to support the above points.

- _____
- _____

(c) **Explanation:** Give **one** reason for each point.

- _____
- _____

(You don't need to use the 'Link' technique for 4-mark questions. But you'll learn more about how to use 'Link' when you're answering 6- and 9-mark questions on pages 56–91).

> **Tip** Aim for quality not quantity! 4-mark answers are not only based on the number of points you make, but also on the overall quality of your answer. This means including content from the figure and your own knowledge, and giving good reasons.

Max your marks

Excelling at 4-mark questions

2. Mark this answer

Activity 2

> **Question recap**
> Using **Figure 1** and your own understanding, suggest **two** reasons why tropical storms have such a big impact in low-income countries (LICs).

Read through the sample answer below and decide whether it's a good answer or not. Do this by following these steps.

(a) Pick out whether it includes any good points, evidence and explanations. Highlight or underline any:

- points in red
- evidence in blue
- explanations in orange.

The photo shows a wooden building which has fallen down, probably during the high winds in a tropical storm which will have destroyed it. The people who live there are probably poor and have no resistance to storms like this.

In the photo, the different building materials (bits of wood, bamboo) show the building was probably cheap to build, but weak. This is typical of developing countries where many people might be very poor.

(b) Use the mark scheme below (just like examiners do) to decide what mark to give. 4-mark questions are not marked using individual points, but by choosing a level and a mark based on the quality of the answer as a whole.

Level	Marks	Descriptor	Examples
2 (Clear)	3–4	• Shows accurate understanding of impacts by applying relevant knowledge and understanding to the photo. • Makes clear and effective use of the photo to explain the impacts of a tropical storm.	• 'Many buildings in developing countries are weak and would collapse during a strong tropical storm. This is because they have few building regulations.' • 'The photo shows poor-quality housing built from wood, which could not stand up to the high winds in a tropical storm.'
1 (Basic)	1–2	• Shows some limited understanding of impacts by applying some knowledge and understanding to the photo. • Makes limited use of the photo to explain the impacts of a tropical storm.	• 'Houses in many poorer countries are built from cheap materials which would fall down in a storm.' • 'Many people living in developing countries do not have money to build houses with proper materials.'
	0	No relevant content.	

(c) Fill in the marking table below showing the strengths and weaknesses of the answer.

Strengths of this answer	
Ways to improve this answer	
The level I would give this answer is…	The mark I would give this answer is…

Max your marks

Resource questions: 'suggest'

Worked example

The sample answer in Activity 2 is marked below. The text has been coloured to show the strengths of the answer, showing:

- points in red
- evidence in blue
- explanations in orange.

Evidence: wooden buildings visible in the photo

Point: the building has fallen down, an essential part of the answer

Explanation: suggests that high winds have destroyed this building and makes the link to tropical storms

The photo shows a wooden building which has fallen down, probably during the high winds in a tropical storm which will have destroyed it. The people who live there are probably poor and have no resistance to storms like this.

Explanation: suggests people are poor with no resistance to tropical storms

In the photo, the different building materials (bits of wood, bamboo) show the building was probably cheap to build, but weak. This is typical of developing countries where many people might be very poor.

Evidence: specific building materials from the photo

Point: the building was cheap to build, which links to the previous point

✓ Examiner feedback

This is a good example of a top Level 2 answer.

- The answer explains the link between the high winds in a tropical storm and the quality of the building. This shows that the candidate has used evidence in the photo.
- The answer explains the weather conditions found during a tropical storm, and how this might affect houses built from cheap, weak building materials. This shows the candidate's understanding.
- In both parts of the answer, the candidate refers directly to the photo.

By meeting the descriptors for Level 2 fully, the answer earns all 4 marks.

3. Mark a different answer

✏️ Activity 3

Now you've marked an answer with some guidance, try marking the answer below (this is answering the same question that can be found on page 42).

- Use the mark scheme and highlight the answer like you did before, using the same colours.
- The mark that the answer got from the examiner is in the answers section at the back of this book.

Wooden shacks like the one in the photo would not be able to stand up to strong hurricane winds so they would fall down.

People in poor countries often live in houses like this on land that isn't theirs.

Max your marks 45

Excelling at 4-mark questions

Questions using 'explain'

Now use the BUG and PEEL stages from pages 42–43 to tackle a different 4-mark question.

Figure 1 shows three measures of development for three countries.

Figure 1

Country	HDI	Death rate per 1000 population	Percentage of population with access to safe water
Japan	0.891	9.51	100
Brazil	0.755	6.58	98
Zimbabwe	0.509	10.13	77

Explain the strengths and limitations of any **one** of the indicators in **Figure 1** in seeking to understand a country's level of development.

[4 marks]

For this 4-mark 'explain' question, you will:
1. Plan your answer
2. Write your answer
3. Mark your answer
4. Mark a different answer
5. Improve an answer

1. Plan your answer

Activity 4

BUG your answer!

Before attempting to answer the question, remember to **BUG** it. Use the guidelines on page 43 to annotate the question in the boxes below.

Evidence:

Box and explain the command word:

Explain the strengths and limitations of any **one** of the indicators in **Figure 1** in seeking to understand a country's level of development.

[4 marks]

Focus:

What you have to write:

46 Max your marks

Resource questions: 'explain'

Activity 5

PEEL your answer!

Use the PEEL guidance on page 43 to help you structure your answer.

(a) **Point:** Make **two** points.

- _____
- _____

(b) **Evidence:** Include **one** advantage of the chosen indicator and **one** disadvantage.

- _____
- _____

(c) **Explanation:** Give **one** reason for each point.

- _____
- _____

(You don't need to use the 'Link' technique for 4-mark questions.)

2. Write your answer

Activity 6

Explain the strengths and limitations of any **one** of the indicators in **Figure 1** in seeking to understand a country's level of development.

[4 marks]

_____
_____
_____
_____
_____
_____
_____
_____

> **Tip**
> Read over your answer, and check that you have:
> a) mentioned examples or data from **Figure 1**
> b) showed some of your own understanding of the data.

Max your marks 47

Excelling at 4-mark questions

3. Mark your answer

Activity 7

(a) To help you to identify if your answer includes well-structured points, highlight the:
- points in red
- explanations in orange
- evidence in blue.

(b) Use the mark scheme below to decide what mark to give your answer.

Remember, 4-mark questions are not marked using individual points. Instead, choose a level and a mark based on the quality of the answer as a whole.

Level	Marks	Descriptor	Examples
2 (Clear)	3–4	• Shows a good understanding of one measure of development, with one clear advantage and one clear disadvantage. • Shows a good understanding of how that measure of development can show a positive or negative picture of a country.	• 'The percentage of people with access to safe water is a useful measure since it shows water quality, which would probably result from higher spending on water.' • 'Water quality shows a country is developing well because, generally, the higher a country's GNI, the better its water, and in turn this would lead to better health.'
1 (Basic)	1–2	• Shows limited understanding of one measure of development, and struggles to give advantages and disadvantages. • Shows limited understanding of how that measure of development can show a positive or negative picture of a country.	• 'Death rate data helps to show how good a country is because if people have good health then they don't die.' • 'Death rates are high in developing countries because living conditions aren't good.'
	0	No relevant content.	

(c) Fill in the marking table below, showing the strengths and weaknesses of the answer.

Strengths of my answer	
Ways to improve my answer	
The level I would give my answer is…	The mark I would give my answer is…

> **Tip** To reach the top marks in Level 2, you must:
>
> a) show that you know the meaning of the development indicator that you have chosen
>
> b) be able to explain one advantage and one disadvantage of the development indicator.
>
> If you cover only one of these, you won't get beyond Level 1.

48 Max your marks

Resource questions: 'explain'

4. Mark a different answer

Activity 8

Read through this sample answer to the same question.

(a) Annotate the answer with the three colours used in Activity 7.

> HDI is a good measure of a country's development, because it shows how well developed a country is socially as well as economically. It is a single figure that combines GDP (to show how wealthy a country is) with literacy (which shows the level of education) and infant mortality (which shows the level of healthcare). So it is a good way of showing how much money is spent on health and education. HDI has a disadvantage because wealthy countries might not have a high HDI figure if wealth is concentrated in the hands of a few wealthy people (like Saudi Arabia), and so does not get spent on most of the population.

> **Question recap**
> Explain the strengths and limitations of any **one** of the indicators in **Figure 1** (page 46) in seeking to understand a country's level of development.

(b) Use the mark scheme in Activity 7 to decide how many marks the answer is worth.

(c) Fill in the marking table below, showing the strengths and weaknesses of the answer.

Strengths of the answer	
Ways to improve the answer	
The level I would give the answer is…	The mark I would give the answer is…

5. Improve this answer

Activity 9

One candidate wrote this answer to the same question. It earns 1 mark.
Continue writing so that the answer earns 4 marks.

Death rate can measure some things about a country's development, because if people's health is poor then they will die.

_____
_____
_____
_____
_____

Max your marks

Excelling at 4-mark questions

Now try this!

Figure 1 shows a map of the geology and rock resistance of a part of the Dorset coast in southern England.

Figure 1

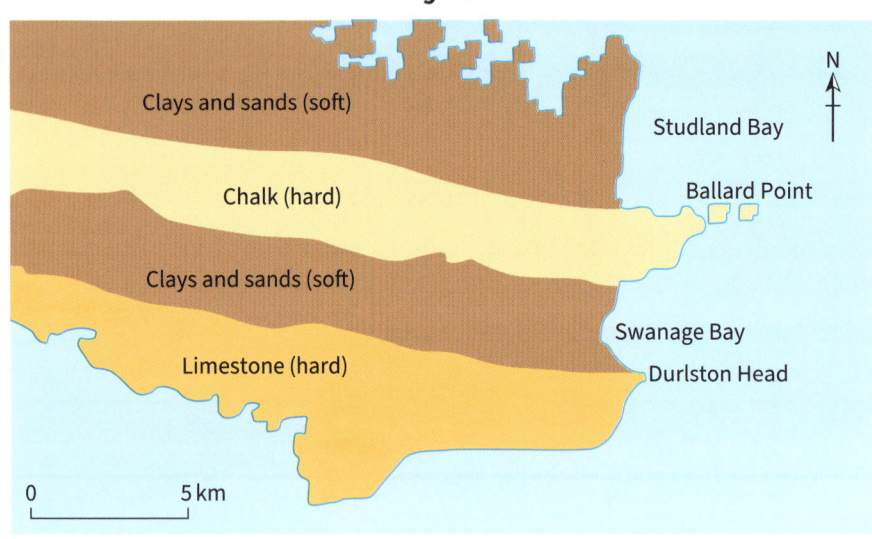

- Clays and sands (soft)
- Chalk (hard)
- Clays and sands (soft)
- Limestone (hard)
- Studland Bay
- Ballard Point
- Swanage Bay
- Durlston Head

0   5 km

Suggest how geology has influenced coastal landforms along the coast shown in **Figure 1**. Use **Figure 1** and your own understanding.

[4 marks]

Tip Follow each stage in Activities 4 and 5 on pages 46–47 to help you tackle this 4-mark question.

Tip To answer this question fully, check that you know the meanings of these words or phrases:
- 'geology'
- 'influenced'
- 'coastal landforms'.

Also, check where you can see coastal landforms on the map.

Max your marks

Knowledge & understanding questions

4-mark questions testing your knowledge and understanding

In this section you'll learn how to maximise marks on 4-mark questions that do not use a resource. They depend on your own knowledge and understanding for a successful answer.

Like other 4-mark questions, they:
- involve short paragraphs of writing
- usually involve explaining a sequence of processes, as the question below shows.

Examiners set this kind of question when they want you to explain how one process leads to another, which leads to another, and so on.
- This kind of explanation is called a 'chain of reasoning'.
- You can learn how to write chains of reasoning by following the steps below.

Worked example

Explain how volcanoes may be formed along constructive plate boundaries.
[4 marks]

To answer this question, you would need to plan a **sequence of statements**. The sequence might look like this:

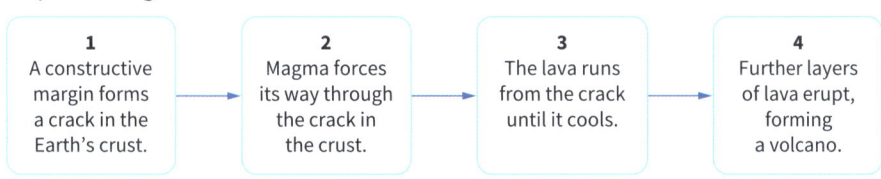

1	2	3	4
A constructive margin forms a crack in the Earth's crust.	Magma forces its way through the crack in the crust.	The lava runs from the crack until it cools.	Further layers of lava erupt, forming a volcano.

The sequence is made up of four statements, written in order. All you need to do is write it out for a perfect 4-mark answer!

Get to know the mark scheme

For the question above, you have to demonstrate:
- knowledge and understanding of a constructive margin
- that you can apply a sequence of processes until you have explained how a volcano forms along a constructive margin.

In the mark scheme below, notice how Level 2 rewards clear understanding of a constructive margin, with a sequence of processes leading to the formation of a volcano.

A Level 1 answer would show some knowledge of the term 'constructive margin', but would not really connect it to the processes leading to a volcano.

Level	Marks	Descriptor	Examples
2 (Clear)	3–4	• Demonstrates a clear understanding of a constructive margin and the processes by which magma reaches the surface. • Application is accurate, with a clear sequence of the processes leading to the formation of a volcano.	• 'A constructive margin forms a crack in the Earth's crust, which magma forces its way through.' • 'The lava runs from the crack until it cools, with later layers of lava forming a volcano.'
1 (Basic)	1–2	• Shows some limited understanding of a constructive margin and the processes by which magma reaches the surface. • Application is weak, with little or no sequencing of the processes leading to the formation of a volcano.	• 'A constructive margin is a crack in the Earth's surface.' • 'Volcanoes form along this crack when hot lava erupts.'
	0	No relevant content.	

Max your marks

Excelling at 4-mark questions

Questions using 'explain'

> Explain how **one** hard method of coastal engineering can protect the coastline.
>
> [4 marks]

For two 4-mark 'explain' questions, you will:
1. Plan your answer
2. Mark an answer
3. Answer a different question
4. Mark your answer

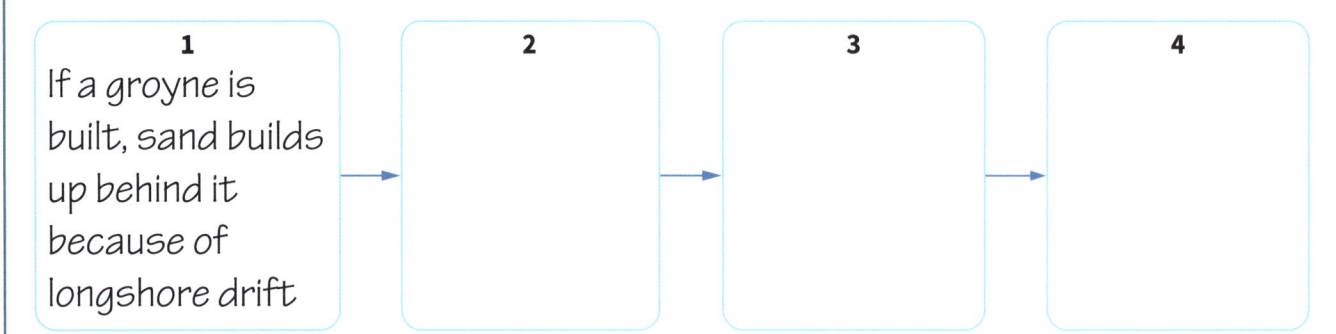

1. Plan your answer

Activity 1

(a) Using the flowchart below, write out the chain of four statements needed to answer this question.

1	2	3	4
If a groyne is built, sand builds up behind it because of longshore drift			

(b) Write four examples in the mark scheme below that you would look for in an answer to this question – 1 and 2 for Level 2, 3 and 4 for Level 1. You could use your chain of reasoning to help you.

Level	Marks	Descriptor	Examples
2 (Clear)	3–4	• Demonstrates a clear understanding of one hard method of coastal engineering and its purpose. • Application is accurate, with a clear sequence of the processes leading to a problem further along the coast.	1 2
1 (Basic)	1–2	• Shows some limited understanding of one hard method of coastal engineering and its purpose. • Application is weak, with little or no sequencing of the processes leading to a problem further along the coast.	3 4
	0	No relevant content.	

2. Mark an answer

Activity 2

Mark this answer using your mark scheme above. Annotate the answer with your own 'Examiner's feedback'.

The job of beach groynes is to trap sand brought by longshore drift. However, by stopping longshore drift, they starve other places of sand further along the coast. Where this happens, there is less beach so the sea can reach the cliff foot and erode it more easily.

Knowledge & understanding questions: 'explain'

3. Answer a different question

Activity 3

Use the steps in Activity 1 on page 52 to help you write your own answer to a different 4-mark question.

> Explain how a change of land use could lead to an increased risk of flooding.
> [4 marks]

_____

_____

_____

_____

_____

_____

_____

_____

_____

4. Mark your answer

Activity 4

(a) Write four examples in the mark scheme that you would look for in an answer to this question.

Level	Marks	Descriptor		Examples	
2 (Clear)	3–4	• Demonstrates a clear understanding of how changes of land use can affect rivers and the likelihood of flooding.	1		
		• Application is accurate with a clear sequence of the processes leading to flooding.	2		
1 (Basic)	1–2	• Shows some limited understanding of how changes of land use can affect rivers and the likelihood of flooding.	3		
		• Application is weak with little or no sequencing of the processes leading to flooding.	4		
	0	No relevant content.			

(b) Mark your answer to Activity 3 using this mark scheme.

The level I would give the answer is…		The mark I would give the answer is…	
Comments			

Max your marks

Excelling at 4-mark questions

Extra practice questions

Now try this!

1. Study **Figure 1**, which shows the location of derelict land and the most deprived areas of Glasgow.

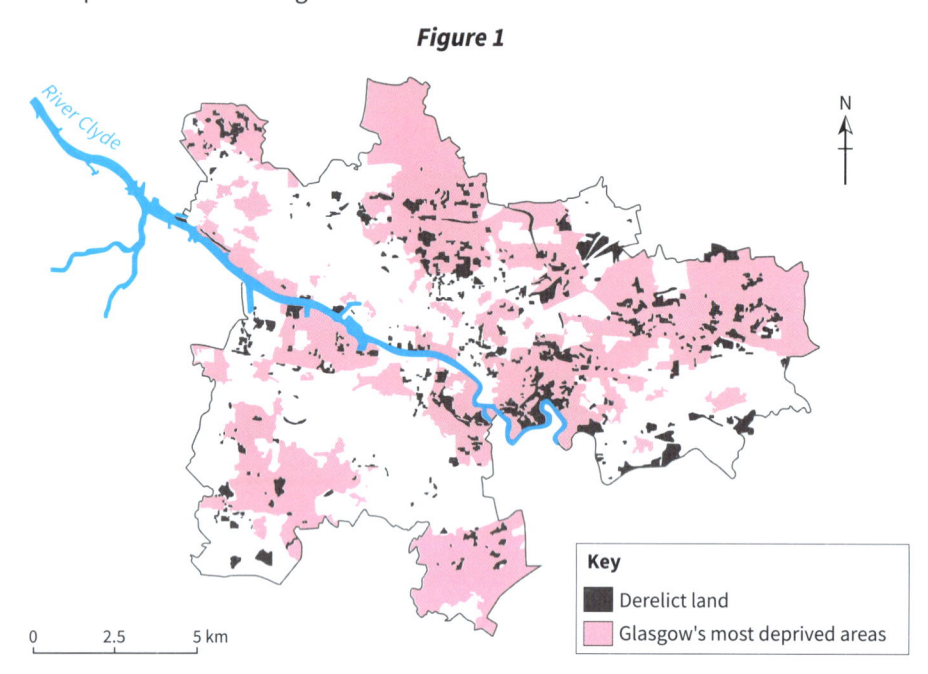

Figure 1

Key
- Derelict land
- Glasgow's most deprived areas

Tip Use the steps in Activity 1 on page 52 to help you answer these questions.

Using **Figure 1**, suggest reasons why derelict land and the most deprived areas of Glasgow can be found in similar parts of the city.

[4 marks]

Strengths of my answer	
Ways to improve my answer	
The level I would give my answer is…	The mark I would give my answer is…

Max your marks

Extra practice questions

2. Study **Figure 2**, showing a slum area in a megacity in one of the world's low-income countries (LICs) or newly emerging economies (NEEs).

Figure 2

Using **Figure 2**, explain how urban growth in low-income countries (LICs) or newly emerging economies (NEEs) has affected quality of life.

[4 marks]

Strengths of my answer	
Ways to improve my answer	
The level I would give my answer is…	The mark I would give my answer is…

Max your marks 55

Max your marks
Stepping up to 6-mark questions

In this section you'll learn how to tackle 6-mark questions that use 'explain', 'suggest' or 'discuss' as a command word.

6-mark questions differ from 4-mark ones:

- They are marked using three levels, not two.
- Levels 1 and 2 are the same standard as Levels 1 and 2 in the 4-mark questions, but Level 3 is more challenging, worth 5–6 marks.

Explain or suggest – what's the difference?

- With 'explain', you're expected to **know**, as these questions test you on what you've been taught in the specification. You could be asked to explain a statement, for example.
- With 'suggest', examiners accept you might **not know**, but are confident that you could make intelligent suggestions, based on what you understand.

What are the common mistakes?

Many 6-mark questions begin 'Using **Figure 1** and your own understanding…'.

- Many candidates use one or the other, but not both!
- If you only use **either** Figure 1 **or** your own understanding, you can only get Level 2 in the mark scheme. That means a maximum of 4 marks.

To succeed, mention features from the figure **as well as** your own understanding.

Questions using 'explain'

First, look at the question below.

> Study **Figure 1**, showing deposition of sediment at Hurst Castle, Hampshire
>
> **Figure 1**
>
> Using **Figure 1** and your own understanding, explain how different landforms may be created by the deposition of sediment.
>
> [6 marks]

Tip Practise aiming for Level 3 on the 6-mark mark schemes. It's easier to earn 3–4 marks just by explaining what you know, but hitting Level 3 every time could see you on your way to a grade 7, 8 or 9!

Tip A 4-mark question might ask:

'Explain two economic impacts of a volcanic eruption.'

A 6-mark question might ask:

'"Volcanic eruptions can have major economic impacts."

Using evidence, explain this statement.'

Tip Note that this question is about Coasts. If you have studied River landscapes and Glacial landscapes, you can still work through this chapter but use a different photo from the *GCSE 9-1 Geography AQA Student Book*.

- For River landscapes, use Photo A on page 134.
- For Glacial landscapes, use Photo C at the top of page 153.

Max your marks

Questions using 'explain'

1. Plan your answer

Before attempting to answer the question, remember to **BUG** it. That means:

✓ **Box** the command word, as shown below.

✓ **Underline** the following:
- The focus of the question
- The evidence you need to answer the question
- The number of reasons you need to give for 6 marks.

✓ **Glance** back over the question to make sure you included everything in your answer.

> For this 6-mark 'explain' question, you will:
> 1. Plan your answer
> 2. Mark an answer
> 3. Mark a different answer

Worked example

Use 'BUGs' like this one to plan your own answers.

Evidence: Support one part of your answer with evidence from the photo, and the second part from what you know. You must do both to get 6 marks.

Box and explain the command word: 'Explain' means you have to give reasons for what happens.

Using Figure 1 and your own understanding, [explain] how **different landforms** may be created by **deposition** of sediment. **[6 marks]**

Focus: The question asks for landforms created by **deposition**, not erosion!

What you have to write: The question asks for 'different landforms'. For 6 marks, you must write about two in detail, or three in less detail.

Use the **PEEL** technique to help you draft your answer.

Activity 1

Answer the questions below (which are based on the exam question above).

(a) **Point:** Make **two** points about how **two** different landforms are created by deposition.

- _____
- _____

(b) **Evidence:** Include **one** piece of evidence from the photo and **one** from your own understanding to support the above points.

- _____
- _____

(c) **Explanation:** Give **two** reasons that show how the landforms have formed.

- _____
- _____

(d) **Link:** Round each point off by linking back to the question (start with a phrase like 'This shows how deposition has…'). It helps you to stay with the question.

- _____
- _____

> 💡 **Tip** If the question asks you to explain, it wants you to give **reasons** why something happens. Don't just describe. For example, this question would want you to say **how** deposition processes lead to particular landforms, not just give a description of the landform.

Max your marks 57

Stepping up to 6-mark questions

2. Mark this answer

Activity 2

Read through the sample answer below and decide how well the student has answered the question on page 56. Do this by following these steps.

(a) Pick out whether it includes any good points, evidence and explanations. Highlight or underline the text to show the following strengths of the answer:

- Points in red
- Evidence in blue
- Explanations in orange
- Links back to the question underlined

The photo shows a spit that has been formed from sand washed up by the waves on the beach. The waves approach at an angle and the swash takes the sand up the beach, then it runs back down in a zig-zag pattern. Then another wave picks it up, and deposits it further along the beach, and so on, until it forms an extension of land as shown in the photo. The sand moves along the beach until it reaches a river, and the photo shows how the river current has shaped it where the water runs out to sea. It looks like the river in the photo has shaped the spit into a hook as it has grown.

Another landform formed by deposition is a sand bar, which is just like a spit except that there is no river to stop the movement of sand. The sand keeps on moving until it cuts off a lake or lagoon. So this shows how important deposition is to forming this landform.

Question recap

Using **Figure 1** and your own understanding, explain how different landforms may be created by the deposition of sediment.

(b) Use the mark scheme below to decide what mark to give. 6-mark questions are not marked using individual points, but by choosing a level and a mark based on the quality of the answer as a whole.

Level	Marks	Descriptor	Examples
3 (Detailed)	5–6	• Shows thorough application of knowledge and understanding to analyse information, giving detailed explanation of the formation of coastal features. • Makes full analysis of the photo, using evidence to support the answer.	• 'The coastal spit shown has been formed by two sets of processes. The main one is longshore drift, caused by winds creating waves which hit the shore at an angle and deposit sand.' • 'Figure 1 shows a coastal spit that has forced the river to divert from where it used to reach the sea.'
2 (Clear)	3–4	• Demonstrates specific and accurate knowledge of coastal processes and landforms. • Shows thorough understanding of the links between coastal processes and landforms.	• 'Coastal spits are formed when waves break on the shore at an angle and take sediment along the coast, forming a long sandy headland into the water.' • 'Figure 1 shows how the river stops the spit from forming a bar, that would join the two bits of coast together.'
1 (Basic)	1–2	• Demonstrates some knowledge of coastal processes and landforms. • Shows limited geographical understanding of the links between coastal processes and landforms.	• 'The spit comes from waves that break on the beach and longshore drift takes place.' • 'The photo shows a long sandy beach that has been deposited by waves.'
	0	No relevant content.	

Questions using 'explain'

(c) Fill in the marking table below showing the strengths and weaknesses of the answer.

Strengths of this answer	
Ways to improve this answer	
The level I would give this answer is…	The mark I would give this answer is…

Worked example

The sample answer in Activity 2 is marked below, so you can compare your marking with this. The text has been coloured and underlined to show the following strengths of the answer:

- Points in red
- Evidence in blue
- Explanations in orange
- Links back to the question underlined

Point: the candidate names a correct landform and states that it's formed of sand

Explanation: the process of how the spit begins to form is described

Evidence: the candidate supports the process with evidence from the photo. This kind of evidence is important when you need to explain processes as a sequence of stages.

The photo shows a spit that has been formed from sand washed up by the waves on the beach. The waves approach at an angle and the swash takes the sand up the beach, then it runs back down in a zig-zag pattern. Then another wave picks it up, and deposits it further along the beach, and so on, until it forms an extension of land as shown in the photo. The sand moves along the beach until it reaches a river, and the photo shows how the river current has shaped it where the water runs out to sea. It looks like the river in the photo has shaped the spit into a hook as it has grown.

Evidence: the photo supports the part in the process played by the river

Evidence: the photo supports how the river is affected by the spit

Another landform formed by deposition is a sand bar, which is just like a spit except that there is no river to stop the movement of sand. The sand keeps on moving until it cuts off a lake or lagoon. So this shows how important deposition is to forming this landform.

Point: the candidate names a second depositional landform

Link: this is where the candidate links back to the original question

Explanation: the process of bar formation is explained

Max your marks 59

Stepping up to 6-mark questions

> **Examiner feedback**
>
> This answer gets a Level 3 – but only just! The strengths are that this candidate:
> - describes landform formation in some detail
> - names two landforms accurately
> - explains the formation as a sequence of events
> - explains the difference between a spit and a bar
> - uses the photo well, recognising and naming landforms, and explaining the impact of the spit on the route taken by the river.
>
> To reach the top of Level 3, the candidate would need to spend more time explaining the second landform so that the two are treated equally.
>
> The answer is a low Level 3 in quality, so it's worth 5 marks.

3. Mark a different answer

Activity 3

Now mark this answer in just the same way as in the example above. Use the mark scheme in Activity 2 to list the strengths and weaknesses of the answer in the table below.

> **Question recap**
>
> Using **Figure 1** and your own understanding, explain how different landforms may be created by the deposition of sediment.

Coastal spits are formed by a number of processes. The main process is longshore drift. This happens when prevailing winds reach the coast at an angle. The waves break on the shore at an angle and then run back down the beach in a kind of zig-zag. This is then repeated many times. Each time a wave breaks, it takes sand and pebbles up the beach, which move in the direction of the waves. Gradually, more sand gets taken along the beach, sometimes blocking off a small inlet to form a sand bar (also called a tombolo) across its mouth. But the one in the photo is where a river cuts through the bar and this forms a spit.

Strengths of this answer	
Ways to improve this answer	
The level I would give this answer is…		The mark I would give this answer is…	

Max your marks

Questions using 'suggest'

Questions using 'suggest'

Now use the stages you followed to answer the question on page 56 to tackle a different 6-mark question.

This time, the command word is 'suggest'. This means that you should look at **Figure 1** and think about what you know about rainforest clearance. Then make suggestions about what could happen based on **Figure 1** and what you know and understand.

> **For this 6-mark 'suggest' question, you will:**
> 1. Plan your answer
> 2. Write your answer
> 3. Mark your answer
> 4. Mark different answers

Study **Figure 1**. It shows a rainforest in Borneo, Indonesia that has been cleared to make way for a plantation for farming.

Figure 1

Using **Figure 1** and your own understanding, suggest the impacts of rainforest clearance in Indonesia.

[6 marks]

---

1. Plan your answer

Activity 1

Before attempting to answer the question, remember to **BUG** it. There are some hints about what to write in the boxes on page 57, and you should use these to annotate the boxes below.

Evidence:	Box and explain the command word:

Using **Figure 1** and your own understanding, suggest the impacts of rainforest clearance in Indonesia.

[6 marks]

Focus:	What you have to write:

Max your marks

Stepping up to 6-mark questions

Activity 2

Use the **PEEL** guidance on page 57 to help you structure your answer.

(a) **Point:**

- _____
- _____

(b) **Evidence:**

- _____
- _____

(c) **Explanation:**

- _____
- _____

(d) **Link:**

- _____
- _____

2. Write your answer

Activity 3

> Using **Figure 1** (page 61) and your own understanding, suggest the impacts of rainforest clearance in Indonesia. **[6 marks]**

_____
_____
_____
_____
_____
_____
_____
_____
_____
_____
_____

Max your marks

Questions using 'suggest'

3. Mark your answer

Activity 4

(a) To help you to identify the strengths of your answer, highlight the:
- points in red
- explanations in orange
- evidence in blue
- and underline any links back to the question.

(b) Use the mark scheme below to decide what mark to give your answer. Remember, 6-mark questions are not marked using individual points. Instead, choose a level and a mark based on the quality of the answer as a whole.

Level	Marks	Descriptor	Examples
3 (Detailed)	5–6	• Provides a range of reasons and impacts which are well developed. There is detailed understanding of these impacts. • Shows thorough identification of the evidence for the impacts of forest clearance in the photo, and understands potential impacts.	• 'The removal of forest cover would expose the soils to heavy tropical rains, which would erode the soil, making the land useless for farming.' • 'The bare soil in the photo shows how exposed it would be to wind or rain, or tropical sun.'
2 (Clear)	3–4	• Gives one to two reasons with some development of points. There is a generally accurate understanding of the impacts. • Makes clear and effective use of the photo to explain the impacts of clearing the forest.	• 'Removing the trees would mean less protection for the soil from heavy rain – runoff would occur and probably take the soil with it.' • 'The photo shows little vegetation to protect the soil so it would probably be lost.'
1 (Basic)	1–2	• Shows some limited understanding of the impacts by applying some knowledge and understanding to the photo. • Makes limited use of the photo to explain the impacts of clearing the forest.	• 'The land is all bare and there are no trees there. The rain would wash it away.' • 'The photo shows all the trees have been cut and burned and there's nothing there.'
	0	No relevant content.	

(c) Fill in the marking table below, showing the strengths and weaknesses of your answer.

Strengths of my answer	
Ways to improve my answer	
The level I would give my answer is…	The mark I would give my answer is…

Max your marks 63

Stepping up to 6-mark questions

4. Mark these different answers

Activity 5

Read through the two sample answers below. This answers the same question.

(a) Annotate each answer using the three colours and underlining as explained in Activity 7 above.

(b) Use the mark scheme in Activity 7 to decide on a level and how many marks each answer is worth.

(c) Fill in the marking table for each answer.

Question recap

Using **Figure 1** and your own understanding, suggest the impacts of rainforest clearance in Indonesia.

Sample answer 1

The forest looks like it has been cleared by burning. The land looks full of tree roots, meaning that it will not be easy to plant crops. The soil is black, which is probably ash from all the burnt trees after the fires have gone out. The next time it rains, the ash will probably get washed away because it looks like the land is sloping a bit, and farmers might find there is no soil left by the time they get to plant their crops. There is no wildlife, which probably got killed in the fires. Lots of rainforests get cleared by burning like this.

Strengths of the answer	
Ways to improve the answer	
The level I would give the answer is…	The mark I would give the answer is…

Sample answer 2

The impacts of burning on this area of rainforest cannot be underestimated. It has probably been cleared for farming but the tree roots will make that difficult. However, it is helpful that they have been left because otherwise the soil would be eroded, now that it is exposed. Tropical rains are heavy so erosion would be serious and the sloping land would make this worse. The ash of the burnt trees in the photo is probably the only fertile part of the soil as rainforest soils are generally infertile once the forest is removed – there are no leaves to maintain fertility any more. The rainforest fauna have deserted or been killed by the fires so their role in the ecosystem is lost forever.

Strengths of the answer	
Ways to improve the answer	
The level I would give the answer is…	The mark I would give the answer is…

Max your marks

Questions using 'discuss'

Questions using 'discuss'

Here is a new 6-mark question for you to tackle.

This time, the command word is 'discuss'. This means you should look at **Figure 1** and think about what you know about the impacts of international migration on a major UK city that you have studied.

Then make suggestions about the impacts based on **Figure 1** and on what you know and understand.

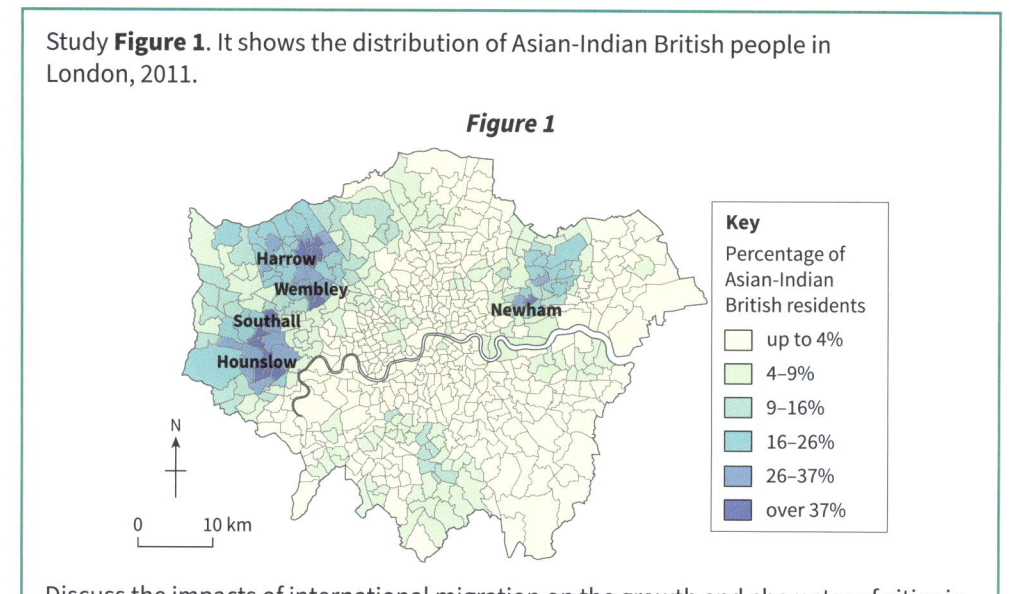

> Study **Figure 1**. It shows the distribution of Asian-Indian British people in London, 2011.
>
> **Figure 1**
>
> Key: Percentage of Asian-Indian British residents
> - up to 4%
> - 4–9%
> - 9–16%
> - 16–26%
> - 26–37%
> - over 37%
>
> (Areas labelled: Harrow, Wembley, Southall, Hounslow, Newham)
>
> Discuss the impacts of international migration on the growth and character of cities in the UK. Use **Figure 1** and a major UK city you have studied.
>
> [6 marks]

Tip

'Discuss' means using a range of examples, in this case to cover a range of impacts. Don't just describe and explain! For example, the question 'Discuss the impacts of rainforest clearance' would want you to say whether impacts are positive or negative, or perhaps whether they are economic, social or environmental.

For this 6-mark 'discuss' question, you will:
1. Plan your answer
2. Write your answer
3. Mark your answer
4. Mark different answers

1. Plan your answer

Activity 1

Before attempting to answer the question, remember to **BUG** it. There are some hints about what to write in the boxes on page 57, and you should use these to annotate the boxes below.

Evidence:

Box and explain the command word:

> Discuss the impacts of international migration on the growth and character of cities in the UK. Use **Figure 1** and your case study of a major city in the UK.
>
> [6 marks]

Focus:

What you have to write:

Max your marks 65

Stepping up to 6-mark questions

Activity 2

Use the **PEEL** guidance on page 57 to help you structure your answer.

(a) **Point:**

- _____
- _____

(b) **Evidence:**

- _____
- _____

(c) **Explanation:**

- _____
- _____

(d) **Link:**

- _____
- _____

2. Write your answer

Activity 3

Discuss the impacts of international migration on the growth and character of cities in the UK. Use **Figure 1** (page 65) and a major UK city you have studied. **[6 marks]**

_____
_____
_____
_____
_____
_____
_____
_____
_____
_____

Max your marks

Questions using 'discuss'

3. Mark your answer

Activity 4

(a) To help you to identify the strengths of your answer, highlight the:
- points in red
- explanations in orange
- evidence in blue
- and underline any links back to the question.

(b) Use the mark scheme below to decide what mark to give your answer. Remember, 6-mark questions are not marked using individual points. Instead, choose a level and a mark based on the quality of the answer as a whole.

Level	Marks	Descriptor	Examples
3 (Detailed)	5–6	• Shows thorough understanding of the impacts of international migration on the growth and character of a named UK city. • Shows thorough application of knowledge and understanding in interpreting the map about the impacts of international migration.	• 'The impacts of immigration have been great, especially on the culture of UK cities. In Manchester, the Curry Mile attracts tourists as well as increasing the range of foods in the city.' • 'Figure 1 shows that immigrants from particular countries, religions or cultures tend to live in areas close to each other, creating suburbs like Southall in west London.'
2 (Clear)	3–4	• Shows sound understanding of the impacts of international migration on the growth and character of a named UK city. • Shows sound application of knowledge and understanding in interpreting the map about the impacts of international migration.	• 'Immigration has been the reason for half the recent growth of cities such as Bristol. In Bristol there are over 50 languages spoken in the city now.' • 'Figure 1 shows that immigrants often settle in suburbs where there are cultural or ethnic groups like their own.'
1 (Basic)	1–2	• Shows limited understanding of the impacts of international migration on the growth and character of a named UK city. • Shows limited application of knowledge and understanding in interpreting the map about the impacts of international migration.	• 'Bristol has a lot of immigrants living there so the city is growing.' • 'Immigrants often live in the same sorts of areas where they have shops and places of worship they are familiar with, and they like living there.'
	0	No relevant content.	

(c) Fill in the marking table below, showing the strengths and weaknesses of the answer.

Strengths of my answer	
Ways to improve my answer	
The level I would give my answer is…	The mark I would give my answer is…

Max your marks

Stepping up to 6-mark questions

4. Mark these different answers

Activity 5

Read through the two sample answers below. This answers the same question.

(a) Annotate each answer using the three colours and underlining as explained in Activity 4.

(b) Use the mark scheme in Activity 4 to decide on a level and how many marks each answer is worth.

(c) Fill in the marking table showing the strengths and weaknesses of each answer.

Sample answer 1

Half of Bristol's population growth in recent years has been due to migrants from overseas, from countries such as Poland, because of the jobs available there such as in construction and the NHS. International migration has affected Bristol because people from over 50 countries have settled there. Over 6000 people live in Bristol who were born in Poland.

Like the map in Figure 1, many immigrants have changed the character of the parts of the city where they live by introducing new shops or places of worship. This changes the culture in cities and there are festivals like the Notting Hill Carnival in London. So immigration has had a big effect on cities.

> **Question recap**
> Discuss the impacts of international migration on the growth and character of cities in the UK. Use **Figure 1** (page 65) and a major UK city you have studied.

Strengths of the answer	
Ways to improve the answer	
The level I would give the answer is…	The mark I would give the answer is…

Sample answer 2

Much of Bristol's growth in recent years has been because of migrants from overseas. They have come here for jobs in things such as hotels or bus driving, or working in the NHS. International migration changes Bristol because people have come from all over the world. They have set up restaurants here and made cities livelier places to live in. There are all sorts of festivals like the Notting Hill Carnival in London that would not have happened if it wasn't for immigrant communities.

Strengths of the answer	
Ways to improve the answer	
The level I would give the answer is…	The mark I would give the answer is…

Max your marks

Extra practice questions

Extra practice questions

Now try this!

1. **Tectonic hazards**

    Figure 1 shows how the impact of a tectonic hazard is managed.

    Figure 1

    > Two strategies are important in managing the impact of tectonic hazards.
    >
    > 1. **Reduce the impact of the hazard**
    >   - Different equipment can help to predict and identify major events.
    >   - Hazard mapping can identify areas at risk from hazards.
    >   - Setting up evacuation zones can help to reduce the impact of a hazard.
    >
    > 2. **Improve ways of coping with the hazard**
    >   - Educating people about what to do and having regular earthquake drills.
    >   - Having well-trained and well-equipped emergency service teams.
    >   - Designing buildings to better withstand earthquakes.

    'Different methods can be used to reduce the effects of a tectonic hazard.'

    Using **Figure 1** and your own understanding, explain this statement.

    [6 marks]

The level I would give the answer is…		The mark I would give the answer is…	
Comments			

Max your marks

Stepping up to 6-mark questions

2. **Tropical storms**

   Figure 2 shows predictions about the future impacts of tropical storms.

   Figure 2

   > Climate scientists predict that the impacts of tropical storms could become more severe in the future, because of:
   > - warmer ocean surface temperatures
   > - higher sea levels
   > - greater wind speeds
   > - higher rainfall brought by such storms.

   'Climate change might affect the distribution, frequency, intensity and impact of tropical storms.'

   Using **Figure 2** and your own understanding, suggest how the impacts of tropical storms might change.

   [6 marks]

The level I would give the answer is…		The mark I would give the answer is…	
Comments			

Max your marks

Extra practice questions

3. **The changing economic world**

Study **Figure 3**, a photo of one of the companies that manufactures Apple products in China.

Figure 3

'TNCs bring a mixture of advantages and disadvantages to a host country.'

Using **Figure 3** and your own understanding, discuss this statement.

[6 marks]

The level I would give the answer is…		The mark I would give the answer is…	
Comments			

Max your marks

Stepping up to 6-mark questions

4. **Economic futures in the UK**

   Figure 4 is a map the University of Southampton Science Park (highlighted in yellow).

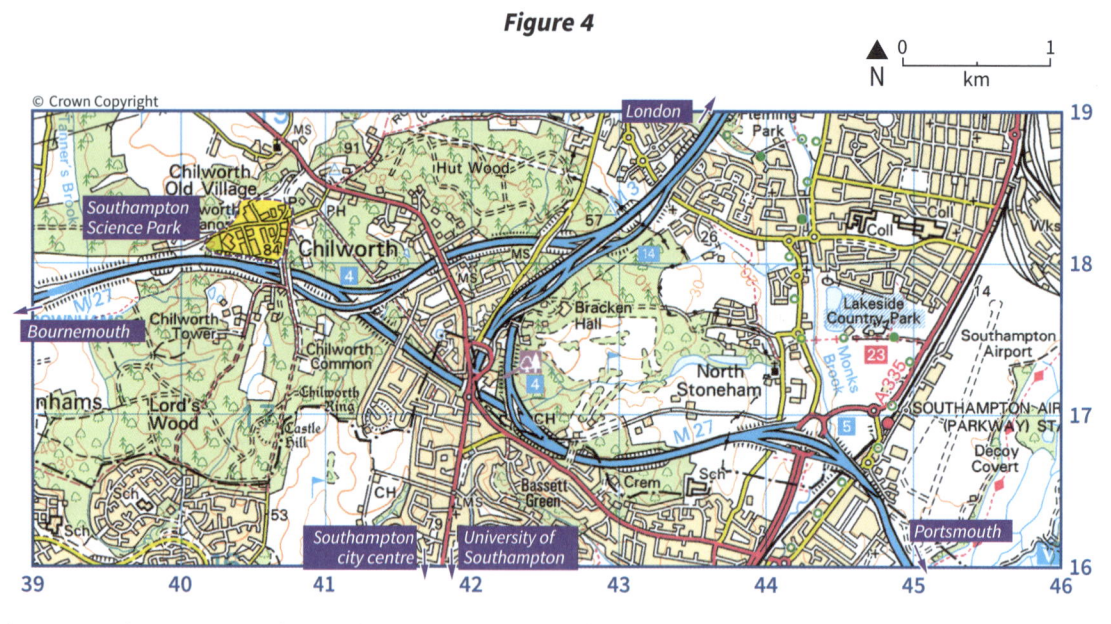

   Figure 4

   Using **Figure 4** and your own understanding, suggest reasons for the location of the Science Park.

   [6 marks]

The level I would give the answer is…		The mark I would give the answer is…	
Comments			

Max your marks

Extra practice questions

5. Urban issues and challenges

Figure 4 shows push and pull factors in the growth of megacities.

Figure 5

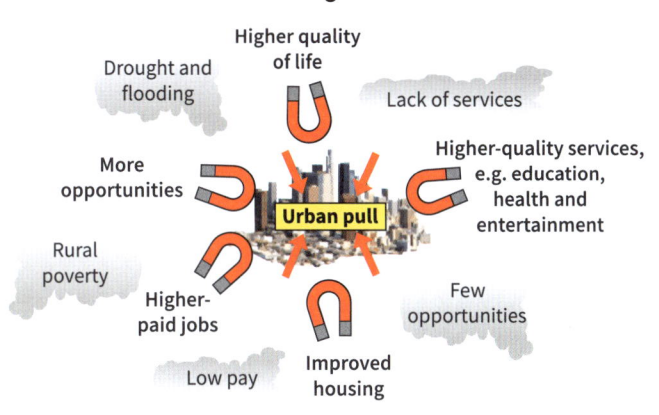

Higher quality of life
Drought and flooding
Lack of services
More opportunities
Higher-quality services, e.g. education, health and entertainment
Urban pull
Rural poverty
Higher-paid jobs
Few opportunities
Low pay
Improved housing

'The growth of large megacities in LICs or NEEs has brought advantages to the millions of migrants who move to such cities each year.'

Using **Figure 5**, suggest why some might disagree with this statement.

[6 marks]

The level I would give the answer is…		The mark I would give the answer is…	
Comments			

Max your marks 73

Max your marks
Hitting the heights on 9-mark questions

In this section you'll learn how to tackle 9-mark questions that use 'evaluate', 'do you agree?', 'assess' or 'to what extent' as command words.

9-mark questions differ from 6-mark questions:

- 9 marks are available, not 6 – so you must write more.
- The levels in the mark scheme are tougher. This is reflected in the marks: Level 1 ranges from 1 to 3 marks, Level 2 from 4 to 6 marks, and Level 3 from 7 to 9 marks.
- Command words are more demanding. Nine-mark questions use some of the same command words as 6-mark ones (e.g. 'discuss'), but they also use 'evaluate' and 'to what extent' and 'do you agree…?'.
- 9-mark questions may give you a statement and ask whether you agree with it or not. That means you have to develop an argument to support or reject the statement.

> **Tip** Don't leave out the 9-mark questions just because they're tough. You can earn 3–4 marks just by explaining what you know, even though you might not be sure how to set up an argument.

Questions using 'evaluate'

What does 'evaluate' mean?

Examiners may use 'evaluate' instead of 'explain' as the command word for 9-mark questions. Here's the key difference:

- With 'explain', you're expected to **know**, as these questions test you on what you've been taught in the specification.
- With 'evaluate', examiners are asking you to **make judgements** about different opinions. There will usually be two sides to an argument, so make sure you acknowledge both sides.
- Remember, 'evaluate' is all about **weighing up evidence and making a judgement** – do you agree or not?

Don't forget SPaG

One of the 9-mark questions on each of Papers 1 and 2 will assess your accuracy of spelling, punctuation, grammar and the use of specialist terminology (known as SPaG). You can be awarded up to 3 marks for SPaG for these questions.

What are the common mistakes?

Questions that use 'evaluate' as a command word are setting you up for an argument. Many candidates do not do this; instead, they just describe or explain. To reach top marks, you need to:

- Show your knowledge and understanding that supports the argument. Use phrases such as 'I agree with the statement because…'.
- Show your knowledge and understanding of the other side of the argument. Use phrases such as 'On the other hand…' or 'However, there is another side…'.
- Write a one-sentence conclusion to say whether you think the statement is wrong or right, and why.

> **Tip** Examiners mark SPaG based on:
> - the accuracy of your spelling
> - how well you use paragraphs
> - the accuracy of your punctuation (the use of commas, full stops and semi-colons, etc.).
>
> Try reading your practice answers aloud and see if they leave you gasping for breath – if they do, you need more punctuation!

Questions using 'evaluate'

In this section we will look at how to plan and write an answer to a 9-mark question, and also consider how an examiner would mark it. First, look at the question below.

Study **Figure 1**, which shows estimated increases in global temperatures (°C) 1960–2100.

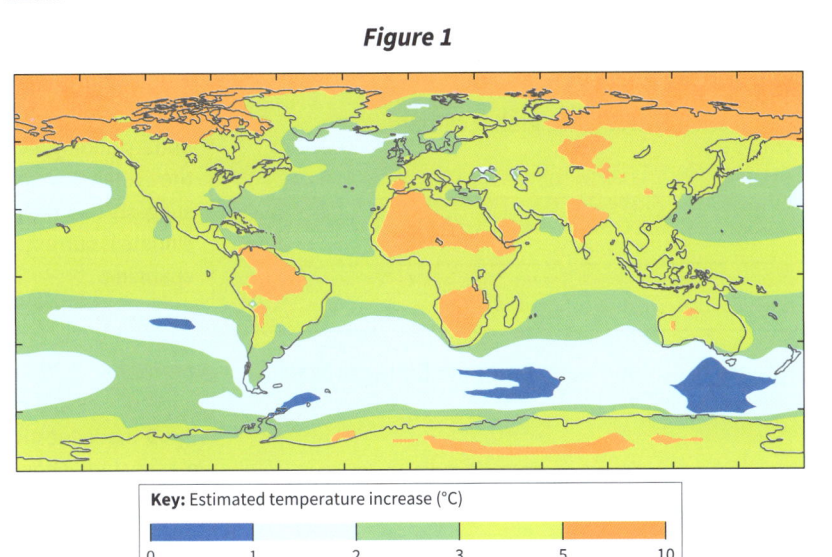

Figure 1

Key: Estimated temperature increase (°C)

0   1   2   3   5   10

Using **Figure 1** and your own understanding, evaluate the evidence which suggests that the global climate is currently changing.

[9 marks] [+3 SPaG marks]

For this 9-mark 'evaluate' question, you will:
1. Plan your answer
2. Mark an answer
3. Mark a different answer

1. Plan your answer

Before attempting to answer the question, remember to **BUG** it. That means:

✓ **Box** the command word, as shown below.

✓ **Underline** the following:
- The focus of the question
- The evidence you need to answer the question
- The number of reasons you need to give for 9 marks.

✓ **Glance** back over the question to make sure you have included everything in your answer.

Worked example

Use 'BUGs' like this one to plan your own answers.

Box and explain the command word: 'Evaluate' means you need to weigh up the evidence – is it strong or weak?

Focus: The question asks for evidence that the global climate is changing, **and** you have to weigh it up!

Using **Figure 1** and your own understanding, ⬚evaluate⬚ the **evidence** which suggests that the **global climate is currently changing**.

[9 marks] [+3 SPaG marks]

What you have to write: The question asks for evidence of global climate change.

Evidence: In one part of your answer, give evidence that the global climate is changing. Then weigh it up in the second part – how strong is it? You must do both to get 9 marks.

Max your marks

Hitting the heights on 9-mark questions

Use the **PEEL** technique to help you draft your answer. **PEEL** will help you in your GCSE exam to write answers in the clearest way. Note that, whereas you would normally make two statements for each of Point, Evidence, Explanation and Link for a 6-mark question, you need to write three of each for a 9-mark question.

Activity 1

Answer the questions below. They demonstrate the four stages of PEEL.

(a) **Point:** Make **three** points about evidence for a changing global climate.

- _____
- _____
- _____

(b) **Evidence:** Include **one** piece of evidence to support each point (including at least one reference to **Figure 1**).

- _____
- _____
- _____

(c) **Explanation:** Weigh up each piece of evidence to show how strong it is as evidence for a changing global climate.

- _____
- _____
- _____

(d) **Link:** Link back to the question to show the importance or strength of each piece of evidence. Start with a phrase like 'This evidence is very reliable in the argument about climate change because…'.

- _____
- _____
- _____

Question recap

Using **Figure 1** (page 75) and your own understanding, evaluate the evidence which suggests that the global climate is currently changing.

Tip

'Evaluate' in this 9-mark question means stating how strong each piece of evidence is.

- To hit the highest marks, select a piece of evidence first and make a judgement about how strong it is (that's your **point**).
- Then give your **evidence**. For example, evidence for a changing global climate might be shrinking glaciers in the Arctic.
- Then you need to say whether this is strong evidence or not, and why (your **explanation**).
- Then draw it together in a mini-conclusion that **links** back to the question – it need only be a sentence or so.

Hitting Level 3

1 **Include detail**, e.g. how scientific research shows average global sea level has risen by 10–20 cm since 1920.

2 **Explain processes clearly**, step-by-step, e.g. how rising global temperatures have melted ice caps and glaciers, meaning that more water goes into the sea.

3 **Apply what you know** to answer the question, e.g. how the evidence for climate change is reliable as it comes from the world's best climate scientists.

Max your marks

Questions using 'evaluate'

2. Mark this answer

Activity 2

Read through the sample answer below and decide whether it's a good answer or not. Do this by following these steps.

(a) Pick out whether it includes any good points, evidence and explanations. Highlight or underline the text to show the following strengths of the answer:
- Points in red
- Evidence in blue
- Explanations in orange
- Links back to the question underlined

Globally the climate is warming, with evidence to prove that this is the case. Everywhere in the world is warmer, though seas are warming less than land. This is because greenhouse gas emissions have increased. It is hard to know exactly what temperatures were like in 1900 and more people and organisations record the weather now than at that time, so there were fewer thermometers back then. So some of the evidence could be questionable just because there were fewer recordings previously.

Even if temperature recordings are not completely reliable, there is a lot of evidence to show that sea levels are rising globally by about 20 cm in 100 years, partly because ocean water expands when it warms and so it rises. Many coastal areas are flooding more now, so it is a global process and not just evidence from one place.

Other evidence which shows that temperatures are rising comes from retreating glaciers and ice sheets because they are melting, especially on land areas where there is expected to be an increase at least 5°C by 2100, as shown in Figure 1. Many glaciers have been photographed for over 100 years, and many in the Alps and on Greenland show that they have retreated a long way from where they were.

(b) Use the mark scheme below to decide what mark to give. Remember, 9-mark questions are not marked using individual points. Instead, choose a level and a mark based on the quality of the answer as a whole.

Level	Marks	Descriptor	Examples
3 (Detailed)	7–9	• Shows detailed knowledge of the evidence for a changing climate. • Shows thorough geographical understanding of the processes by which the climate may be changing globally. • Shows application of knowledge and understanding in a coherent and reasoned way in evaluating the evidence for climate change.	• 'Figure 1 shows that everywhere in the world is affected by a changing climate to varying degrees.' • 'Sea level is increasing due to rising global temperatures, which melt ice caps, from which more water goes into the sea.' • 'This is likely to be reliable evidence as the IPCC consists of thousands of the world's best scientists.'
2 (Clear)	4–6	• Shows clear knowledge of the evidence for a changing climate. • Shows some geographical understanding of the processes by which the climate may be changing globally. • Shows reasonable application of knowledge and understanding in evaluating the evidence for climate change.	• 'Figure 1 shows that the global climate is changing and getting warmer.' • 'Global sea levels have risen due to global warming, which increases temperatures and melts ice caps and glaciers, which go into the sea.' • 'We know sea levels are rising because countries with coastlines are getting flooded.'
1 (Basic)	1–3	• Shows limited knowledge of the evidence for a changing climate. • Shows slight geographical understanding of the processes by which the climate may be changing globally. • Shows limited application of knowledge and understanding in evaluating the evidence for climate change.	• 'World temperatures are going up all the time and winters are getting warmer like in Figure 1.' • 'Global warming is making the seasons different and there are more floods.' • 'Scientists think more floods and storms are because of global warming.'
	0	No relevant content.	

Max your marks

Hitting the heights on 9-mark questions

(c) Fill in the marking table below, showing the strengths and weaknesses of the answer.

Strengths of this answer	
Ways to improve this answer	
The level I would give this answer is…	The mark I would give this answer is…

Worked example

The sample answer in Activity 2 is marked below, so you can compare your marking with this. The text has been coloured and underlined to show the following strengths of the answer:

- Points in red
- Evidence in blue
- Explanations in orange
- Links back to the question underlined

Globally the climate is warming, with evidence to prove that this is the case. Everywhere in the world is warmer, though seas are warming less than land. This is because greenhouse gas emissions have increased. It is hard to know exactly what temperatures were like in 1900 and more people and organisations record the weather now than at that time, so there were fewer thermometers back then. So some of the evidence could be questionable just because there were fewer recordings previously.

Point: the candidate makes the point that the climate is warming

Evidence: the candidate shows how temperatures are warmer

Explanation: the candidate briefly explains the increase

Link (evaluation): the candidate gives one reason why temperature readings may not be accurate

Link (evaluation): the candidate extends the evaluation by referring to the volume of temperature recordings

Point: the candidate makes a second point about temperature recordings and reliability

Even if temperature recordings are not completely reliable, there is a lot of evidence to show that sea levels are rising globally by about 20 cm in 100 years, partly because ocean water expands when it warms and so it rises. Many coastal areas are flooding more now, so it is a global process and not just evidence from one place.

Evidence: the candidate shows evidence of sea levels rising

Explanation: the candidate gives a reason for this

Link (evaluation): the candidate shows that this evidence is probably reliable as many places experience the same thing

Evidence/point: the candidate makes the point about retreating glaciers.

Other evidence which shows that temperatures are rising comes from retreating glaciers and ice sheets because they are melting, especially on land areas where there is expected to be an increase of at least 5°C by 2100, as shown in Figure 1. Many glaciers have been photographed for over 100 years, and many in the Alps and on Greenland show that they have retreated a long way from where they were.

Explanation: the candidate explains this

Link (evaluation): the candidate refers to the reliability of photos taken over a long time to show change

78 Max your marks

Questions using 'evaluate'

3. Mark a different answer

Activity 3

Now mark the answer below in just the same way as the example opposite. Use the mark scheme in Activity 2 and list the strengths and weaknesses of the answer in the table below.

Many sources of evidence show how the climate is changing. Temperatures have risen globally since the 19th century by about 0.8 degrees and Figure 1 shows this is even more now. This is probably due to carbon emissions of greenhouse gases like CO_2 from the burning of fossil fuels.

Temperatures in Figure 1 seem to be getting warmer all the time, so that sea levels will carry on rising. Already some islands in the Pacific have been flooded and countries like Bangladesh have severe floods because much of the country is very low-lying. Glaciers in mountains like the Himalayas have been melting because temperatures are rising, so this all goes to the sea via rivers and makes sea levels rise.

Another piece of evidence is that the seasons seem to be changing, so that spring is earlier and winters are not so cold as they were and have less snow. Birds now migrate earlier than they did and their nests are being built 9 days earlier than 40 years ago. So that all seems to mean that there is a lot of evidence that climate is changing.

Question recap

Using **Figure 1** (page 75) and your own understanding, evaluate the evidence which suggests that the global climate is currently changing.

Strengths of this answer	
Ways to improve this answer	
The level I would give this answer is…	**The mark I would give this answer is…**

How to recognise Level 3 in an answer

Can you see evidence of the following in the answer above? If so, the answer is Level 3 – if not, it's Level 2 or even Level 1. You would need all three qualities to reach Level 3.

1 Does the candidate know the detail?
A Level 3 answer would contain plenty of detail, e.g. precise data about temperatures, years.

2 Are there clear explanations of processes?
A Level 3 answer would contain clear explanations about the link between warming global climates and the ways in which this can lead to rising sea levels.

3 Is there a clear answer to the question?
A Level 3 answer would give clear explanations about whether or not the evidence was reliable, and why.

Max your marks

Hitting the heights on 9-mark questions

Questions using 'do you agree?'

Below is a different 9-mark question for you to tackle.

- This time, the command phrase is 'do you agree?'
- It's just like 'evaluate' – it means that you should weigh up the evidence, and whether that evidence means the statement is true or not.

Look at the question below.

> 'For those who live in the poorest areas of cities in one of the world's low-income countries (LICs) or newly emerging economies (NEEs), life presents far more problems than benefits.'
>
> Do you agree with this statement? Using one or more examples, explain your answer.
>
> [9 marks] [+3 SPaG marks]

For this 9-mark 'evaluate' question, you will:
1. Plan your answer
2. Write your answer
3. Mark your answer
4. Mark different answers

1. Plan your answer

Activity 1

Before attempting to answer the question, remember to **BUG** it. That means:

✓ **Box** the command word, as shown below.

✓ **Underline** the following:
- The focus of the question
- The evidence you need to answer the question
- The number of reasons you need to give for 9 marks.

✓ **Glance** back over the question to make sure you included everything in your answer.

Box and explain the command word:

Evidence:

> 'For those who live in the poorest areas of cities in one of the world's low-income countries (LICs) or newly emerging economies (NEEs), life presents far more problems than benefits.'
>
> To what extent do you agree with this statement?
>
> [9 marks] [+3 SPaG marks]

Focus:

What you have to write:

80 Max your marks

Questions using 'do you agree?'

Activity 2

Use the **PEEL** technique to help you draft your answer.

(a) **Point:** Make **three** points in support of or against the fact that life presents far more problems than benefits for the poorest.

- _____
- _____
- _____

(b) **Evidence:** Include **one** piece of evidence to support each point.

- _____
- _____
- _____

(c) **Explanation:** Weigh up each piece of evidence to show how strong it is.

- _____
- _____
- _____

(d) **Link:** Link back to the question to show the importance or strength of each piece of evidence. Start with a phrase like 'This point supports/is against the fact that life presents far more problems than benefits for the poorest…'.

Hitting Level 3

1 Know some detail
A Level 2 answer might say:

- *Emerging cities like Rio often have few services such as water or sewerage*

whereas Level 3 would say:

- *In Rio, a third of homes have no electricity and half have no sewage connections.*

2 Explain processes clearly, step-by-step
A Level 2 answer might say:

- *There are few services because most people cannot afford to pay for water or electricity*

whereas Level 3 would say:

- *The rapid growth of favelas means that the city authorities cannot keep pace with population growth and demand for services.*

3 Apply what you know to answer the question
A Level 2 answer might say:

- *The statement is true because there are insufficient services for people and quality of life is poor*

whereas Level 3 would say:

- *This shows the statement is generally true because there are too few basic services for a decent quality of life. But there are benefits, such as education that is widely available.*

Hitting the heights on 9-mark questions

2. Write your answer

Activity 3

> 'For those who live in the poorest areas of cities in one of the world's low-income countries (LICs) or newly emerging economies (NEEs), life presents far more problems than benefits.'
>
> Do you agree with this statement? Using **one** or **more** examples, explain your answer.
>
> [9 marks] [+3 SPaG marks]

Level 3 checklist

1 Have you included detail?
A Level 3 answer would contain plenty of detail – e.g. data about quality of life. ☐

2 Have you given clear explanations of processes?
A Level 3 answer would explain clearly why life presents problems for people in the poorest areas. ☐

3 Have you given a clear answer to the question?
A Level 3 answer would give a clear answer to the question – perhaps showing that there are ways in which life benefits the poorest, as well as problems. ☐

Max your marks

Questions using 'do you agree?'

3. Mark your answer

Activity 4

(a) To help identify if your answer includes well-structured points, highlight any:
- points in red
- evidence in blue
- explanations in orange
- and underline any links back to the question.

(b) Use the mark scheme below to decide what mark to give. Remember, 9-mark questions are not marked using individual points. Instead you should choose a level and a mark based upon the quality of your answer as a whole.

Level	Marks	Descriptor	Examples
3 (Detailed)	7–9	• Shows comprehensive and specific knowledge of the problems and benefits of one or more cities. • Shows thorough and accurate understanding of the problems and benefits of one or more cities. • Shows effective application of knowledge and understanding in making a judgement and reaching a substantiated conclusion. Justification is detailed and balanced.	• 'In Rio, a third of homes have no electricity (or have illegal hook-ups from power cables) and half have no sewerage connections.' • 'One reason is that favelas like Rocinha are growing so quickly that the city council cannot keep pace with population growth.' • 'This shows the statement is true because electricity and sewerage connections are basics for a reasonable life. But there are benefits, such as provision of schooling.'
2 (Clear)	4–6	• Shows reasonable knowledge of the problems and benefits of one or more cities. • Shows clear geographical understanding of the problems and benefits of one or more cities. • Shows reasonable application of knowledge and understanding in making a judgement and reaching a conclusion. Justification is clear and well supported.	• 'Cities like Rio often have no water or sewerage connections, and electricity supplies can be unsafe and irregular.' • 'This is because people are poor and cannot afford water or electricity bills.' • 'So the statement is true because most people do not have a decent lifestyle with basics that we would take for granted.'
1 (Basic)	1–3	• Shows limited knowledge of the problems and benefits of one or more cities. Answers may be largely generic. • Shows some geographical understanding of the problems and benefits of living in cities. • Shows limited application of knowledge and understanding in making a judgement and/or reaching a conclusion. Justification is limited to one or more simple points.	• 'Developing cities have no water or sewerage pipes and have many health problems from drinking bad water.' • 'There are so many people that the city cannot keep pace with them all.' • 'So the statement is right because life there is very hard and the city cannot support all those people.'
	0	No relevant content.	

(c) Fill in the marking table below, showing the strengths and weaknesses of the answer.

Strengths of this answer	
Ways to improve this answer	
The level I would give this answer is…	The mark I would give this answer is…

Max your marks 83

Hitting the heights on 9-mark questions

4. Mark these different answers

Activity 5

Read through these two sample answers to the same question.

(a) Annotate each answer using the three colours and underlining as explained in Activity 4.

(b) Use the mark scheme in Activity 4 to decide on a level and how many marks each answer is worth.

(c) Fill in the marking table showing the strengths and weaknesses of each answer.

Sample answer 1

I agree with the statement. Rio's favelas are growing so quickly that it is hard to keep pace with services needed like water. Rocinha has grown three times its size since 2010. It is better than it was because now houses are being built out of brick instead of timber and odd bits of metal, and they also have water and electricity. There are shops there and many services like health facilities that you would expect. But I agree with the statement because Rocinha is probably one of Rio's best favelas and there are many worse that do not have half the benefits that it has. You wouldn't choose to live there if you had more money so areas like that are still for low-income people, so I still think the statement is true.

Elsewhere Rio has squatter settlements, which are places where people just put together their own shacks illegally. Some of these shacks are on sloping land because nobody else wants to live there and they can be a long way from jobs in the city centre. When rains come, people are vulnerable, because in 2010 over 200 people were killed in a landslide. Again, this shows that the statement is true, because it's the poor who have to live there – people with jobs and decent incomes would never choose to live in places like that.

> **Question recap**
>
> 'For those who live in the poorest areas of cities in one of the world's low-income countries (LICs) or newly emerging economies (NEEs), life presents far more problems than benefits.'
>
> Do you agree with this statement? Using one or more examples, explain your answer.

Strengths of this answer	
Ways to improve this answer	
The level I would give this answer is…	**The mark I would give this answer is…**

84 Max your marks

Questions using 'do you agree?'

Sample answer 2

I don't agree with the statement. It is true that people living in squatter settlements have a lot of problems, like they don't have water supply or sewerage connections, and when you walk down the street you might be electrocuted as power cables can be hanging down everywhere. But cities have many jobs for people and so the people who have moved there from the countryside are often employed more than if they had stayed in rural areas. Many rural areas do not have schools and cities like Rio have plenty of schools for all ages, maybe universities too. There are often hospitals and medical treatment in cities that you don't have in the countryside. So it's not perfect living in Rio but it can be better than a lot of places so I don't agree with the statement.

Strengths of this answer	
Ways to improve this answer	
The level I would give this answer is…	The mark I would give this answer is…

Level 3 checklist

1 Has it included detail?
Explain what other detail might have been included.

Yes ☐   No ☐   Partly ☐

2 Has it explained processes clearly?
Explain how explanations might have been clearer.

Yes ☐   No ☐   Partly ☐

3 Is there a clear answer to the question?
Explain where the answer is or is not clear.

Yes ☐   No ☐   Partly ☐

Max your marks

Hitting the heights on 9-mark questions

Questions using 'assess'

Below is a different 9-mark question for you to tackle.

- 'Assess' is similar to 'evaluate' because you have to weigh up evidence, but different in that you have to rank the evidence in terms of severity or importance.
- Like 'evaluate' and 'to what extent …?', 'assess' also requires a brief conclusion at the end of your answer.

Look at the question below.

> Using a case study of an LIC/NEE, assess the importance of the country's location in its economic development.
>
> [9 marks] [+3 SPaG marks]

For this 9-mark 'assess' question, you will:

1. Plan your answer
2. Write your answer
3. Mark your answer
4. Mark a different answer

1. Plan your answer

Activity 1

Use the format shown on page 75 to **BUG** the question in the space below.

- Remember that you must 'assess'. This means that you need to judge how far location is important in the economic development of your chosen country. Are other factors important as well?
- Also remember that you need to plan for SPaG.

Box and explain the command word:

Evidence:

> Using a case study of an LIC/NEE, assess the importance of the country's location in its economic development.
>
> [9 marks] [+3 SPaG marks]

Focus:

What you have to write:

86 Max your marks

Questions using 'assess'

2. Write your answer

Activity 2

Using a case study of an LIC/NEE, assess the importance of the country's location in its economic development.

[9 marks] [+3 SPaG marks]

___

Hitting Level 3

1 Include some detail about the LIC/NEE's location, e.g.
- *Nigeria's location near the Equator means that farming produces tropical crops.*

2 Explain processes clearly to show how the LIC/NEE's development has been affected by its location, e.g.
- *Its exports used to go mainly to Europe which was the closest wealthy market for Nigerian crops.*

3 Apply what you know to assess how important each factor had been in the LIC/NEE's development, e.g.
- *Oil has been much more important than location in developing Nigeria because it's a product in global demand.*

Max your marks

Hitting the heights on 9-mark questions

3. Mark your answer

Activity 3

(a) To help identify if your answer includes well-structured points, highlight any:

- <mark style="background-color:#fcd5d5">points</mark> in red
- <mark style="background-color:#cfe2f3">evidence</mark> in blue
- <mark style="background-color:#fce5cd">explanations</mark> in orange
- and <u>underline</u> any links back to the question.

(b) Use the mark scheme below to decide what mark to give. Remember, 9-mark questions are not marked using individual points. Instead you should choose a level and a mark based upon the quality of your answer as a whole.

Level	Marks	Descriptor
3 (Detailed)	7–9	• Shows comprehensive and specific knowledge about the location of the chosen country. • Shows thorough and accurate understanding of how its location and other factors have affected the development of the country. • Shows effective application of knowledge and understanding in assessing the importance of each factor, making a judgement, and reaching a substantiated conclusion.
2 (Clear)	4–6	• Shows reasonable knowledge about the location of the chosen country. • Shows clear geographical understanding of how its location and other factors have affected the development of the country. • Shows reasonable application of knowledge and understanding in assessing the importance of each factor, making a judgement, and reaching a conclusion.
1 (Basic)	1–3	• Shows limited knowledge about the location of the chosen country. Answers may be largely generic. • Shows some limited geographical understanding of how its location and other factors have affected the development of the country. • Shows limited or no application of knowledge and understanding in assessing the importance of each factor, making a judgement and reaching a conclusion.
	0	No relevant content.

(c) Fill in the marking table below, showing the strengths and weaknesses of the answer. Remember to give a SPaG mark.

Strengths of this answer	
Ways to improve this answer	
The level I would give this answer is…	The mark I would give this answer is…

Max your marks

Questions using 'assess'

4. Mark a different answer

Activity 4

Read through the sample answer below.

(a) Use colours and underlining as in Activity 3 to highlight the strengths of the answer.

India's location is really important in its economic development. To the east are the Arabian Sea and the rich Gulf states, e.g. the UAE. This helps India to trade as it exports products from ports such as Mumbai and imports oil to further its economic development. To the west lies the Bay of Bengal and beyond that the emerging economies of South-East Asia, which are also important for trade. To the north are the Himalayas, which have greatly limited trade with China in the past. India's location is now attractive for TNCs such as BT in Bangalore. India's location and time-difference encourages call centres. This shows how important the English language has been as well as location in India's development – English is taught across schools and in all universities.

In some ways India's location has prevented any major economic development. India faces climate extremes and some inland areas experience harsh droughts, which have restricted economic development due to a lack of water.

Other significant factors have affected India's development. India's colonisation by Britain led to the construction of railways and ports to develop and export natural resources for low prices. Although this might be a benefit, its poor trading terms have been very significant in restricting India's development. Political relationships are tense with some neighbours such as conflicts with Pakistan. Kashmir is still a disputed region with limited economic development. Overall, location has been important, but other factors influence India's development to almost as great an extent.

> **Question recap**
>
> Using a case study of an LIC/NEE, assess the importance of the country's location in its economic development.

(b) Use the level descriptions in the mark scheme in Activity 3 to decide how many marks this answer is worth.

(c) Fill in the marking table, showing the strengths and weaknesses of the answer. Remember to give a SPaG mark.

Strengths of this answer	
Ways to improve this answer	
The level I would give this answer is…	The mark I would give this answer is…

Max your marks 89

Hitting the heights on 9-mark questions

Extra practice questions

Now try this!

- **BUG** and **PEEL** these questions.
- After you write each answer, review it yourself or ask one of your peers to review it while you review theirs.
- Use the mark schemes in this chapter to help you judge its quality.
- Remember that you will be given 2 lines per mark, so that means 18 answer lines for a 9-mark question, although you can write more if necessary.

1. **Urban regeneration**

   To what extent has a named example of an urban regeneration project in a major city in the UK brought benefits to the area?

> **Tip** 'To what extent' is very similar to 'evaluate' – you should weigh up evidence, and judge how successful or important something is.

[9 marks] [+3 SPaG marks]

Max your marks

Extra practice questions

2. **Extreme weather**

   Assess the severity of impacts of one named extreme weather event in the UK.

   [9 marks] [+3 SPaG marks]

3. **Desertification** *Answer this question on a separate sheet of paper.*

   EITHER OPTION 1

   Evaluate the extent to which desertification has mainly physical causes.

   [9 marks] [+3 SPaG marks]

   OR OPTION 2

   Evaluate the attempts that have been used to balance the needs of economic development and conservation in cold environments.

   [9 marks] [+3 SPaG marks]

Focus on Paper 3: Geographical applications
Section A: Issue evaluation

Paper 3

Time: 1 hr 15 min

Structure: Section A   Issue evaluation (34 marks + 3 SPaG)

               Section B   Fieldwork (36 marks + 3 SPaG)

Assessment:

- There are no options so you should attempt every question. And remember, never leave a question blank!
- There are two 9-mark questions, one at the end of each section. In Section A, this question is about decision-making. In Section B, it is a question based on your own fieldwork.
- There are no marks for factual recall. The bulk of the marks are available for the application of your knowledge and understanding. There are quite a lot of marks available for skills.

Resources booklet

Section A provides an opportunity to demonstrate your geographical skills and apply your knowledge and understanding to a particular issue using secondary sources.

You will be provided with a resources booklet containing a range of resources to focus your attention on a particular issue (e.g. a proposal to construct a new reservoir). The issue will be drawn from a compulsory section of the specification.

Questions in Section A will focus on the resources in the booklet, although you will be expected to use your wider knowledge and understanding of the specification to support your answers.

When do I get the resources booklet?

Your teacher will decide when to give you a copy of the resources booklet. It may be after Easter when you have completed the course. Your teacher will guide you through the booklet and you should annotate the resources, using labels and highlighters to pick out the key points in each resource.

Do I get a new resources booklet in the exam?

Yes. You will have a fresh copy of the resources booklet in the exam. You will **not** be allowed to take your original annotated version into the exam with you. Don't forget to take a pen, pencil, ruler, rubber and calculator!

Do I need to do any additional research?

No. You should **not** do any additional research as you will only be credited with supporting evidence that is taken from the resources booklet. Don't waste your time trawling the internet!

Section A: Issue evaluation

Using the resources booklet

> The resources booklet contains three figures and there are six pages of resources in total. Go to pages 103–108 to see what a resources booklet looks like. Each figure will have a particular focus and may involve different types of resources (see below).

What should I do with the resources booklet?

In preparation for the exam, it is important that you are confident in using the resources booklet. You need to make sure that you understand **all** of the resources. When you first get your resources booklet:

1. Have a quick look through the booklet to identify the topic being studied.
2. Find this topic in your textbook or revision book. You will need to revise this prior to the exam to support your background knowledge and understanding.
3. For each resource, use labels/annotations and highlighters to pick out the key points:

- **For a graph**, identify the main trends and pick out some key points (highs, lows, anomalies). Make sure you understand the axes and the scales. Consider manipulating the data to provide you with comparative figures. Use fractions or percentages to describe change (e.g. 'In October, there were three times as many tourists as there were in June.').
- **For a map**, draw rings to pick out patterns of areas with the highest and lowest values. Look for any causal reasons, such as latitude with the distribution of tropical cyclones. What's in the key? Remember to use the scale and north arrow. Use your geographical knowledge to identify locations, regions and names of oceans and continents.
- **For a photo**, be prepared to examine it forensically, picking out as many features as you can. Add labels or draw rings to help focus your attention. Remember to use locational terms such as 'foreground' and 'background'. Also, be prepared to infer the consequences of your observations. What may happen next? What are the short-term and long-term social, economic and environmental consequences?
- **For a text article**, use a highlighter to pick out key facts and figures. Consider the purpose of the article. For example, is it presenting different points of view or advantages and disadvantages? Identify and look up any words that you do not understand. Look for the presence of concepts, such as scale (spatial and temporal), development and sustainability. This will help you to achieve Level 3 marks.

Activity 1

The map below is from **Figure 1** in the sample resources booklet (pages 103–108).

Write labels onto the map to help you describe the distribution of tropical storms. One has been done for you.

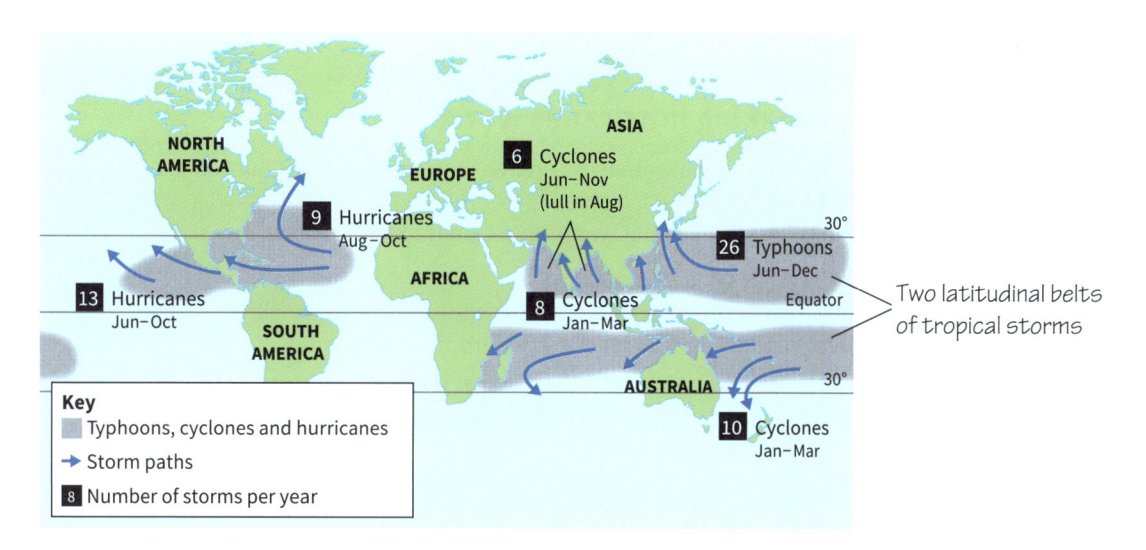

Map labels:
- 9 Hurricanes Aug–Oct (North America)
- 13 Hurricanes Jun–Oct (South America)
- 6 Cyclones Jun–Nov (lull in Aug) (Asia)
- 26 Typhoons Jun–Dec
- 8 Cyclones Jan–Mar (Africa)
- 10 Cyclones Jan–Mar (Australia)
- Two latitudinal belts of tropical storms

Key
- Typhoons, cyclones and hurricanes
- → Storm paths
- 8 Number of storms per year

Section A: Issue evaluation

Activity 2

The photo below is from **Figure 2** in the sample resources booklet (pages 103–108). It shows the effects of Hurricane Dorian on the Bahamas.

Write annotations to suggest the likely social, economic and environmental effects of the hurricane on the people of the Bahamas.

Worked example

Here is a section of text taken from **Figure 1** in the sample resources booklet (pages 103–108). It has been highlighted to pick out the key points.

Storm surge

This is a surge or 'wall' of high water up to about 3 m in height that floods low-lying coastal areas. It can cause enormous devastation and is responsible for the greatest loss of life from tropical storms. In 2005, Hurricane Katrina caused a 7.6 m storm surge that inundated much of the city of New Orleans, causing immense damage and loss of life. Freshwater became contaminated by saltwater, agricultural land was ruined and property destroyed.

Activity 3

Use a highlighter to pick out the key points in the extract below, taken from **Figure 1** in the sample resources booklet (pages 103–108).

Is climate change making hurricanes worse?

'Scientists cannot say whether climate change is increasing the number of hurricanes, but the ones that do happen are likely to be more powerful and more destructive because of our warming climate,' says BBC Weather's Tomasz Schafernaker. Here's why:

- An increase in sea surface temperatures strengthens the wind speeds within storms and also raises the amount of precipitation from a hurricane.
- Sea levels are expected to rise by 30 cm to 120 cm over the next century, with the potential of far worse damage from sea surges and coastal flooding during storms.

Section A: Issue evaluation

Tackling the exam questions

In Section A, you will need to answer a series of questions based on the issue in the resources booklet. To answer the questions you should use evidence from the resources together with your background knowledge and understanding.

Low-mark questions

There will be a few short-answer questions, probably worth 1 or 2 marks each. They may be skills-based (e.g. making a calculation) or may ask you to 'explain' or 'suggest'. You will probably be asked to complete a diagram. Be careful not to miss out a question and double-check your answers.

> **Tip**
> It's a recognised fact that top students often lose marks on the low-mark questions! They can rush what are considered (often wrongly) to be 'easy' questions. Be careful.

Now try this!

Attempt the following questions based on the sample resources booklet (pages 103–108).

1.1 In **Figure 1**, calculate the total number of recorded hurricanes between 1851 and 2018. **[1 mark]**

_____

1.2 Explain the pattern of tropical storms shown in **Figure 1**. **[2 marks]**

_____

_____

_____

_____

1.3 In **Figure 1**, the graph showing the total number of hurricanes by month (1851–2018) is a bar graph. Outline one advantage of a bar graph for displaying this data. **[1 mark]**

_____

_____

Extended-answer questions

There will probably be three 6-mark questions in Section A (or two 6-mark and one 4-mark). They are likely to involve some form of discussion or evaluation, using command words such as 'discuss' or 'to what extent'.

- Treat these questions seriously – they are often challenging but are worth a lot of marks.
- Take time to make a plan before you start to write.
- Make sure you refer to supporting evidence from the resources.
- If you can, try to refer to one or more of the 'threshold' concepts, such as scale (spatial and temporal), development and sustainability. This will help to move you into Level 3 in a 6-mark question.

> **Tip**
> It is a good idea to use short extracts from text articles to support a point you are making. Write them in quote marks (e.g. 'immense damage and loss of life') and give a reference to the article if appropriate. Be selective – avoid simply copying out huge chunks of text!

Focus on Paper 3: Geographical applications 95

Section A: Issue evaluation

Worked example

'A storm surge is the greatest threat associated with a tropical storm.' Discuss this statement with reference to **Figure 1** (pages 103–104) and your own understanding.

[6 marks]

A storm surge is a surge of high water that floods low-lying coastal areas. While the other threats from tropical storms – strong winds over 120 km/h and very heavy rain (over 200 mm in a few hours) – can have significant effects (particularly locally), storm surges are generally considered to cause much more widespread devastation and destruction. For example, in 2005, a 7 m storm surge associated with Hurricane Katrina inundated much of New Orleans causing 'immense damage and loss of life'. Scientists expect the threat of storm surges to increase as sea levels rise in the future due to climate change, though this might also lead to strong winds and heavy rain which may be more destructive locally.

Examiner feedback

This is a Level 3 answer and earns 5 of the 6 marks. The answer:

- shows good understanding of a storm surge and its impacts
- makes excellent use of resources (refers to Hurricane Katrina, tropical storm hazards and climate change)
- refers to the concept of scale
- does include some discussion but doesn't gain the final mark as there is room for this to be developed, perhaps using the candidate's 'own understanding'.

Now try this!

Attempt the following question based on the sample resources booklet (pages 103–108).

2. To what extent did the forecast track of Hurricane Dorian (30 August 2019) prove to be accurate?

[6 marks]

_____
_____
_____
_____
_____
_____
_____
_____
_____
_____

Section A: Issue evaluation

Tackling the 9-mark decision-making question

The final question in Section A requires you to make and then justify a decision. You will need to consider the points of view of the stakeholders involved, appraise the advantages and disadvantages, and evaluate alternatives. In reaching and justifying your decision, you will consider physical and human interrelationships, and reflect on the impacts on people and the physical environment. A synoptic approach (see pages 22–23) is one key aspect of this final question.

Here are some important points to remember:

- There is no right or wrong answer, but you have to make a decision from the options given and then justify it using evidence from the resources booklet.
- Do not leave this question blank! Focus on the geography, write something sensible using evidence from the booklet, and try to offer more than one point of view (a discussion).
- SPaG provides three additional marks for this question, so try to write with care and precision.

> **Tip** Remember that SPaG includes geographical terminology, so try to include appropriate geographical terms to boost your SPaG mark.

Before the exam

You will probably have a good idea about what the question is likely to be. This will enable you to make some basic preparations.

Look at **Figure 3** in the sample resources booklet (pages 103–108). It focuses on a proposal to construct a storm surge barrier to help protect New York from future flooding associated with tropical storms. There is information about the advantages and disadvantages of the proposal.

Given this information, it seems likely that the 9-mark question will focus on whether or not the proposal should go ahead.

> **Tip** Don't try to guess the precise wording of the question beforehand. If you do, you may be tempted to simply rewrite the answer you have already practised. Be confident with the resources booklet and answer the question that is set in the exam.

Activity 4

Use a table to summarise information and help you prepare for the decision-making question. Notice that the table below has been split into social, economic and environmental factors. This will give you a clear structure for your answer.

(a) Complete the table below to identify advantages and disadvantages of the proposal in **Figure 3** of the sample resources booklet (pages 107–108). Try to include two points in each box.

	Advantages	Disadvantages
Social		
Economic		• Hugely expensive ($20–25 billion)
Environmental	• Impacts will be minimal (according to the Storm Surge Working Group)	

Focus on Paper 3: Geographical applications 97

Section A: Issue evaluation

(b) Use a highlighter to pick out what you consider to be the most important points (some points are more important than others!).

(c) Now consider the concept of scale, both spatial and temporal. Remember that this is a higher-level concept that will help you to achieve a high-level mark. Try to complete as many boxes as you can.

	Advantages	Disadvantages
Local		• Very expensive ($20–25 billion)
National		
Global	• The barrier system could be a template for other countries threatened by sea level rise	
Short-term		
Long-term		• The barrier could have long-term impacts on coastal processes, affecting patterns of erosion and deposition

In the exam

You have about 35 minutes for Section A. Try to leave yourself about 10 minutes to answer this final 9-mark question. Do not be tempted to go beyond this time limit as it will affect your performance in Section B.

- Plan your answer – use a table or make a list of the key points you want to include.
- Support your decision with evidence, using clear paragraphs (use PEEL).
- Make explicit links to the evidence in the booklet to support your argument.
- Try to refer to higher-level concepts (scale, sustainability, development), especially in your conclusion.
- Write a conclusion ('In conclusion…'). Don't simply repeat what you have said before. Focus on the factor that is most important in your decision-making.

Now try this!

Try this question on a separate sheet of paper.

3. 'The City of New York authority has decided not to go ahead with the storm surge barrier system.'
Do you think this was the right decision?

Yes ◯
No ◯

Tick the box to show your choice

Use evidence from the resources booklet and your own understanding to explain your choice.

[9 marks + 3 SPaG marks]

98 Focus on Paper 3: Geographical applications

Focus on Paper 3: Geographical applications
Section B: Fieldwork

Part 1: short-answer questions based on unfamiliar fieldwork

Here you will be presented with information about fieldwork enquiries. This might take the form of photos, sketch maps, diagrams and tables of data. The questions will focus on the six stages of enquiry, shown in the table below.

	Stage of enquiry	Don't forget to revise…
1	Question selection	• Primary and secondary sources • Risk assessments (including how to reduce risks)
2	Data collection (methodology) including sampling techniques	• Primary and secondary data • Sampling methods (random, stratified and systematic)
3	Data presentation	• Selection of methods (focus on **why** they are appropriate for the data collected)
4	Data analysis	• Use of appropriate statistical tests (e.g. central tendency, percentages, best fit lines)
5	Conclusions	• Links between conclusions and the original aim of enquiry
6	Evaluation	• Problems/limitations with data collection • Suggestions for other data sources • Reliability of conclusions

Be prepared to:

complete a diagram such as a bar chart or scattergraph

calculate using data (e.g. median, mean, percentage)

describe patterns on diagrams

suggest suitable alternatives to data collection or presentation (and give reasons)

assess the methods of data collection or reliability of conclusions

suggest options or alternatives, giving reasons.

Now try this!

1. Using a questionnaire, students asked 100 people at random what they thought was the main problem in their local town centre. The survey was conducted at 9 a.m. on a rainy Saturday morning. The graph in **Figure 1** shows the results of the survey.

   1.1 Complete the graph using this information:

   Lack of free parking = 24 people
   [2 marks]

   1.2 Suggest **one** adaptation to the method used that might provide the students with more appropriate data.

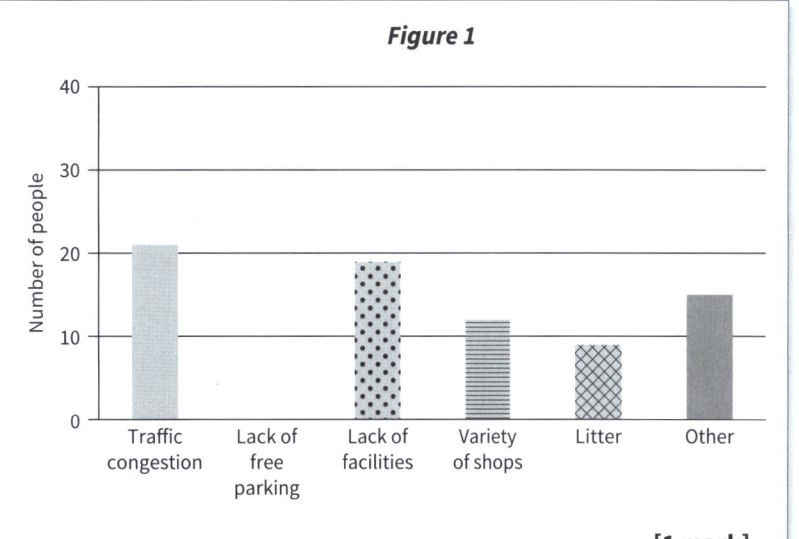

   Figure 1

   [1 mark]

   _____
   _____

Section B: Fieldwork

Part 2: questions based on own fieldwork

In this part of the exam you will be asked questions on your physical and human enquiries. It's a great opportunity to write about something that you actually experienced, so make the most of it!

> **Tip** Know the titles of your physical and human enquiries. You will be expected to write the titles before answering the questions.

What questions will I be asked?

Figure 2 shows the questions that you are most likely to be asked. Notice that there are no questions asking you to describe what you did. Instead, the questions will ask you to **explain** why you did certain things (such as the collection of data or the selection of a presentation technique). You may be asked to **assess** or **evaluate** your results and conclusion. You could be asked to **discuss** problems and limitations or **suggest** possible improvements outlined in your evaluation.

Figure 2

- Why was the question suitable for geographical study?
- Why did I choose the locations?
- What were the potential risks and how were they reduced?
- What data did I collect?
- What sampling methods did I use and why were they appropriate?
- Why did I choose the presentation techniques?
- Why did I use statistical techniques?
- Why did I get the results/conclusion?
- Why were there issues with the enquiry (evaluation)?

How to succeed in the fieldwork enquiry questions

Revise your fieldwork enquiries thoroughly. Make sure you know what you did and, most importantly, why you did it.

Complete revision grids (see page 101) for both fieldwork enquiries.

Be prepared to use simple sketches to support your answers (don't forget to annotate them).

You do not need to learn lots of facts and figures. The examiner has no way of knowing if these are correct, so you cannot be awarded marks. However, you may wish to refer to anomalies or trends.

Focus on Paper 3: Geographical applications

Section B: Fieldwork

How to cope with the final 9-mark question

For the final question, you have to select one of your enquiries to write about. Think carefully about which enquiry is best suited to the question.

The question is most likely to focus on the interrelationships between data collection, results, conclusions and evaluation. It is one of the most challenging questions in the entire exam, so take time to revise and prepare for it.

Look at **Figure 3**, which shows interrelationships in a fieldwork enquiry. Notice how 'Data collection', 'Results' and 'Conclusion' are all linked, and how evaluation considers all three enquiry strands. Notice the role of feedback in the enquiry process, which leads back to the initial question. Sometimes in the light of conclusions, a different aim can emerge. Try to discuss these interrelationships when answering the 9-mark question.

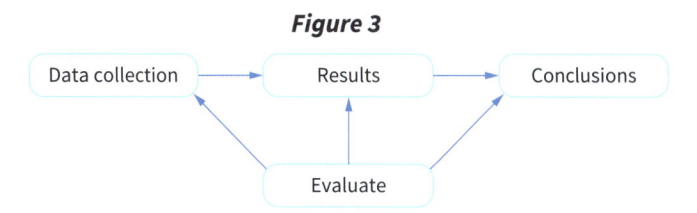

Figure 3

Data collection → Results → Conclusions

Evaluate

> **Tip**
> When evaluating your conclusion, consider internal and external validity.
> - **Internal validity:** how valid (reliable) are your conclusions in the context of the study area (e.g. stretch of river or coast)? Would you expect to get the same results and draw the same conclusions on all occasions?
> - **External validity:** how valid (reliable) are your conclusions *beyond* the study area (e.g. for other rivers or stretches of coastline)?

Activity

Use the table below to help you write a plan to answer this question:

> For **one** of your enquiries, to what extent did the data that you collected allow you to make reliable conclusions? **[9 marks + 3 SPaG marks]**

Title of fieldwork enquiry: _____

What data did you collect?	
What were your conclusions?	
How reliable were your conclusions? Do you think they would always be the same for your study area (internal validity)? Would they apply to areas outside your study area (external validity)?	
Did your data allow you to make reliable conclusions?	
Consider 'to what extent' your data allowed you to make reliable conclusions. Place a cross on the line and use this to help you in your discussion.	No ─────────────── Yes 0% 100%

Focus on Paper 3: Geographical applications 101

Section B: Fieldwork

> **Now try this!**
>
> 2. Now attempt to answer the question in the Activity on page 101 using a separate sheet of paper.

Fieldwork enquiry revision template

	Physical enquiry	**Human enquiry**
Investigation title		
1. Question selection		
Why is the question suitable for geographical study?		
What are the risks and how were they reduced?		
Why were the locations chosen?		
2. Data collection (methodology) including sampling techniques		
Explain the collection of **one** form of primary data (sampling, methods, location, etc.)*		
Explain a **second** method of data collection (primary or secondary)		
3. Data presentation		
For **one** presentation method, why did you choose it to present fieldwork data?*		
For a **second** presentation method, why did you choose it to present fieldwork data?		
4. Data analysis		
What statistical techniques did you use and why?		
What were your main results? Were there any anomalies?		
5. Conclusions		
What were your conclusions?		
6. Evaluation		
What were the problems/limitations with data collection? (Methods, locations, timings, actual data, etc.)		
What other data might have been useful in answering the question?		
How reliable were the conclusions? Consider internal and external validity.		

* You will probably only be asked to write about **one** primary data collection method and **one** method of data presentation. However, it is useful to prepare **two** so that you can select the best one to use when answering a question.

Focus on Paper 3: Geographical applications
Issue evaluation resources booklet

Figure 1

Tropical storm development, distribution and impacts

What is a tropical storm?

A tropical storm is a huge storm that develops in the tropics. In the USA and the Caribbean these are commonly called **hurricanes**. In South-East Asia and Australia they are usually called **cyclones**, but in Japan and the Philippines they are called **typhoons**.

Distribution of tropical storms

The world map shows the regions where most tropical storms form, as well as their principal months of occurrence and the most common tracks they follow. Tropical storms do not develop within about 5° of the Equator because the effect of the Earth's rotation, which triggers the 'spin' of a tropical storm, is too weak. Surface ocean temperatures exceeding 26.5°C are required for them to form and, for this reason, they seldom form poleward of 30° latitude nor over the cool waters of the South Atlantic and the eastern South Pacific.

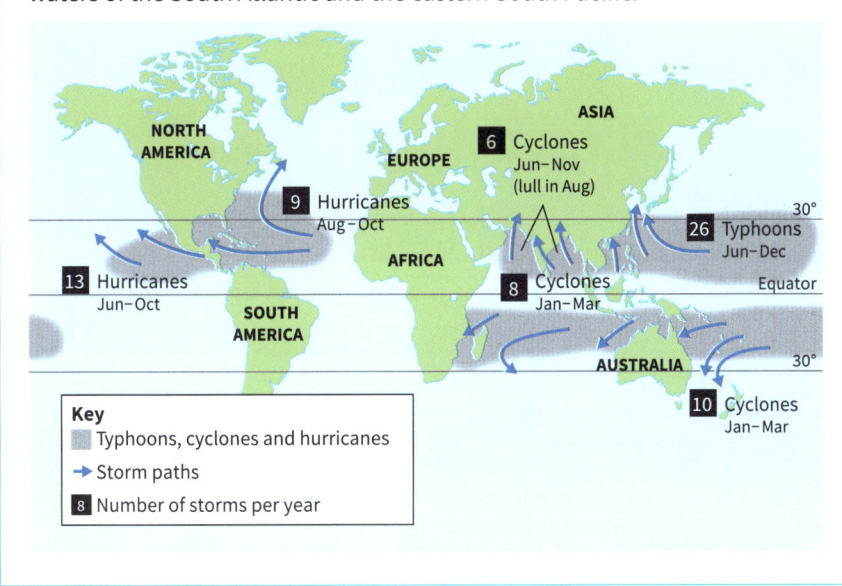

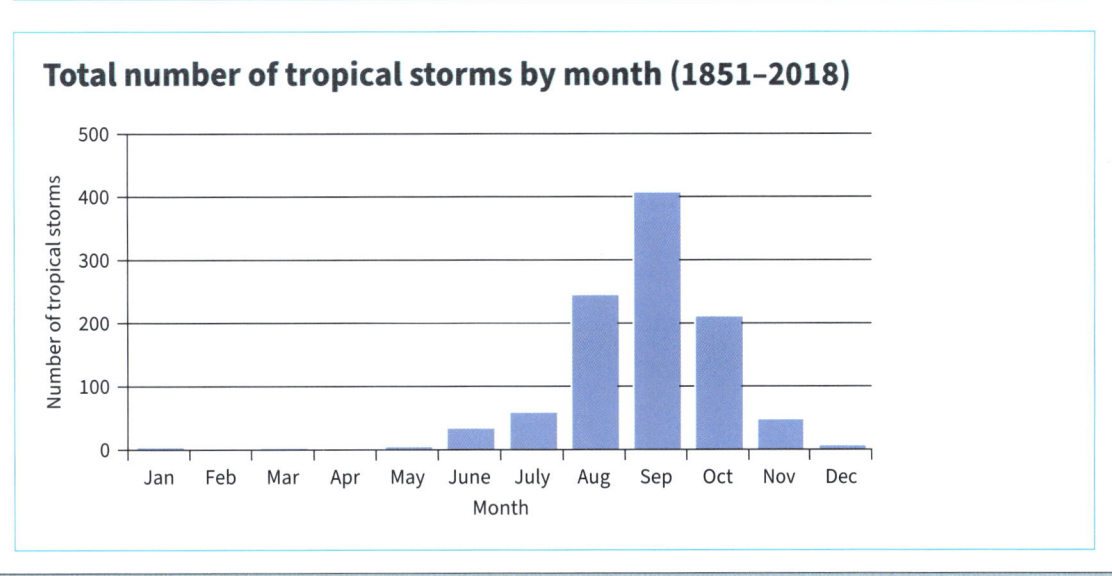

- 6 Cyclones Jun–Nov (lull in Aug)
- 9 Hurricanes Aug–Oct
- 26 Typhoons Jun–Dec
- 13 Hurricanes Jun–Oct
- 8 Cyclones Jan–Mar
- 10 Cyclones Jan–Mar

Key
- Typhoons, cyclones and hurricanes
- → Storm paths
- 8 Number of storms per year

Total number of tropical storms by month (1851–2018)

Bar chart showing number of tropical storms (y-axis 0–500) by month (Jan–Dec). Values approximately: Jan ~0, Feb 0, Mar 0, Apr 0, May ~5, June ~35, July ~60, Aug ~245, Sep ~410, Oct ~210, Nov ~50, Dec ~5.

Focus on Paper 3: Geographical applications 103

Issue evaluation resources booklet

Tropical storm hazards

Tropical storms bring a deadly mix of high seas, strong winds and torrential rain. A huge proportion of the world's population lives near the coast, so there is a significant potential for loss of life and property damage.

Strong winds

Average wind speeds exceed 120 km/h (75 mph). The strongest winds occur at the eyewall (the outer edge of the eye) where they can reach 250 km/h. The strong winds are capable of causing significant damage and disruption by tearing off roofs, breaking windows and damaging communication networks, often causing power cuts.

Storm surge

This is a surge or 'wall' of high water up to about 3 m in height that floods low-lying coastal areas. It can cause enormous devastation and is responsible for the greatest loss of life from tropical storms. In 2005, Hurricane Katrina caused a 7.6 m storm surge that inundated much of the city of New Orleans, causing immense damage and loss of life. Freshwater became contaminated by saltwater, agricultural land was ruined and property destroyed.

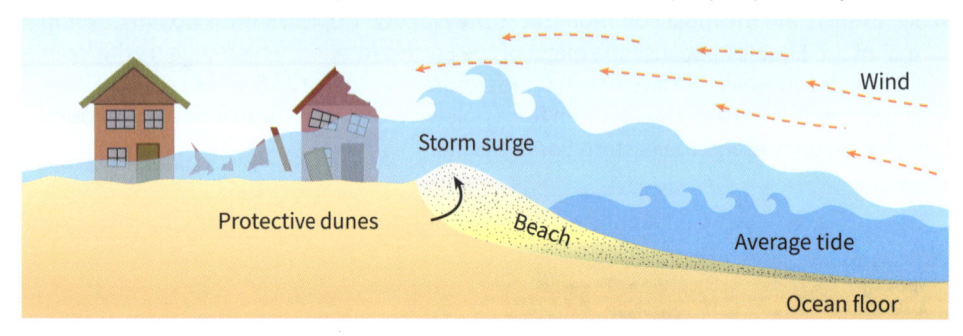

Torrential rainfall

The warm, humid air associated with a tropical storm can trigger huge quantities of rainfall, often exceeding 200 mm in just a few hours. This can inundate coastal regions and lead to catastrophic flooding inland as rivers burst their banks.

Is climate change making tropical storms worse?

'Scientists cannot say whether climate change is increasing the number of hurricanes, but the ones that do happen are likely to be more powerful and more destructive because of our warming climate,' says BBC Weather's Tomasz Schafernaker. Here's why:

- An increase in sea surface temperatures strengthens the wind speeds within storms and also raises the amount of precipitation from a tropical storm.
- Sea levels are expected to rise by 30 cm to 120 cm over the next century, with the potential of far worse damage from sea surges and coastal flooding during storms.

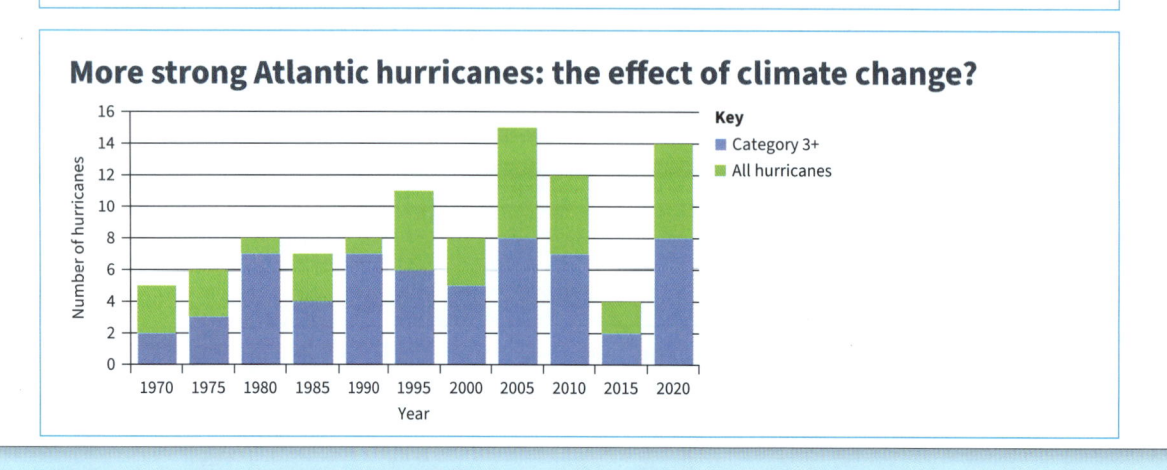

More strong Atlantic hurricanes: the effect of climate change?

Focus on Paper 3: Geographical applications

Issue evaluation resources booklet

Figure 2

Hurricane Dorian, the Bahamas, 2019

The impacts of Hurricane Dorian

Tropical storms are incredibly powerful and can cause devastation to small islands and coastal regions. In 2019, the Bahamas was struck by Hurricane Dorian, the most powerful hurricane to hit the islands on record. Regarded as the worst natural disaster in the country's history, Hurricane Dorian killed over 50 people and devastated huge swathes of the country, causing damage worth over $7 billion.

The hurricane made landfall on 1 September and battered the Abaco Islands and Grand Bahama, in the north of the archipelago, for two days. Winds reaching 165 km/h combined with a powerful storm surge and torrential rainfall caused almost total destruction of harbours, residential property and agricultural land. One of the main reasons for the extensive devastation was the unusually slow speed of movement of the storm, causing huge quantities of rainfall. Many people were evacuated from coastal properties, most of which were destroyed by the storm. Power lines were brought down and roads were flooded, hampering rescue efforts.

Damage caused by Hurricane Dorian on Grand Bahama

Extract from *The Washington Post*

Classified as a Category 5 hurricane, Dorian is the most powerful storm to affect the Bahamas. Its sustained winds – reaching 185 mph – are close to the highest ever recorded in the Atlantic Ocean.

Satellite images reveal Hurricane Dorian to be almost perfectly symmetrical, with its distinctive eye surrounded by towering, swirling thunderstorm clouds. The clouds surrounding the eye resemble the fiery streaks of a Catherine wheel firework.

Dorian's winds are unusually strong for a storm so far north in the Atlantic Ocean. Its central pressure, recorded at 911 mb, is lower than Hurricane Andrew's, the last great storm to strike southern Florida in 1992. Since 1950, the strength of Dorian's winds is surpassed only by the 190 mph winds associated with Hurricane Allen in 1980.

Satellite image of Hurricane Dorian approaching the northern Bahamas and threatening Florida

Issue evaluation resources booklet

Tracking Hurricane Dorian

The map below shows the predicted track and strength of Hurricane Dorian, forecast on 30 August 2019. Forecasters expected the hurricane to intensify rapidly as it headed towards the Bahamas. It was then expected to make landfall in central Florida, threatening strong winds (over 85 mph), torrential rain and a storm surge.

Hurricane Dorian forecast track (30 August 2019)

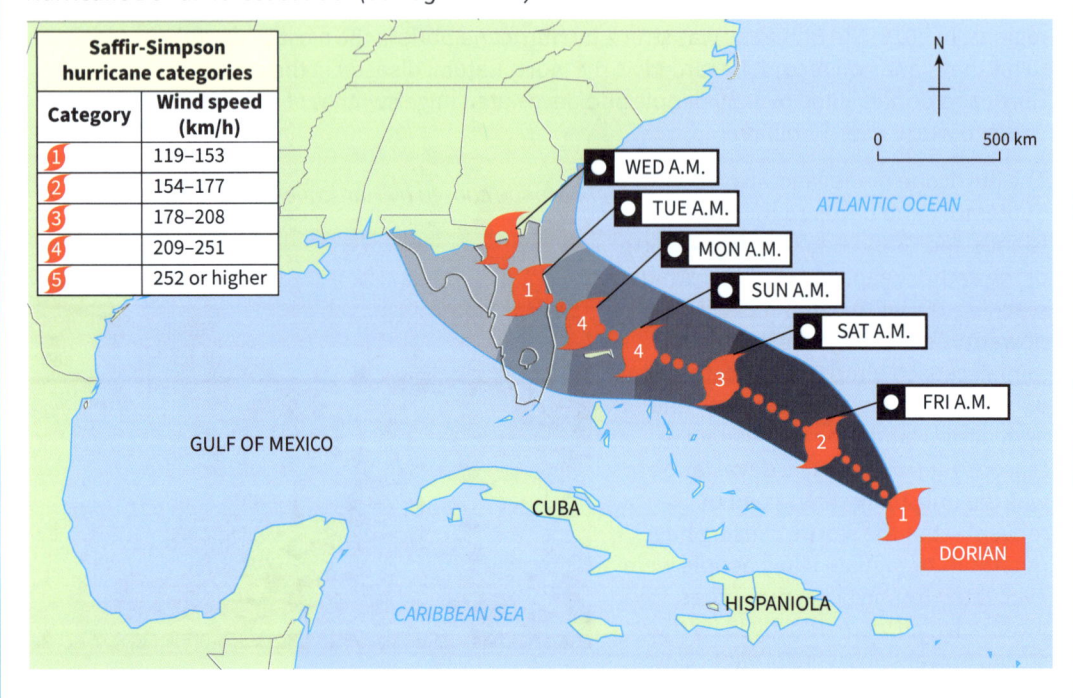

| Saffir-Simpson hurricane categories ||
Category	Wind speed (km/h)
1	119–153
2	154–177
3	178–208
4	209–251
5	252 or higher

Threats to the USA's East Coast and New York

By 1 September, forecasters amended the predicted track of Hurricane Dorian, suggesting that it would not make landfall in Florida but would instead track parallel to the coastline.

This turned out to be an accurate forecast, with the storm passing close to the coastline of Florida and North Carolina. The storm then passed dangerously close to the coast of New Jersey and Delaware, with heavy rain falling on New York City.

This rekindled memories of the devastating impacts of Hurricane Sandy on the New Jersey coast and New York City in 2012. Had the hurricane tracked a little further west, the impacts could have been considerable.

Hurricane Dorian eventually made landfall in Nova Scotia, Canada on 7 September 2019.

Issue evaluation resources booklet

Figure 3

New York: under threat from hurricanes

The East Coast of the USA, from Florida in the south to New England in the north, is vulnerable to the effects of hurricanes. Much of the coastline is flat and low-lying, comprising sandy barrier islands, wide beaches and extensive river estuaries. To combat the threat of hurricanes, most communities rely upon prediction and planning, evacuating people away from coastal areas to temporary shelters.

In 2012, Hurricane Sandy struck the New Jersey coast, devastating several coastal communities and driving a storm surge into New York Bay that caused significant damage and financial losses in New York City itself. This was just a year after Hurricane Irene had struck the city, causing widespread flooding.

Impacts of Hurricane Sandy in New York (2012)
• 53 people died and thousands were evacuated.
• Thousands of homes and 250 000 vehicles were destroyed.
• $19 billion damage caused; the Stock Exchange closed for two days.
• Fire at Breezy Point, caused by an exploding transmitter, destroyed over 100 buildings.
• Subways and road tunnels were flooded; international airports were closed.
• Several hospitals were temporarily closed due to flooding.

With sea levels rising due to climate change and an increase in hurricane intensity, large parts of New York and New Jersey are likely to be at risk in the future. The National Oceanic and Atmospheric Administration (NOAA) has recorded a sea level rise of about 30 cm per century. By the end of the century, sea level is expected to rise by 100–200 cm.

The New York/New Jersey Metropolitan Storm Surge Working Group's proposal

In the wake of Hurricane Sandy, a group of scientists, business leaders, engineers, lawyers and civic leaders established the New York/New Jersey Metropolitan Storm Surge Working Group. They have proposed a series of storm surge barriers to protect vulnerable seaports, international airports, subway and road tunnels, hospitals and millions of low-income residents living on low-lying land.

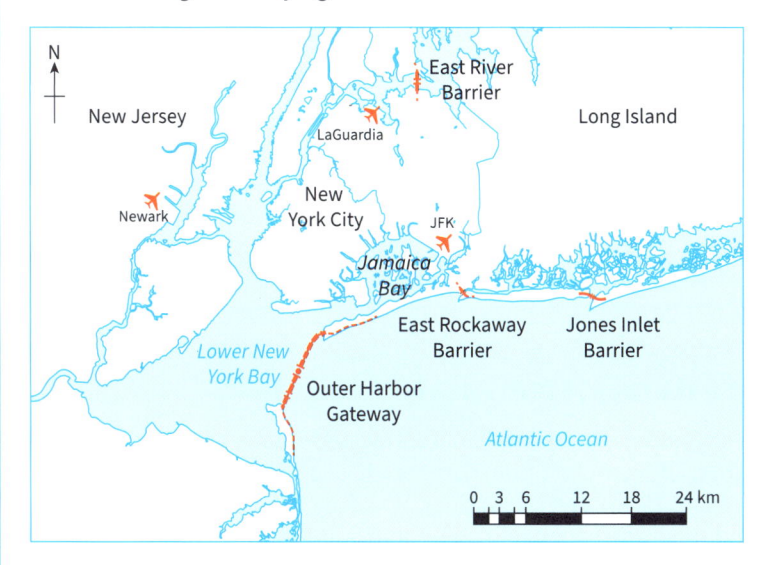

Focus on Paper 3: Geographical applications

Issue evaluation resources booklet

Research has suggested that rising sea levels and more powerful hurricanes will increase the flood risk significantly. Floods of a magnitude that used to occur on average once every 500 years pre-1800 now occur once every 24 years and, by 2050, are predicted to occur once every 5 years.

Storm surge barriers have been constructed elsewhere. Three barriers have operated successfully in New England and, in Europe, the Thames Barrier (UK), Delta Project (the Netherlands) and St Petersburg Dam (Russia) have prevented the flooding of vulnerable areas.

Part of the St Petersburg Dam, Russia

The Aerts' Report on the storm surge barrier system

Unconvinced by the plans and concerned about costs, New York City commissioned a report by Dr Jeroen Aerts of the University of Amsterdam. Asked to compare the barrier system with less ambitious improvements such as raising levées (river banks), relocating subway stations, constructing smaller local barriers and raising key buildings, Aerts concluded that the costs/benefits were roughly equal.

Despite the report, the City authorities dismissed the large-scale project on the following grounds:

- The system of barriers would be hugely expensive ($20–25 billion).
- The sheer scale of the barriers could mean that they take decades to construct.
- The impact on fish migration, water quality and shoreline processes are unknown.
- Massive levées would dramatically affect local communities and the character of natural beaches.
- Spending on barriers would divert money from other schemes to mitigate sea level rise.

Aerts reacted to the decision with surprise, suggesting that planning should start now to protect the city in the future. 'As a Dutchman,' Aerts said, 'you are quite surprised to see a large city like New York – so many people exposed – and no levées, no protection at all. [That] was astonishing to me. Don't rule out the barriers yet... you need a barrier.'

Storm Surge Working Group responses to the decision

- The small-scale projects have yet to be designed, let alone constructed.
- The impact on natural systems will be minimal as most of the time the barriers would be open. Environmental impacts will be minimal as long as the floodgates are open 60–80% of the time.
- Local plans already involve the construction of levées, affecting the character of beaches.
- The project could be expanded in the future to protect Long Island and the New Jersey coast.

Can the restoration of natural systems protect the coast?

Local environmentalists have suggested that restoring natural systems, such as oyster beds, coastal wetlands and sand dunes, could protect from rising sea levels and storm surges. This would be a cheap, more naturalistic alternative to a barrier. However, scientists have suggested that these environments would simply be overwhelmed by storm surges so would be largely ineffective.

Specification checklist

Tick or colour the appropriate box to indicate your confidence level with the key ideas from each specification topic listed below.

Specification topic	Key ideas	🙂	😐	☹️
1 Natural hazards	Natural hazards pose major risks to people and property			
2 Tectonic hazards	Earthquakes and volcanic eruptions are the result of physical processes			
	The effects of, and responses to, tectonic hazards vary between areas of contrasting levels of wealth			
	Management can reduce the effects of tectonic hazards			
3 Weather hazards	Global atmospheric circulation helps to determine patterns of weather and climate			
	Tropical storms (hurricanes, cyclones, typhoons) develop as a result of particular physical conditions			
	Tropical storms have significant effects on people and the environment			
	The UK is affected by a number of weather hazards			
	Extreme weather events in the UK have impacts on human activity			
4 Climate change	Climate change is the result of natural and human factors and has a range of effects			
	Managing climate change involves both mitigation (reducing causes) and adaptation (responding to change)			
5 Ecosystems	Ecosystems exist at a range of scales and involve the interaction between living and non-living components			
6 Tropical rainforests	Tropical rainforests have distinctive environmental characteristics			
	Deforestation has economic and environmental impacts			
	Tropical rainforests need to be managed to be sustainable			
7 Hot deserts	Hot desert ecosystems have distinctive environmental characteristics			
	Development of hot desert environments creates opportunities and challenges			
	Areas on the fringe of hot deserts are at risk of desertification			
8 Cold environments	Cold environments (polar and tundra) have distinctive characteristics			
	Development of cold environments creates opportunities and challenges			
	Cold environments are at risk from economic development			
9 UK landscapes	The UK has a range of diverse landscapes			
10 Coastal landscapes	The coast is shaped by a number of physical processes			
	Distinctive coastal landforms are the result of rock type, structure and physical processes			
	Different management strategies can be used to protect coastlines from the effects of physical processes			
11 River landscapes	The shape of river valleys changes as rivers flow downstream			
	Distinctive fluvial (river) landforms result from different physical processes			
	Different management strategies can be used to protect river landscapes from the effects of flooding			

Specification checklist

12 Glacial landscapes	Ice was a powerful force in shaping the physical landscape of the UK			
	Distinctive global landforms result from different physical processes			
	Glaciated upland areas provide opportunities for different economic activities, and management strategies can be used to reduce land use conflicts			
13 The urban world	A growing percentage of the world's population lives in urban areas			
	Urban growth creates opportunities and challenges for cities in lower income countries and newly emerging economies			
14 Urban change in the UK	Urban change in cities in the UK leads to a variety of social, economic and environmental opportunities and challenges			
15 Sustainable urban development	Urban sustainability requires management of resources and transport			
16 The development gap	There are global variations in economic development and quality of life			
	Various strategies exist for reducing the global development gap			
17 Nigeria: a newly emerging economy	Some LICs or NEEs are experiencing rapid economic development, which leads to a significant social, environmental and cultural change			
18 The changing UK economy	Major changes in the economy of the UK have affected, and will continue to affect, employment patterns and regional growth			
19 Resource management	Food, water and energy are fundamental to human development			
	The changing demand and provision of resources in the UK create opportunities and challenges			
20 Food management	Demand for food resources is rising globally but supply can be insecure, which may lead to conflict			
	Different strategies can be used to increase food supply			
21 Water management	Demand for water resources is rising globally but supply can be insecure, which may lead to conflict			
	Different strategies can be used to increase water supply			
22 Energy management	Demand for energy resources is rising globally but supply can be insecure, which may lead to conflict			
	Different strategies can be used to increase energy supply			
23 Issue evaluation				
24 Fieldwork	Physical geography topic			
	Human geography topic			
	Unfamiliar fieldwork			

Skills and case studies checklists

Tick or colour the appropriate box to indicate your confidence level with the geographical skills listed below.

	🙂	😐	☹️
Cartographic skills – atlas maps			
Coordinates – latitude and longitude			
Distributions and patterns of human and physical features, e.g. population distribution and movements, transport, settlements, relief, drainage			
Interrelationships between physical and human features and patterns on thematic maps			
Cartographic skills – Ordnance Survey maps			
Interpret at a range of scales, including 1:50 000 and 1:25 000			
Four- and six-figure grid references			
Scale, distance and direction (straight and curved line distances with a variety of scales)			
Gradient, contour and spot height			
Numerical and statistical information			
Basic landscape features and their characteristics			
Major relief features in relation to cross-sectional drawings			
What patterns of relief, drainage, settlement, communication and land use tell us about the physical and human landscape			
Cross-sections and transects of physical and human landscapes			
Physical features of coastlines, river and glacial landscapes			
Human activity, including tourism			
Cartographic skills – maps and photographs			
Compare maps			
Sketch maps: draw, label, understand and interpret			
Photographs: use and interpret ground, aerial and satellite photos			
Describe human and physical landscapes (landforms, vegetation, land use, settlement) and geographical phenomena from photos			
Draw sketches from photos			
Label and annotate diagrams, maps, graphs, sketches and photos			
Graphical skills			
Construct line charts, bar charts, pie charts, pictograms, histograms with equal class intervals, divided bar, scattergraphs and population pyramids			
Suggest an appropriate form of graphical representation for data			
Complete choropleth maps, isoline maps, dot maps, desire lines, proportional symbols and flow lines			
Gradient, contour and value on isoline maps			
Plot information on graphs			
Interpret population pyramids, choropleth maps, flow line maps, dispersion graphs			
Numerical skills			
Understand number, area and scales and the qualitative relationships between units			
Design fieldwork data collection sheets and collect data with an understanding of accuracy, sample size and procedures, control groups and reliability			
Proportion and ratio, magnitude and frequency			
Draw informed conclusions from numerical data			
Statistical skills			
Measures of central tendency, spread and cumulative frequency (median, mean, range, quartiles and inter-quartile range, mode and modal class)			
Calculate percentage change and understand percentiles			

Skills and case studies checklists

Sketch trend lines through scatter plots, draw estimated lines of best fit, identify trends, make predictions			
Identify weaknesses in statistical presentation of data			
Qualitative and quantitative data Obtain, illustrate, communicate, interpret, analyse and evaluate geographical information from primary and secondary sources including:			
Maps			
Fieldwork data			
Geospatial data presented in GIS frameworks			
Satellite imagery			
Written and digital sources			
Visual and graphical sources			
Numerical and statistical information			
Formulate enquiry and argument			
Identify questions and sequences of enquiry			
Write descriptively, analytically and critically			
Communicate your ideas effectively			
Develop an extended written argument			
Draw well-evidenced and informed conclusions			
Literacy			
Communicate information in ways suitable for a range of target audiences			

Fill in your examples and case studies to use as a revision checklist.

Theme	Example (Ex)/case study (CS) needed	My example/case study
Challenge of natural hazards	• **Ex:** Tectonic hazard, two contrasting countries (effects and responses) • **Ex:** Tropical storm (effects and responses) • **Ex:** Recent extreme weather event in the UK (causes, impacts and management)	
The living world	• **Ex:** Small-scale UK ecosystem • **CS:** Tropical rainforest (causes of deforestation, impacts and issues) • **CS:** Development opportunities and challenges in hot deserts or cold environments	
Physical landscapes in the UK	• **Ex (2):** Section of river valley/coastline/glaciated area (landforms of erosion and deposition) • **Ex (2):** River management/coastal management/tourism and management (glaciation)	
Urban issues and challenges	• **CS:** Major city in LIC/NEE (growth, opportunities, challenges) • **Ex:** Urban planning improving urban poor • **CS:** Major city in UK (migration, opportunities, challenges) • **Ex:** UK urban regeneration	
Changing economic world	• **CS:** LIC/NEE country (economic structure, TNCs, trade, aid, debt) • **Ex:** Tourism in one LIC/NEE • **Ex:** UK industrial sustainability	
Challenge of resource management	• **Ex – food (2):** Large-scale agricultural development, local scheme to increase sustainable production • **Ex – water (2):** Large-scale water transfer, local scheme to improve water supply • **Ex – energy (2):** Fossil fuels; local renewable energy	

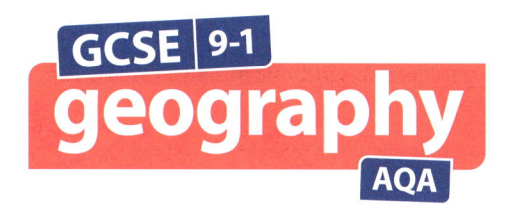

though
GCSE 9-1 Geography AQA
Practice Paper

Paper 1 Living with the physical environment

Time allowed: 1 hour 30 minutes
Total number of marks: 88 (including 3 marks for spelling, punctuation, grammar and specialist terminology [SPaG])

Instructions
Answer **all** questions in Section A and Section B
Answer **two** questions in Section C

Paper 1 Living with the physical environment
Section A The challenge of natural hazards

Answer **all** questions in this section.

Question 1 **The challenge of natural hazards**

0 1 . 1 What is meant by a natural hazard?

[1 mark]

_____

_____

0 1 . 2 Name **three** types of natural hazard.

[3 marks]

1 _____

2 _____

3 _____

0 1 . 3 Explain why people continue to live in areas that are at risk from tectonic hazards.

[4 marks]

_____

_____

_____

_____

_____

_____

_____

_____

Mark schemes for the exam papers can be found at www.oxfordsecondary.com/geog-aqa-answers.

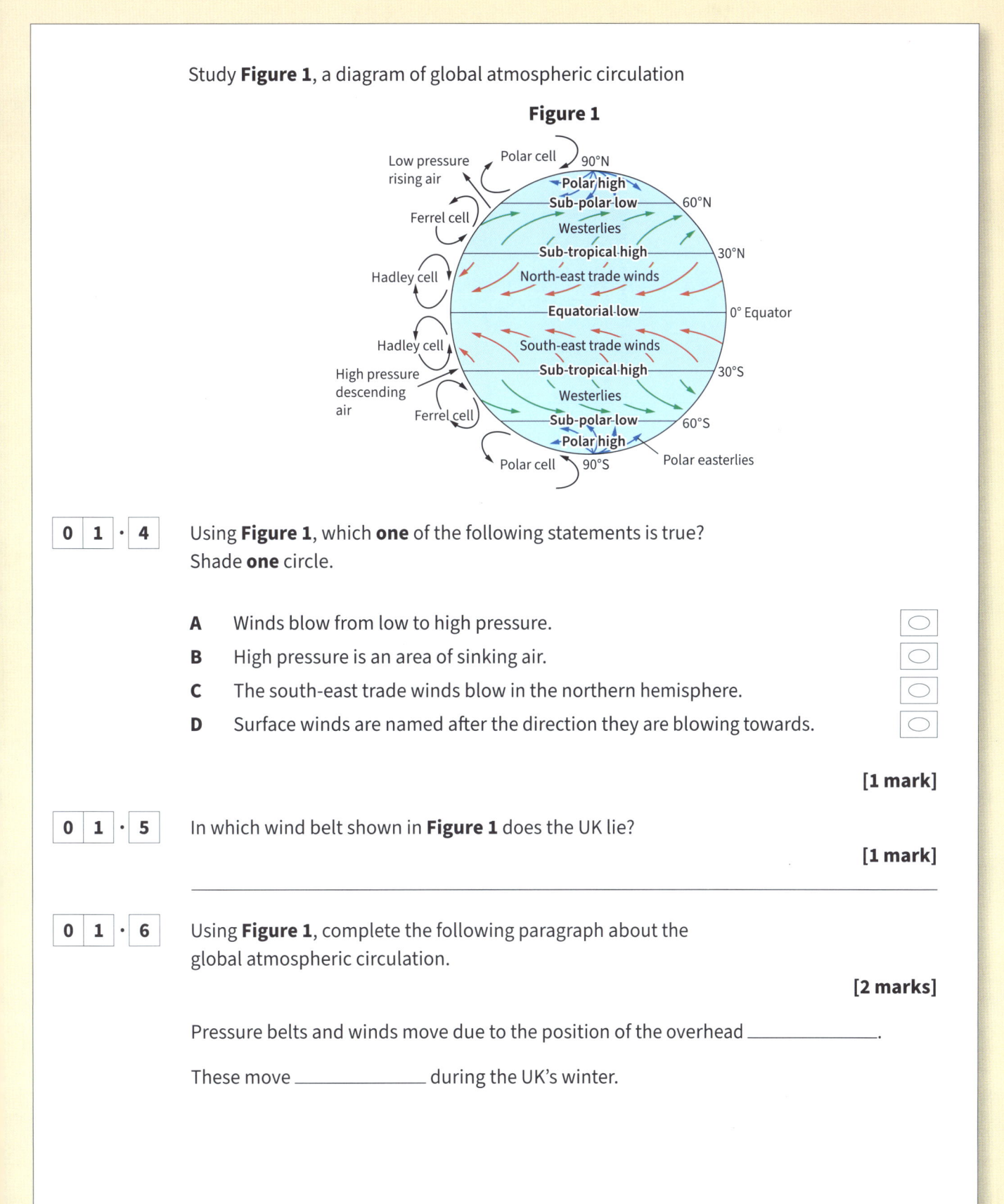

Section A The challenge of natural hazards

Study **Figure 1**, a diagram of global atmospheric circulation

Figure 1

0 1 . 4 Using **Figure 1**, which **one** of the following statements is true?
Shade **one** circle.

- **A** Winds blow from low to high pressure.
- **B** High pressure is an area of sinking air.
- **C** The south-east trade winds blow in the northern hemisphere.
- **D** Surface winds are named after the direction they are blowing towards.

[1 mark]

0 1 . 5 In which wind belt shown in **Figure 1** does the UK lie?

[1 mark]

_____

0 1 . 6 Using **Figure 1**, complete the following paragraph about the global atmospheric circulation.

[2 marks]

Pressure belts and winds move due to the position of the overhead _____.

These move _____ during the UK's winter.

Mark schemes for the exam papers can be found at www.oxfordsecondary.com/geog-aqa-answers.

Paper 1 Living with the physical environment

Study **Figure 2**, a graph showing the number of tropical storms in the Atlantic between 1900 and 2018.

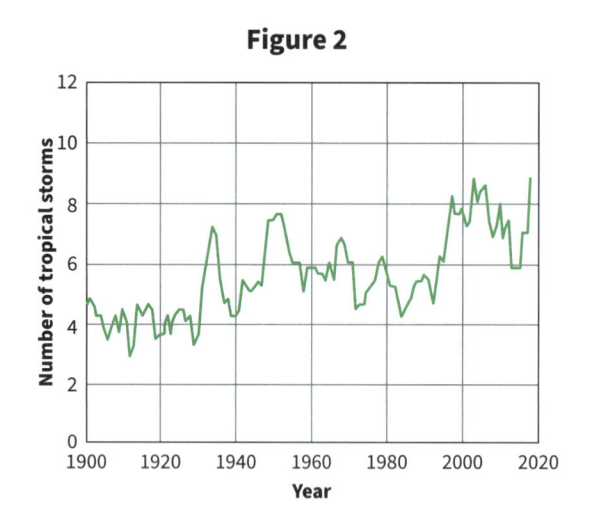

Figure 2

0 1 . 7 Outline the overall change that has occurred in the number of storms experienced in the period shown in **Figure 2**.

[1 mark]

0 1 . 8 Give **two** reasons why most tropical storms develop between 5° and 15° north and south of the Equator.

[2 marks]

1 _____

2 _____

0 1 . 9 Explain how climate change can affect the frequency and intensity of tropical storms.

[6 marks]

Mark schemes for the exam papers can be found at **www.oxfordsecondary.com/geog-aqa-answers**.

Section A The challenge of natural hazards

0 1 . 10 'Managing climate change needs to be a combination of mitigation and adaptation.'
Do you agree with this statement? Explain your answer.

[9 marks]
[+3 SPaG marks]

Mark schemes for the exam papers can be found at **www.oxfordsecondary.com/geog-aqa-answers**.

Exam practice papers, Paper 1   117

Paper 1 Living with the physical environment
Section B The living world

Answer **all** questions in this section.

Question 2   **The living world**

Study **Figure 3**, a photograph taken in the Cambodian tropical rainforests in South-East Asia.

Figure 3

0 2 . 1   Which **one** of the following features of a tropical rainforest is shown in **Figure 3**? Shade **one** circle only.

- **A**   An epiphyte   ○
- **B**   The canopy   ○
- **C**   A buttress root   ○
- **D**   A liana   ○

[1 mark]

0 2 . 2   Explain how the feature selected in **Figure 3** helps the vegetation adapt to the climate of the tropical rainforests.

[2 marks]

_____

_____

_____

_____

Mark schemes for the exam papers can be found at www.oxfordsecondary.com/geog-aqa-answers.

Section B The living world

Study **Figure 4**, a diagram showing the food web in a tropical rainforest.

Figure 4

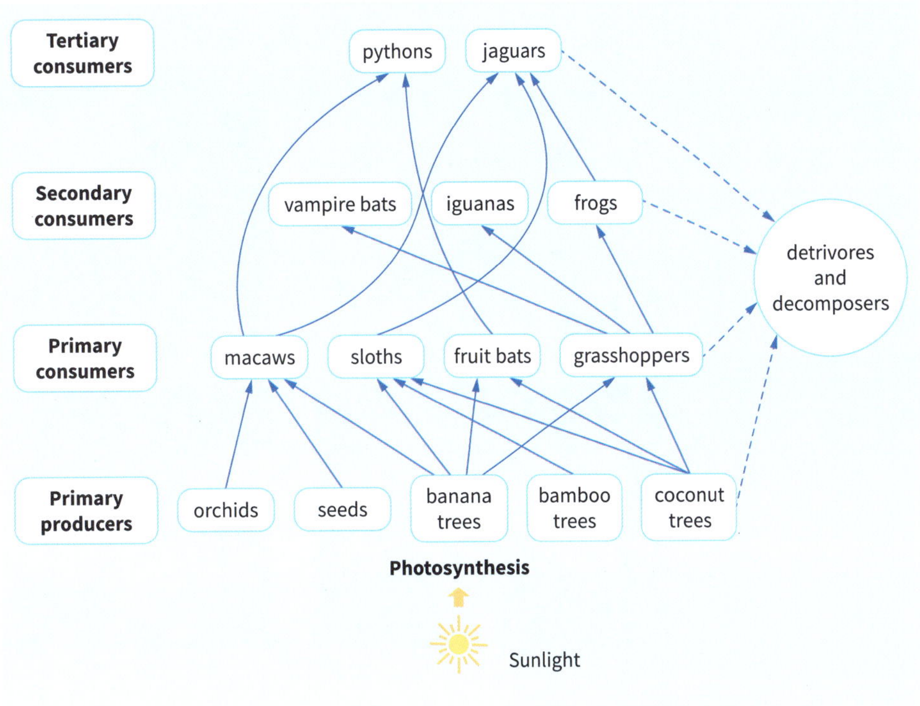

| 0 2 . 3 | With the help of **Figure 4**, which one of the following are primary consumers? Shade one circle only. |

- **A** Herbivores
- **B** Carnivores
- **C** Top carnivores
- **D** Decomposers

[1 mark]

| 0 2 . 4 | Explain why the number of species reduces when moving through the different layers of the food web from the primary producers up to the tertiary consumers, as shown in **Figure 4**.

[2 marks]

_____

_____

_____

_____

Mark schemes for the exam papers can be found at **www.oxfordsecondary.com/geog-aqa-answers**.

Paper 1 Living with the physical environment

Study **Figure 5**, which shows some animals that live in tropical rainforests and a list of some of the ways animals have adapted to living in these areas in order to survive.

Adaptations

- Camouflage
- Sleeping throughout the day
- Having a very specialist diet
- Living in the forest canopy

Figure 5

0 2 . 5 Use **Figure 5** and your own understanding to explain how animals have adapted to the physical conditions of the tropical rainforests.

[6 marks]

Section B The living world

0 2 . 6 Study **Figure 6**, a table showing the amount of forest lost in the Amazon Basin in km^2 2012–2021.

Figure 6

Year	2012	2013	2014	2015	2016	2017	2018	2019	2020	2021
Area (km^2)	4571	5891	5010	6207	7893	6947	7536	9762	8426	10476

Which year saw the smallest amount of forest lost in the period 2012–2021?

[1 mark]

_____

0 2 . 7 What was the percentage increase in the amount of forest lost between 2012 and 2021? Give your answer to the nearest whole percentage.

[2 marks]

Show your working.

Nearest whole percentage =

0 2 . 8 Calculate the mean annual amount of forest lost in km^2 in the Amazon during the period 2012–2021. Give your answer to one decimal point.

[1 mark]

_____

_____

0 2 . 9 Assess the importance of the interdependence of the climate, soils and people in **either** a hot desert environment **or** a cold environment.

[9 marks]

_____
_____
_____
_____
_____
_____
_____
_____

Mark schemes for the exam papers can be found at www.oxfordsecondary.com/geog-aqa-answers.

Paper 1 Living with the physical environment

Extra space

Paper 1 Living with the physical environment
Section C Physical landscapes in the UK

Answer **two** questions from the following:
Question 3 (Coasts), Question 4 (Rivers), Question 5 (Glacial).

Question 3 **Coastal landscapes in the UK**

Study **Figure 7**, a map showing the major upland areas, lowland areas and river systems of the British Isles.

Figure 7

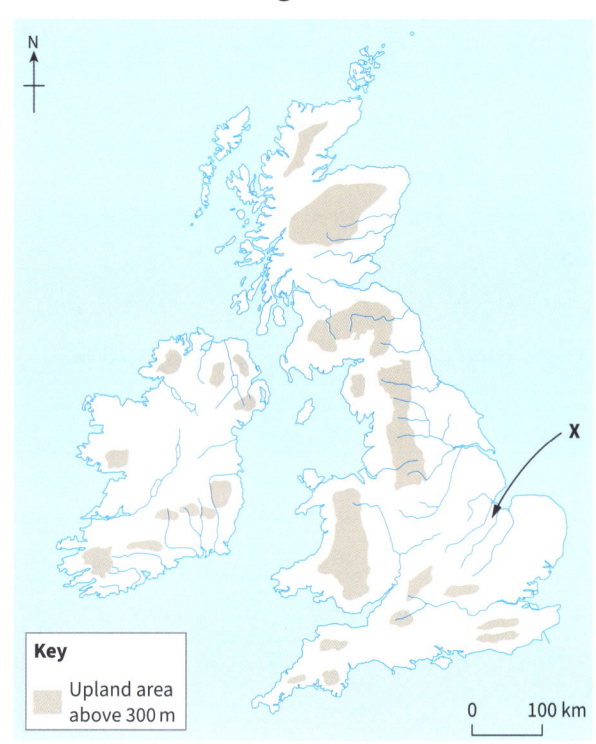

| 0 | 3 | . | 1 | What is the name of lowland area **X** shown in **Figure 7**?
Shade **one** circle only.

- A   Central Lowlands of Scotland   ◯
- B   The Fens   ◯
- C   Vale of York   ◯
- D   Vale of Glamorgan   ◯

[1 mark]

Mark schemes for the exam papers can be found at **www.oxfordsecondary.com/geog-aqa-answers**.

Paper 1 Living with the physical environment

Study **Figure 8**, a diagram of a coastal process.

Figure 8

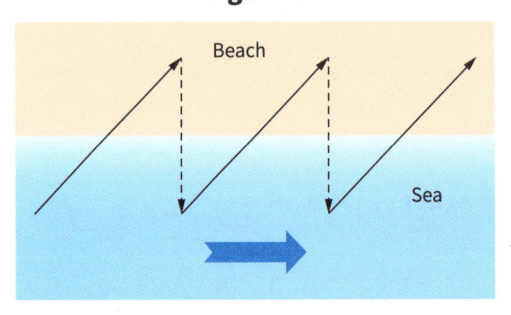

| 0 | 3 | . | 3 | | Give the name of this coastal process.

[1 mark]

_____

| 0 | 3 | . | 3 | | On **Figure 8**, label the following:
- direction of coastal process
- backwash
- swash

[2 marks]

| 0 | 3 | . | 4 | | Name one coastal landform formed as a result of the coastal process shown in **Figure 8**.

[1 mark]

_____

Study **Figure 9**, a photograph of a landslide at West Bay in Dorset.

Figure 9

Mark schemes for the exam papers can be found at **www.oxfordsecondary.com/geog-aqa-answers**.

Exam practice papers, Paper 1

Section C Physical landscapes in the UK

0 3 . 5 Using **Figure 9** and your own understanding, explain how mass movement can affect the shape of the coastline.

[4 marks]

0 3 . 6 Name an example of a coastal management scheme in the UK.

Assess whether the overall benefits outweigh any conflicts that are caused as a result of the scheme.

[6 marks]

Paper 1 Living with the physical environment

Question 4   River landscapes in the UK

Study **Figure 10**, a map showing the major upland areas, lowland areas and river systems of the British Isles.

Figure 10

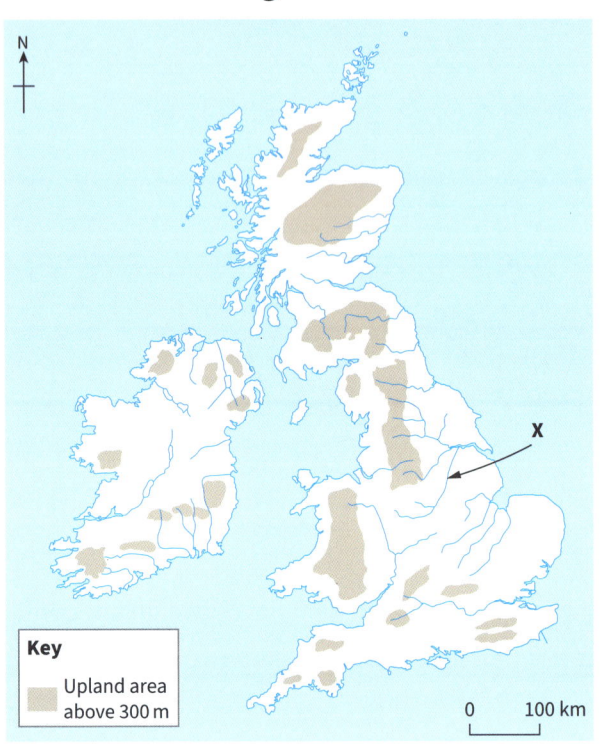

0 4 . 1   What is the name of river **X** shown in **Figure 10**?
Shade **one** circle only.

- A   River Lagan   ○
- B   River Thames ○
- C   River Severn ○
- D   River Trent   ○

[1 mark]

Mark schemes for the exam papers can be found at **www.oxfordsecondary.com/geog-aqa-answers**.

Section C Physical landscapes in the UK

Study **Figure 11**, a diagram showing three river processes.

Figure 11

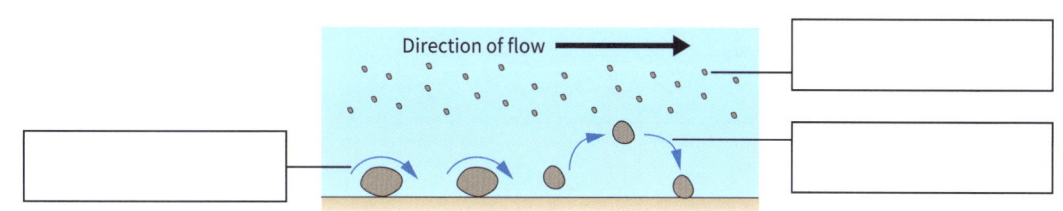

River bed

04.2 On **Figure 11**, label the following:
- saltation
- suspension
- traction

[2 marks]

04.3 Name the river action these three processes perform.

[1 mark]

Study **Figure 12**, a photograph showing part of the lower course of a river.

Figure 12

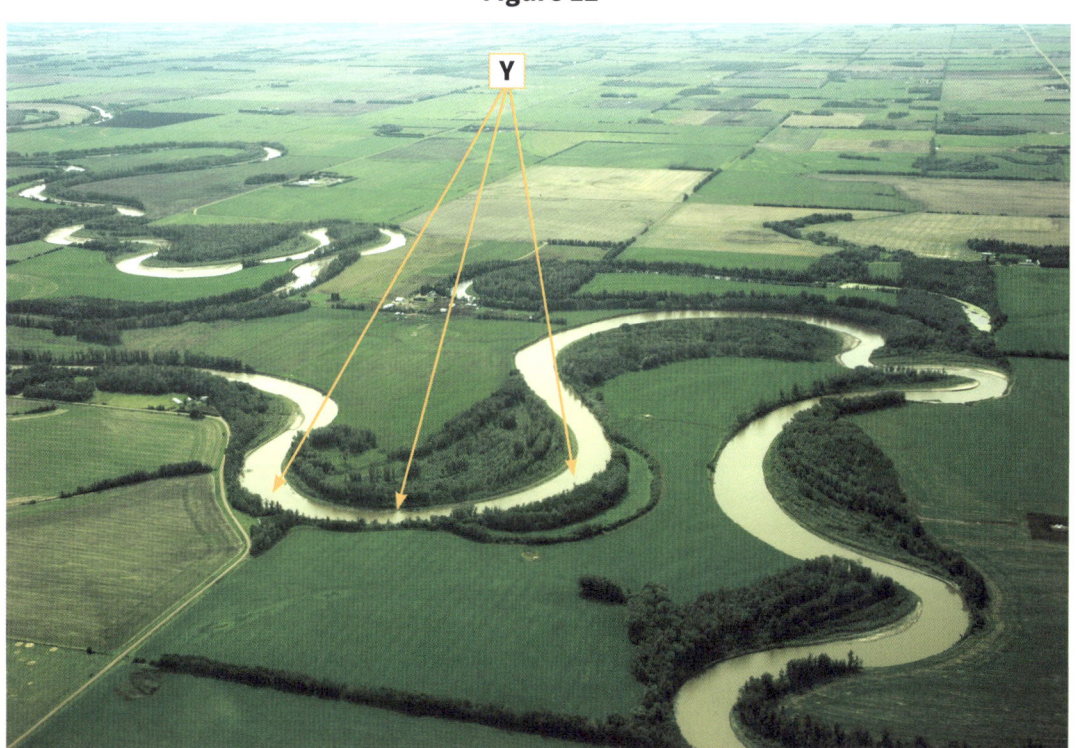

04.4 Name the river feature labelled 'Y' on **Figure 12**.

[1 mark]

Mark schemes for the exam papers can be found at **www.oxfordsecondary.com/geog-aqa-answers**.

Paper 1 Living with the physical environment

0 4 . 5 Using **Figure 12** and your own understanding, explain how the river contributes to the shape of the landscape.

[4 marks]

0 4 . 6 Name an example of a flood management scheme in the UK.

Assess whether the overall benefits outweigh any environmental issues that are caused as a result of the scheme.

[6 marks]

Mark schemes for the exam papers can be found at www.oxfordsecondary.com/geog-aqa-answers.

Section C Physical landscapes in the UK

Question 5 **Glacial landscapes in the UK**

Study **Figure 13**, a map showing the major upland areas, lowland areas and river systems of the British Isles.

Figure 13

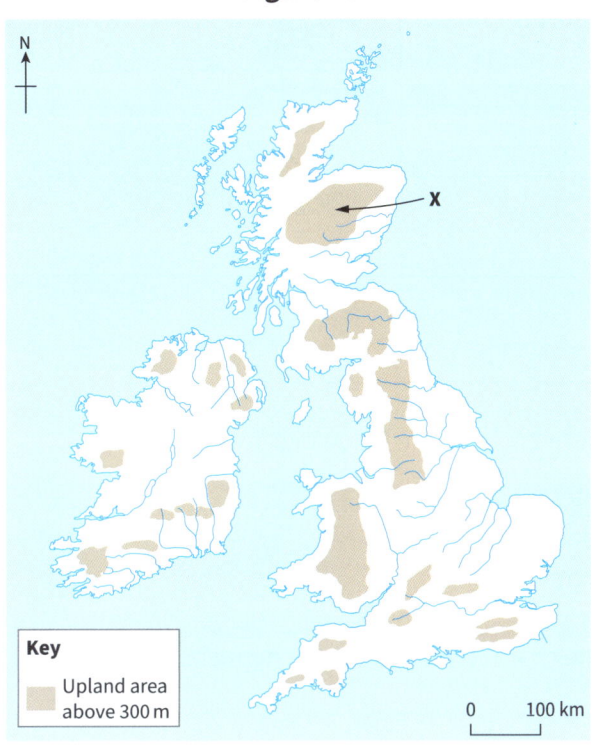

| 0 | 5 | . | 1 |

What is the name of upland **X** shown in **Figure 13**?
Shade **one** circle only.

A   Pennines
B   Lake District
C   Snowdonia
D   Grampians

[1 mark]

Mark schemes for the exam papers can be found at www.oxfordsecondary.com/geog-aqa-answers.

Paper 1 Living with the physical environment

Study **Figure 14**, a diagram showing areas of glacial deposition.

Figure 14

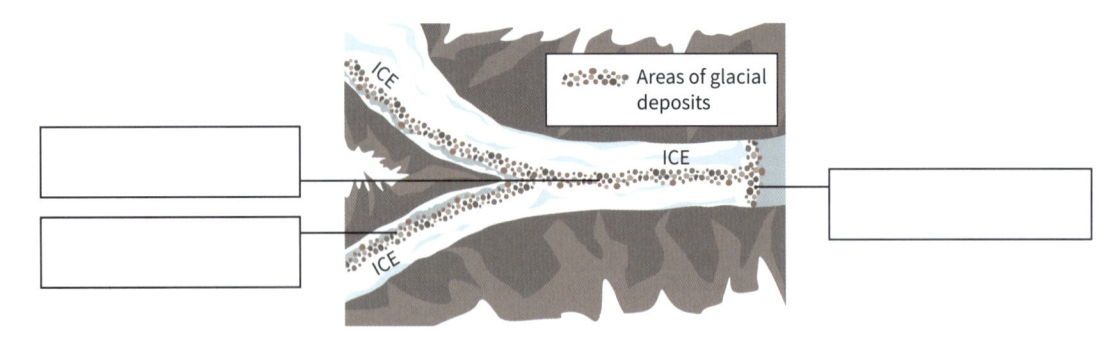

| 0 | 5 | . | 2 | State the name given to the areas of glacial deposits in **Figure 14**.

[1 mark]

| 0 | 5 | . | 3 | On **Figure 14**, label the following glacial deposits:

- lateral
- medial
- terminal

[2 marks]

| 0 | 5 | . | 4 | Give **one** characteristic of glacial deposits.

[1 mark]

Study **Figure 15**, a photograph showing a glaciated highland area.

Figure 15

Mark schemes for the exam papers can be found at **www.oxfordsecondary.com/geog-aqa-answers**.

130 Exam practice papers, Paper 1

Section C Physical landscapes in the UK

0 5 . 5 Using **Figure 15** and your own understanding, explain how glaciation has affected the shape of the landscape.

[4 marks]

0 5 . 6 Name an example of a glaciated upland area in the UK used for tourism.

Assess whether the overall benefits outweigh any environmental damage that is caused as a result of tourism.

[6 marks]

Mark schemes for the exam papers can be found at **www.oxfordsecondary.com/geog-aqa-answers**.

GCSE 9-1 Geography AQA
Practice Paper

Paper 2 Challenges in the human environment

Time allowed: 1 hour 30 minutes
Total number of marks: 88 (including 3 marks for spelling, punctuation, grammar and specialist terminology [SPaG])

Instructions
Answer **all** questions in Section A and Section B
Answer question 3 and **one other** question in Section C

Paper 2 Challenges in the human environment
Section A Urban issues and challenges

Answer **all** questions in this section.

Question 1   **Urban issues and challenges**

Study **Figure 1**, showing the population change in a major world city 1950–2020.

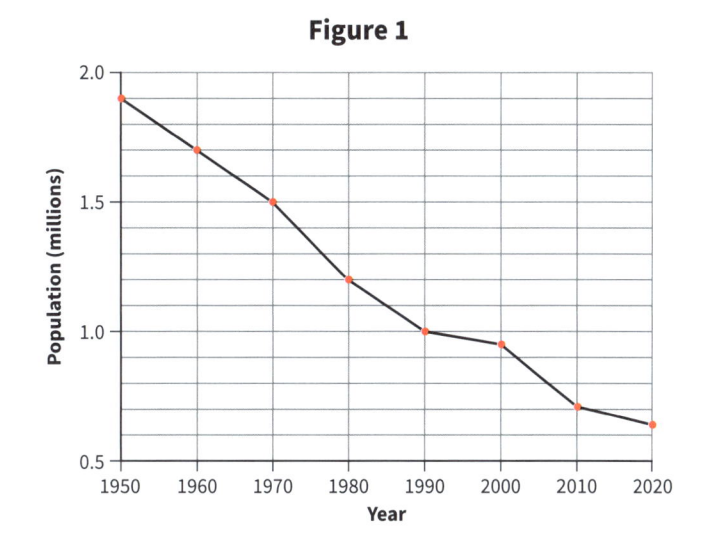

Figure 1

[Line graph showing population (millions) on y-axis from 0.5 to 2.0, and Year on x-axis from 1950 to 2020. Data points: 1950 ≈ 1.9, 1960 ≈ 1.7, 1970 ≈ 1.5, 1980 ≈ 1.2, 1990 ≈ 1.0, 2000 ≈ 0.95, 2010 ≈ 0.7, 2020 ≈ 0.65]

0 1 . 1   What was the population of the city in 1970?

[1 mark]

0 1 . 2   What was the change in the population between 1950 and 2020?

[1 mark]

0 1 . 3   In which type of country is this city likely to be situated? Shade **one** circle only.

- A   Newly emerging economy (NEE)   ○
- B   High-income country (HIC)   ○
- C   Low-income country (LIC)   ○

[1 mark]

0 1 . 4   Which of the following could be a reason for the trend shown in **Figure 1**? Shade **one** circle only.

- A   There has been rural–urban migration.   ○
- B   Birth rates have been higher than death rates.   ○
- C   Deindustrialisation has taken place.   ○
- D   Urbanisation is taking place.   ○

[1 mark]

Mark schemes for the exam papers can be found at www.oxfordsecondary.com/geog-aqa-answers.

Paper 2 Challenges in the human environment

Study **Figure 2**, which gives information about Dharavi, a squatter settlement in the Indian city of Mumbai.

Figure 2

People		Hygiene and health	
Population of Dharavi	Estimated 800 000–1 million	No of individual toilets in Dharavi	1440
Area	2.39 km² (the size of London's Hyde Park)	People per individual toilet	625
Population density	At least 330 000 people per km²	% of women with anaemia*	75%
No of homes in Dharavi	60 000	% of women with malnutrition	50%
People per home	Between 13 and 17	% of women with recurrent gastroenteritis**	50%
Average size of home	10 m² (equivalent to a medium-sized bedroom)	Most common causes of death	Malnutrition, diarrhoea, dehydration, typhoid

* anaemia: a lack of iron leading to tiredness
** gastroenteritis symptoms: diarrhoea, vomiting

0 1 . 5 Using **Figure 2**, explain why urban growth in LICs and NEEs often leads to serious challenges for the city.

[4 marks]

0 1 . 6 Discuss the attempts of a city in an LIC or an NEE to provide sufficient health and education services for its inhabitants.

[6 marks]

Name of city in LIC or NEE _____

Mark schemes for the exam papers can be found at www.oxfordsecondary.com/geog-aqa-answers.

Exam practice papers, Paper 2

Section A Urban issues and challenges

_____
_____
_____
_____
_____
_____
_____
_____
_____

Study **Figure 3**, a map showing the distribution of Asian-Indian British residents in London.

Figure 3

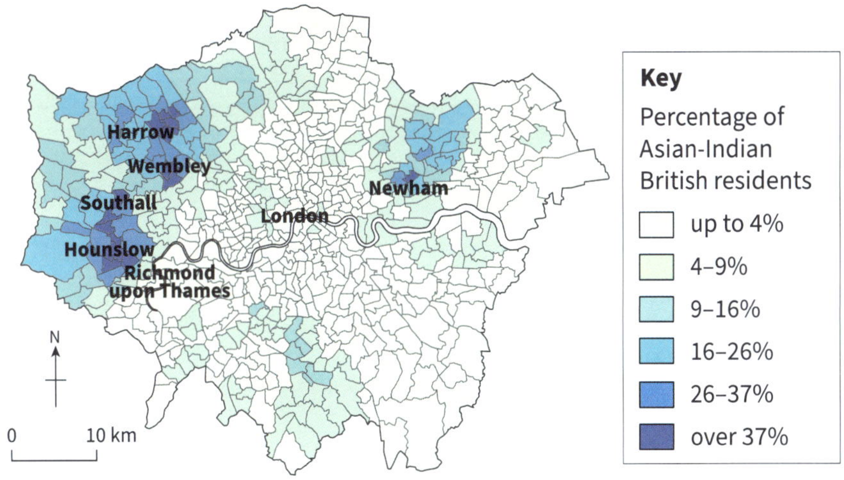

| 0 | 1 | . | 7 | | What kind of map is shown in **Figure 3**?

[1 mark]
_____

| 0 | 1 | . | 8 | | Using **Figure 3**, describe the distribution of Asian-Indian British residents in London.

[2 marks]
_____
_____
_____
_____

Mark schemes for the exam papers can be found at **www.oxfordsecondary.com/geog-aqa-answers**.

Paper 2 Challenges in the human environment

01.9 Explain how migration can affect a city under the following headings:

[4 marks]

Enriching a city's cultural life _____

_____

_____

Challenge of integration into the wider community _____

_____

_____

01.10 To what extent has urban change created social and economic challenges in a UK city you have studied?

[9 marks]

[+3 SPaG marks]

Name of UK city _____

_____

_____

_____

_____

_____

_____

_____

_____

_____

_____

_____

_____

Continue your answer on a separate sheet of paper

Mark schemes for the exam papers can be found at www.oxfordsecondary.com/geog-aqa-answers.

Paper 2 Challenges in the human environment
Section B The changing economic world

Answer **all** questions in this section.

Question 2   **The changing economic world**

Study **Figure 4**, a partly completed diagram of the five stages of the Demographic Transition Model.

Figure 4

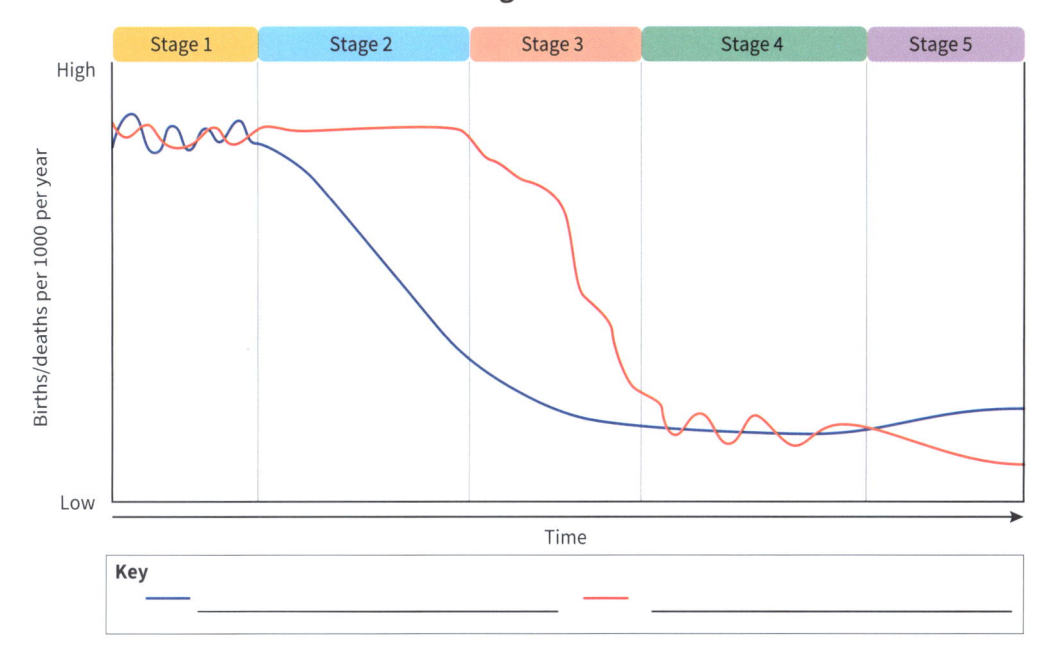

0 2 . 1   On **Figure 4**, complete the key by adding 'Birth rate' and 'Death rate' to the correct line symbol.

[1 mark]

0 2 . 2   On **Figure 4**, which stage has the greatest population increase?

- A   Stage 1
- B   Stage 2
- C   Stage 3
- D   Stage 4

[1 mark]

0 2 . 3   Complete the table to show which is the most likely stage that the following types of country have reached.

Type of country	Stage
HIC	
LIC	
NEE	

[3 marks]

Mark schemes for the exam papers can be found at **www.oxfordsecondary.com/geog-aqa-answers**.

Paper 2 Challenges in the human environment

0 2 . 4 Explain how **physical** factors can cause uneven development.

[4 marks]

0 2 . 5 Describe the location of an LIC or NEE you have studied.

Name of country _____

[2 marks]

0 2 . 6 Complete the following fact file for the LIC or NEE that you have studied.

[2 marks]

Importance regionally	
Importance internationally	

Mark schemes for the exam papers can be found at www.oxfordsecondary.com/geog-aqa-answers.

Section B The changing economic world

Study **Figure 5**, two photographs of contrasting examples of economic development in India, which is an NEE.

Figure 5

0 2 . 7   With reference to your case study of an LIC/NEE and **Figure 5**, assess the environmental impacts of economic development.

[6 marks]

Mark schemes for the exam papers can be found at www.oxfordsecondary.com/geog-aqa-answers.

Paper 2 Challenges in the human environment

Study **Figure 6**, which gives details of the north–south divide in Great Britain.

Figure 6

Government spending per person
Yorkshire = £7623
E. Midlands = £6983
London = £9176

Life expectancy
Liverpool = 75.7 years
Cambridge = 79.5 years

Southern students are more likely to attend a top university

UNEMPLOYMENT	
1 Merthyr Tydfil	30.1%
2 Liverpool	26.8%
3 Port Talbot	26.7%
4 Glasgow	25.7%
5 Hartlepool	25.7%
6 Middlesbrough	25.5%
7 Hastings	24.3%
8 Stoke-on-Trent	24.2%
9 Wolverhampton	24.1%
10 Birmingham	23%
11 Hackney	22.2%
12 Plymouth	17.5%
13 Sheffield	16.3%

0 2 . 8 What is the median value for the unemployment blackspots shown on **Figure 6**?

[1 mark]

0 2 . 9 Why may this measure of central tendency give a misleading impression of unemployment in these towns?

[1 mark]

0 2 . 10 Evaluate the strategies that attempt to remove the differences between the north and south of Great Britain.

Use **Figure 6** and your own understanding.

[9 marks]

Continue your answer on a separate sheet of paper

Mark schemes for the exam papers can be found at **www.oxfordsecondary.com/geog-aqa-answers**.

Paper 2 Challenges in the human environment
Section C The challenge of resource management

Answer Question 3 (Resources) and **either** Question 4 (Food) **or** Question 5 (Water) **or** Question 6 (Energy).

Question 3   **Resource management**

Study **Figure 7**, a tweet sent by the National Grid on 21 April 2017.

Figure 7

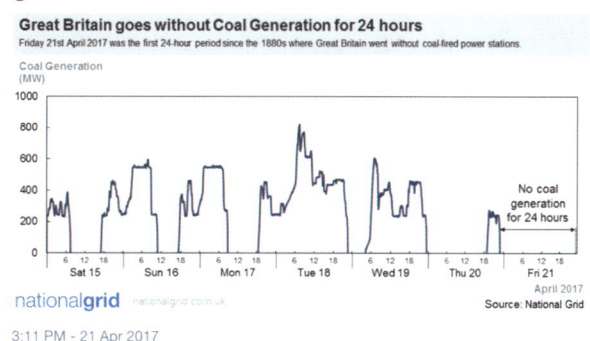

0 3 . 1   What was the highest figure for coal generation in the period 15–21 April 2017?

[1 mark]

0 3 . 2   What was the time and date for this peak of coal generation?

[1 mark]

0 3 . 3   Suggest why Great Britain was able to survive without any coal-generated electricity for 24 hours.

[2 marks]

Mark schemes for the exam papers can be found at **www.oxfordsecondary.com/geog-aqa-answers**.

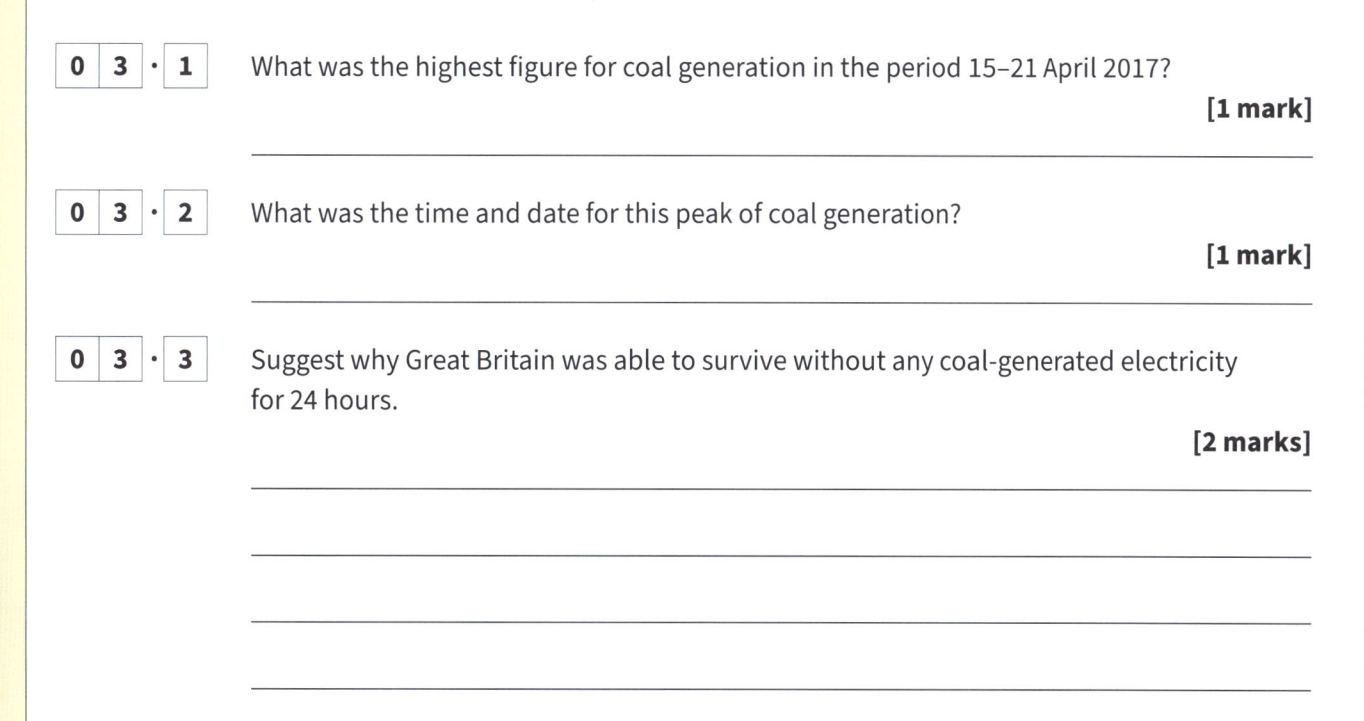

Paper 2 Challenges in the human environment

Study **Figure 8**, a graph showing how farm sizes changed in the UK between 2005 and 2018.

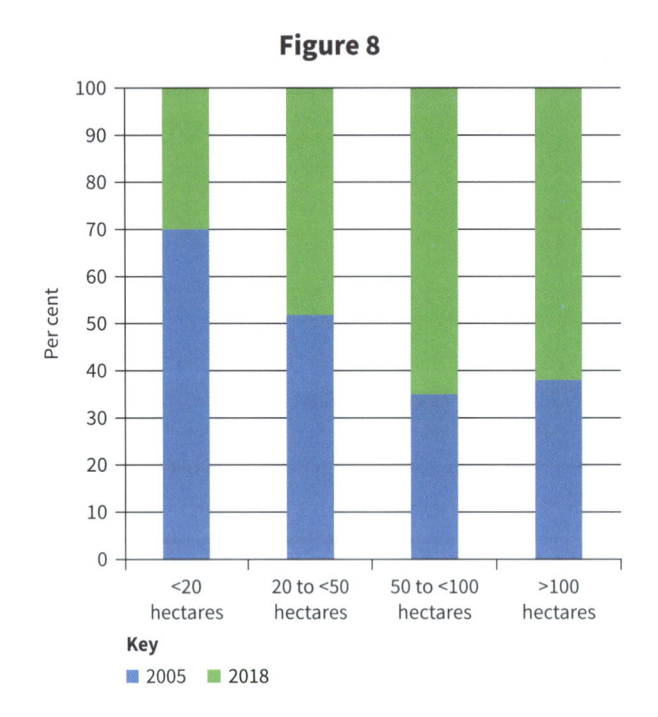

Figure 8

[Stacked bar chart titled "Figure 8" with y-axis "Per cent" from 0 to 100, and x-axis categories: <20 hectares, 20 to <50 hectares, 50 to <100 hectares, >100 hectares. Key: 2005 (blue), 2018 (green). Approximate 2005 values: 70, 52, 35, 38.]

0 3 . 4 What percentage of farms had an area of between 50 and 100 hectares in 2018?

[1 mark]

0 3 . 5 In **Figure 8**, what is the main trend in the size of UK farms between 2005 and 2018?

[1 mark]

0 3 . 6 Suggest how the change in the size of UK farms might affect the provision of food in the UK.

[2 marks]

Mark schemes for the exam papers can be found at www.oxfordsecondary.com/geog-aqa-answers.

Section C The challenge of resource management

Study **Figure 9**, which shows areas of water stress in England.

Figure 9

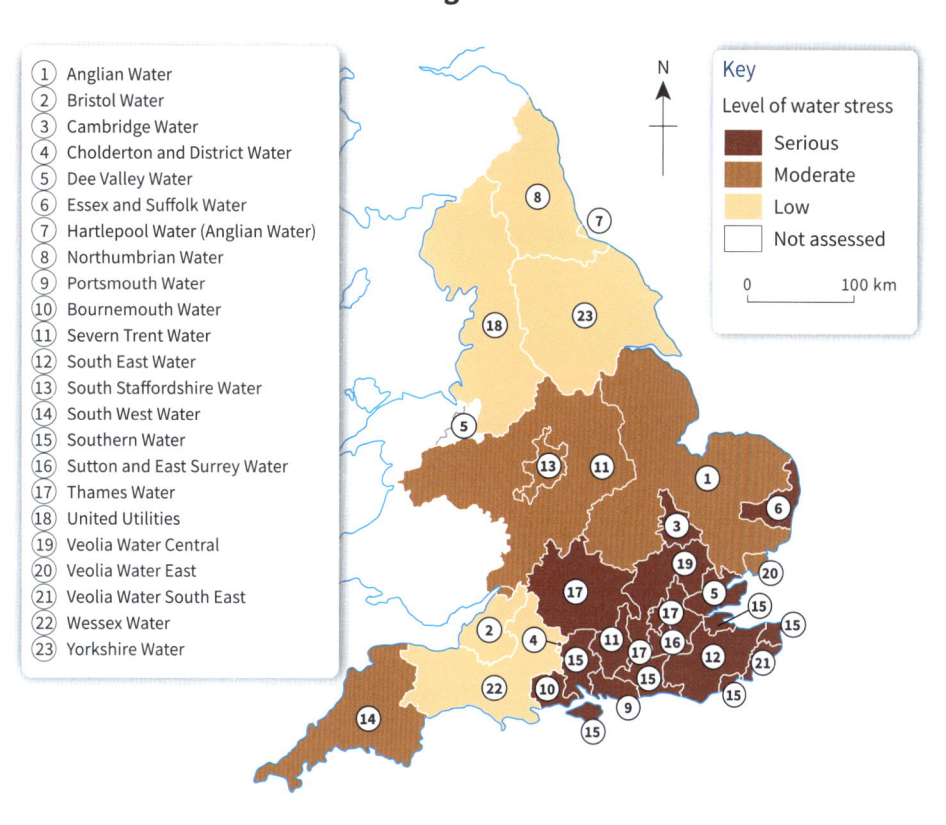

Key:
1. Anglian Water
2. Bristol Water
3. Cambridge Water
4. Cholderton and District Water
5. Dee Valley Water
6. Essex and Suffolk Water
7. Hartlepool Water (Anglian Water)
8. Northumbrian Water
9. Portsmouth Water
10. Bournemouth Water
11. Severn Trent Water
12. South East Water
13. South Staffordshire Water
14. South West Water
15. Southern Water
16. Sutton and East Surrey Water
17. Thames Water
18. United Utilities
19. Veolia Water Central
20. Veolia Water East
21. Veolia Water South East
22. Wessex Water
23. Yorkshire Water

Key — Level of water stress: Serious, Moderate, Low, Not assessed

03.7 Discuss how water transfer may be needed to maintain supplies across England. Use **Figure 9** and your own understanding.

[6 marks]

Mark schemes for the exam papers can be found at **www.oxfordsecondary.com/geog-aqa-answers**.

Exam practice papers, Paper 2

Paper 2 Challenges in the human environment

Answer **either** Question 4 (Food) **or** Question 5 (Water) **or** Question 6 (Energy).

Question 4   **Food**

Study **Figure 10**, which gives information about the country of South Sudan in Africa.

Figure 10

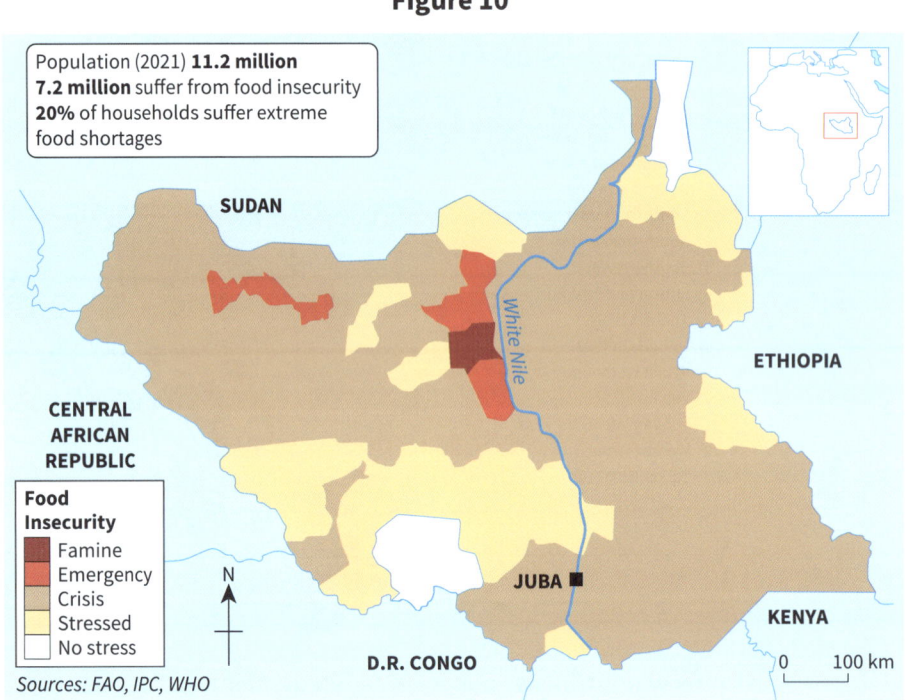

Population (2021) **11.2 million**
7.2 million suffer from food insecurity
20% of households suffer extreme food shortages

Food Insecurity:
- Famine
- Emergency
- Crisis
- Stressed
- No stress

Sources: FAO, IPC, WHO

0 4 . 1   What is meant by food insecurity?

[1 mark]

0 4 . 2   Give **two** pieces of evidence from **Figure 10** that show that South Sudan suffers from food insecurity.

[2 marks]

1 _____

2 _____

0 4 . 3   Suggest the impacts of food insecurity on a country.

[2 marks]

Mark schemes for the exam papers can be found at www.oxfordsecondary.com/geog-aqa-answers.

Section C The challenge of resource management

0 4 . 4 Choose an example of **either** a large-scale agricultural development **or** a local scheme in an LIC or a NEE that aims to increase the supply of food.

For the example chosen, discuss the extent to which it has been able to increase the supply of food.

Name of example _____

Circle the one you have chosen.

    A large scale agricultural development   A local scheme

[6 marks]

Mark schemes for the exam papers can be found at **www.oxfordsecondary.com/geog-aqa-answers**.

Paper 2 Challenges in the human environment

Question 5 Water

Study **Figure 11**, which gives information about the Nile Basin.

Figure 11

While Egypt is entirely dependent on the Nile for its water supply and regards any possible reduction as an issue of national security, some of the world's poorest countries see the river as a vital source for national development.

| 0 5 . 1 | What is meant by water insecurity?

[1 mark]

_____

_____

Mark schemes for the exam papers can be found at www.oxfordsecondary.com/geog-aqa-answers.

Exam practice papers, Paper 2

Section C The challenge of resource management

0 5 . 2 Give **two** pieces of evidence from **Figure 11** that show countries in the Nile Basin could suffer from water insecurity.

[2 marks]

1 _____

2 _____

0 5 . 3 Suggest the impacts of water insecurity on a country.

[2 marks]

_____
_____
_____
_____

0 5 . 4 Choose an example of **either** a large-scale water transfer scheme **or** a local scheme in an LIC or NEE, which aims to increase the supply of water.

For the example chosen, discuss the extent to which it has been able to increase the supply of water.

Name of example _____

Circle the one you have chosen.

    A large-scale water transfer scheme   A local scheme

[6 marks]

_____
_____
_____
_____
_____
_____
_____
_____
_____
_____

Mark schemes for the exam papers can be found at www.oxfordsecondary.com/geog-aqa-answers.

Paper 2 Challenges in the human environment

Question 6 **Energy**

Study **Figure 12**, which gives information about the gas supplies in Europe in 2018.

Figure 12

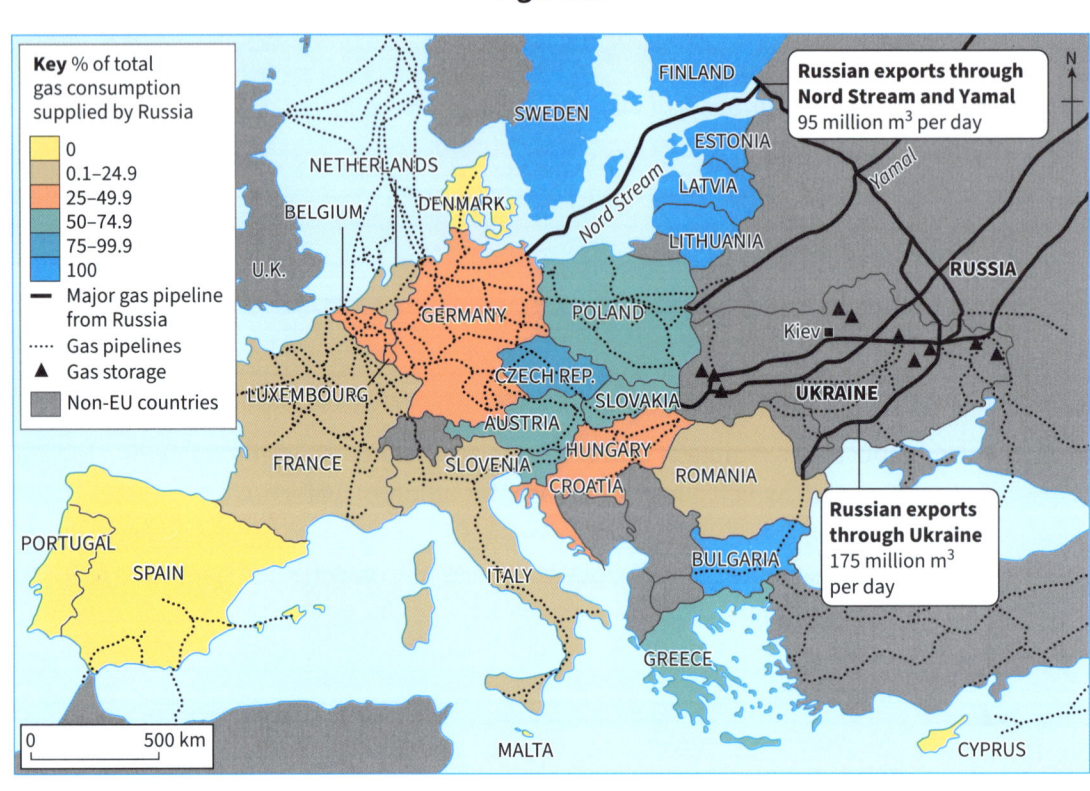

[Map of Europe showing % of total gas consumption supplied by Russia, major gas pipelines from Russia, gas pipelines, gas storage, and non-EU countries. Russian exports through Nord Stream and Yamal: 95 million m³ per day. Russian exports through Ukraine: 175 million m³ per day.]

06.1 What is meant by energy insecurity?

[1 mark]

_____

_____

06.2 Give **two** pieces of evidence from **Figure 12** that could suggest that Russia's war with Ukraine in 2022 will increase energy insecurity in Europe.

[2 marks]

1 _____

2 _____

Mark schemes for the exam papers can be found at www.oxfordsecondary.com/geog-aqa-answers.

Section C The challenge of resource management

0 6 . 3 Suggest the impacts of energy insecurity on a country.

[2 marks]

0 6 . 4 Choose an example of **either** the extraction of a named fossil fuel **or** a local renewable scheme in an LIC or NEE, which aims to increase the supply of energy.

For the example chosen, discuss the extent to which it has been able to increase the supply of energy.

Name of example _____

Circle the one you have chosen.

    The use of a named fossil fuel   A local renewable energy scheme

[6 marks]

Mark schemes for the exam papers can be found at **www.oxfordsecondary.com/geog-aqa-answers**.

Exam practice papers, Paper 2   **149**

GCSE 9-1 Geography AQA
Practice Paper

Paper 3 Geographical applications

Time allowed: 1 hour 15 minutes
Total number of marks: 76 (including 6 marks for spelling, punctuation, grammar and specialist terminology [SPaG])

Instructions
Answer **all** questions
Use a clean copy of the pre-release resources booklet

Paper 3 Geographical applications
Section A Issue evaluation

Answer **all** questions in this section.

Study **Figure 1** in the resources booklet, 'The tropical rainforest global ecosystem'.

0 1 . 1 Describe the annual rainfall pattern of Belém.
[2 marks]

0 1 . 2 Explain how the global atmospheric system causes the rainfall pattern of Belém.
[2 marks]

0 1 . 3 Explain how climate change can affect nutrient cycling in tropical rainforests.
[2 marks]

Mark schemes for the exam papers can be found at **www.oxfordsecondary.com/geog-aqa-answers**.

Paper 3 Geographical applications

0 1 . 4 What percentage of the deforestation in Amazonia is caused by cattle ranching?

Shade **one** circle only.

[1 mark]

- A   40%   ◯
- B   50%   ◯
- C   60%   ◯
- D   70%   ◯

0 1 . 5 Assess the significance of physical and human factors as being responsible for changing the characteristics of tropical rainforests.

Use **Figure 1** and your own understanding.

[6 marks]

Section A Issue evaluation

Study **Figure 2** in the resources booklet, 'Biofuels in Indonesia'.

0 2 . 1 Suggest why Indonesia's rainforests have such high levels of biodiversity.

[4 marks]

0 2 . 2 'The tropical rainforests are important to Indonesia's economy.'

To what extent do you agree with this statement?

[6 marks]

Mark schemes for the exam papers can be found at **www.oxfordsecondary.com/geog-aqa-answers**.

Paper 3 Geographical applications

Study **Figure 3** in the resources booklet, 'The threat to the Indonesian rainforests'.

0 3 . 1 What is the link between palm oil production and the changes happening in Indonesian rainforests?

[2 marks]

_____

_____

_____

_____

The following **three** options have been suggested for how Indonesia could manage the country's rainforests in the future.

Option 1	Continue to expand palm oil production to help Indonesia's economy grow as quickly as possible.
Option 2	Slow further expansion of oil palm plantations by taxing palm oil production and monitoring and policing remaining rainforests.
Option 3	Ban palm oil production and create forest reserves, which can only be used for small-scale farming and other sustainable land uses.

0 3 . 2 Which of the **three** options do you think will benefit Indonesia without causing long-term damage to the country's rainforests?

Use evidence from the resources booklet and your own understanding to explain why you have reached this decision.

[9 marks]

[+ 3 SPaG marks]

Chosen option _____

_____

_____

_____

_____

_____

_____

_____

_____

Continue your answer on a separate sheet of paper

Mark schemes for the exam papers can be found at www.oxfordsecondary.com/geog-aqa-answers.

Paper 3 Geographical applications
Section B Fieldwork

Answer **all** questions in this section.

As part of their investigation of the rural geography in part of the county of Dorset, GCSE students were given a set of secondary data on the facilities in a number of villages in the county.

The data is shown in **Figure 4**.

Figure 4

Village	Population	Church/chapel	Village hall	Primary school	Post office & shop	Food shop	Garage	Bank	Doctor	Pub	Playing field	Cash point	Mobile library	Bus service, daily (D) or weekly (W)
Corfe Castle	980	Yes	1	0	1	2	1	0	1	4	1	1	0	D
East Lulworth	170	Yes	0	0	0	0	0	0	0	1	1	0	1	D
Harmans Cross	340	Yes	1	0	1	0	1	0	0	0	0	1	1	D
Kingston	100	Yes	0	0	0	0	0	0	0	1	0	0	0	W
Langton Maltravers	910	Yes	1	1	1	0	0	0	0	2	1	0	1	D
Ridge	290	No	0	0	0	0	0	0	0	0	0	0	1	W
Steeple	30	Yes	0	0	0	0	0	0	0	0	0	0	0	W
Studland	540	Yes	1	0	1	0	0	0	0	1	1	0	1	D
West Lulworth	770	Yes	1	1	1	0	0	0	0	2	1	1	1	D
Wool	1970	Yes	0	2	1	2	2	0	1	2	1	1	0	D
Worth Maltravers	240	Yes	1	0	1	0	0	0	0	1	0	0	0	D

Date of information: 2006

0 4 . 1 State why this information is an example of secondary data.

[1 mark]

_____

_____

0 4 . 2 What is the modal value for the number of pubs in this survey?

[1 mark]

_____

Paper 3 Geographical applications

04.3 Students carried out a fieldwork enquiry in the same Dorset villages listed in **Figure 4**. **Figure 5** is a scattergraph that shows the link between the number of services and population in each village.

Complete **Figure 5** by plotting the data for Worth Maltravers.

Population **240**, Number of services **3**

[1 mark]

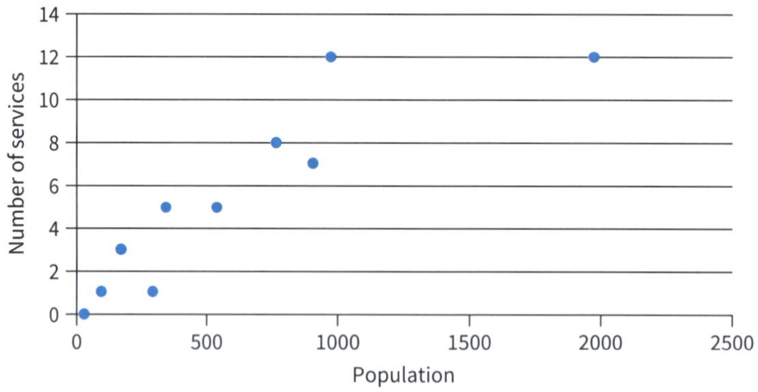

Figure 5

04.4 Draw in and label the best fit line.

[1 mark]

04.5 What conclusion could the students make about the hypothesis, 'There is a link between the number of services in a village and its population size'?

[2 marks]

04.6 Give **two** limitations of this data being used as a basis for a conclusion.

[2 marks]

1 _____

2 _____

Mark schemes for the exam papers can be found at www.oxfordsecondary.com/geog-aqa-answers.

Section B Fieldwork

0 4 . 7 As part of their fieldwork enquiry, the students were told to collect some primary data using a sampling technique to add to the secondary data provided.

Suggest **two** possible sampling techniques they could have used.

[2 marks]

1 _____

_____

2 _____

_____

0 4 . 8 Choose **one** of these sampling techniques.

Give **one** advantage and **one** disadvantage of your chosen technique.

[2 marks]

Chosen technique _____

Advantage _____

_____

Disadvantage _____

_____

Study **Figure 6**, a photograph of part of the coast of Northern Ireland, and **Figure 7**, a photograph of the seafront at Brighton in South East England.

Figure 6

Mark schemes for the exam papers can be found at **www.oxfordsecondary.com/geog-aqa-answers**.

Exam practice papers, Paper 3   157

Paper 3 Geographical applications

Figure 7

04.9 For **one** of the areas shown in **Figures 6** and **7**, suggest a hypothesis or question that could form the title of a fieldwork enquiry in the area.

[1 mark]

Figure number chosen _____

Hypothesis or question _____

04.10 For **one** of the areas shown in **Figures 6** and **7**, suggest **one** data collection technique that could be used to test this hypothesis or question in the area.

[1 mark]

Figure number chosen _____

Data collection technique _____

04.11 Explain why it would be necessary to carry out a risk assessment before carrying out geographical fieldwork in the area you have chosen.

[2 marks]

_____
_____
_____
_____

Mark schemes for the exam papers can be found at www.oxfordsecondary.com/geog-aqa-answers.

158 Exam practice papers, Paper 3

Section B Fieldwork

05.1 State the title of your **physical** geography fieldwork enquiry.

Title of physical fieldwork enquiry _____

Justify **one** of the data presentation techniques used.

[2 marks]

_____
_____
_____

05.2 Describe how the timing of when you collected your data could have affected the validity of your results.

[3 marks]

_____
_____
_____
_____
_____

05.3 State the title of your **human** geography fieldwork enquiry.

Title of human fieldwork enquiry _____

Suggest how your data collection for this enquiry could have been improved to enable your results to be more accurate.

[6 marks]

_____
_____
_____
_____
_____
_____
_____

Mark schemes for the exam papers can be found at www.oxfordsecondary.com/geog-aqa-answers.

Paper 3 Geographical applications

05.4 Assess the extent to which the analysis of the data collected for **either** your human geography enquiry **or** your physical geography enquiry helped your geographical understanding of the topic investigated.

[9 marks]
[+ 3 SPaG marks]

Paper 3 Geographical applications
Resources booklet

Figure 1

The tropical rainforest global ecosystem

The climate of the tropical rainforests

Belém is a city in the north of Brazil. It lies about 100 km from the Atlantic Ocean on the Amazon River. Belém has a tropical rainforest climate and is subject to the Intertropical Convergence Zone with no cyclones – a true equatorial climate.

The sun is high throughout the year without any definite seasons. Belém's annual average temperature is 32 °C, with over 2900 mm of rainfall and 2200 hours of sunshine each year – an average of 6 hours a day. Humidity remains high and average temperatures only vary a little throughout the year.

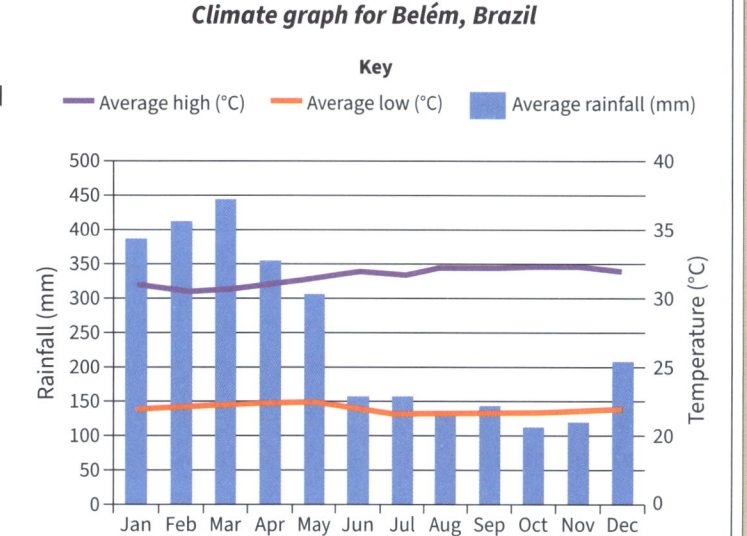

Climate graph for Belém, Brazil

Key
— Average high (°C)   — Average low (°C)   ■ Average rainfall (mm)

The effect of climate change

A major threat to tropical rainforests is global warming. Rising populations and resource consumption add greenhouse gases to the atmosphere, which causes the climate to change. Some scientists think global warming will lead to species extinction at an unprecedented rate.

During drought conditions, rainforests can increase the effects of climate change because they stop absorbing carbon dioxide and emit it instead. This is because plants stop growing and can therefore no longer absorb the gas. Forest fires are more likely

Impact of global warming on tropical rainforests

Temperature rise	Impact on species	Impact on ecosystem
3 °C	20–50% of species face extinction	• Forest gets stressed by drought • Increased danger of fire • Flooding causes the loss of mangrove • Pests and diseases thrive in rising temperatures

in drought conditions, and burning trees release carbon dioxide. Leaf litter dries up, so decomposers die out, which threatens the nutrient cycle. Leaves in the canopy die, reducing the availability of food. This, in turn, affects food webs.

Deforestation adds to the problem. With fewer trees, there is less evaporation and transpiration. This means there are fewer clouds and less rain. This makes droughts more common and more severe.

Mark schemes for the exam papers can be found at **www.oxfordsecondary.com/geog-aqa-answers**.

Paper 3 Geographical applications

Figure 1 continued

Causes of deforestation

Causes of deforestation in Amazonia

Key
- Cattle ranching
- Small-scale subsistence agriculture
- Fires, mining, urbanisation, roads, dams
- Logging (legal and illegal)
- Large-scale commercial agriculture including soya bean production

Farmers in many LICs practise subsistence agriculture, so they have to cut down forest to clear land for growing food and grazing animals. However, research in 2016 showed that the main motive for many farmers in clearing the forest was to grow cash crops. The farmers need the money earned to pay for the rising cost of education and healthcare, and to buy Western goods. It also increases their own status by claiming land as part of their property.

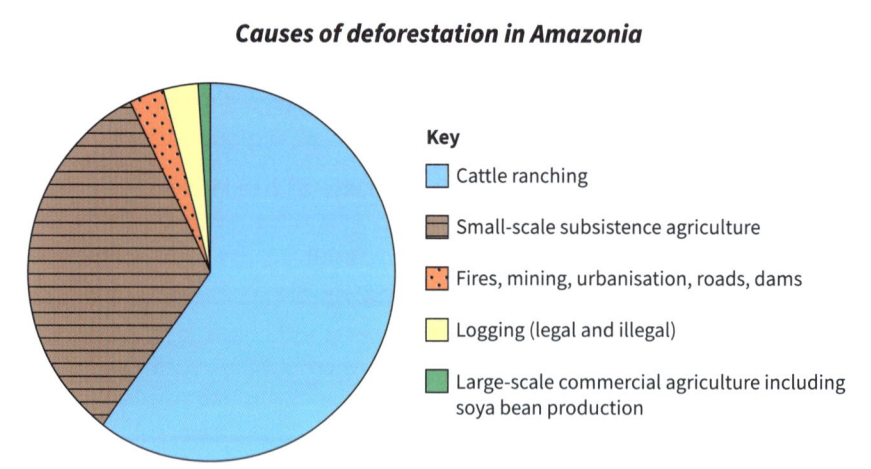

Dependence on firewood for fuel contributes to the steady rate of deforestation. The average household in the Congo Basin in Africa uses 1658 kg of firewood a year. A 70 kg bag of charcoal only lasts a family two weeks. The collection of firewood is traditionally carried out by women.

Governments consider rainforests to be a valuable resource. They are keen to cut the forest down for valuable hard woods that they can sell for export. Many of the countries have large debts and see selling cash crops and timber as a way to reduce their debt. This means that, once cleared, forests are converted into other land uses such as pulp, palm and soya plantations, pastures, settlements and hydroelectric power installations. The tropical rainforests contain raw materials such as oil, gas, iron ore and gold. The impact of mining on rainforests is growing due to rising demand and high mineral prices. Mining projects often come with major infrastructure construction, such as roads, railway lines and power stations, putting further pressure on forests and freshwater ecosystems. To reach these resources, forest has to be destroyed.

Forest degradation and the threats from deforestation

Each year, fires burn millions of hectares of forest worldwide. Fires are a part of nature, but degraded forests are particularly vulnerable. The resulting loss has wide-reaching consequences on biodiversity, climate and the economy.

Illegal logging occurs in all types of forests across all continents, destroying nature and wildlife, taking away community livelihoods and distorting trade. Illegally harvested wood reaches markets such as the USA and EU, which encourages the practice. The commercial trade in charcoal also significantly damages forests.

Rates of deforestation in six countries

Country	Average rate of deforestation (%) 2001–19
Malaysia	−15.7
Indonesia	−9.8
Democratic Republic of Congo	−8.0
Brazil	−6.7
Nigeria	6.0
Burundi	−1.2

Mark schemes for the exam papers can be found at **www.oxfordsecondary.com/geog-aqa-answers**.

Resources booklet

Figure 2

Biofuels in Indonesia

The issue: biofuels in Indonesia's rainforests

- Indonesia's population and economy have each grown rapidly in recent years.
- Some of Indonesia's economic growth has been based on deforesting tropical rainforests. The cleared land is used to grow palm oil plants.
- Indonesia's government sees this as a way to develop the country. They hope it will lift rural people out of poverty and allow major companies to profit from palm oil.

The location of Indonesia in South-East Asia

Getting to know Indonesia

Indonesia is a large country in Asia. It is spread over numerous large and small islands, with half of all Indonesians living in urban areas. The population was 277.1 million in 2021. The capital Jakarta is located on the island of Java. It has a young population – 26% of the population is aged between 1 and 14 years – and life expectancy is quite high at 72 years. Gross incomes average about $13 436 per person per year as, despite rapid industrialisation, in 2019, 28.5% of the population was still employed in farming.

Indonesian rainforests have a very high level of diversity, but are remote and hard to monitor. Indonesia has more species of mammal than any other nation; an incredible 515 species by most counts. Unfortunately, Indonesia also leads the world in the number of threatened mammals at 135 species – nearly a third of all of its native mammals.

Species group	Percentage of all world species found in Indonesia	Percentage of all world species found in the rest of the world
Plant species	10	90
Mammal species	12	88
Reptiles & amphibians	16	84
Birds	17	83
Fish	25	75

Mark schemes for the exam papers can be found at **www.oxfordsecondary.com/geog-aqa-answers**.

Paper 3 Geographical applications

Figure 2 continued

Tropical rainforest in Indonesia

About 10% of the world's remaining tropical rainforest are found in Indonesia, covering 98 million hectares. Yet Indonesia has one of the highest deforestation rates in the world. In the 1960s, about 80% of Indonesia was forested. According to the United Nations, this figure is now down to around 50%. Although the exact figures are not known, it is estimated that more than a million hectares of rainforest are cleared in Indonesia every year.

Rainforest canopy, Kalimantan

Environmental problems
- Many unique species are already extinct and many are endangered, such as the orang-utan.
- Indonesia is the world's third largest emitter of greenhouse gasses, after the USA and China. Most of its emissions are a result of the loss of rainforest (and also peatland). In 2018, Indonesia emitted 1.68% of all global greenhouse gases, more than the combined emissions from the cars, trucks, trains and buses in the USA each year.
- Pesticides used on cleared land pollute waterways and soils.

Social problems
- Burning forests creates smoke that causes problems for air traffic and people's health, which can be affected many hundreds of miles away.

Economic problems
- The 99 million Indonesians who depend on the rainforests for their livelihoods contribute 21% of Indonesia's GDP.
- The livelihoods of the indigenous people who have sustained and been sustained by these forests for centuries are being threatened.

Mark schemes for the exam papers can be found at www.oxfordsecondary.com/geog-aqa-answers.

Resources booklet

Figure 3

The threat to the Indonesian rainforests

The Indonesian palm oil industry

Palm oil production in Indonesia 2000–2020

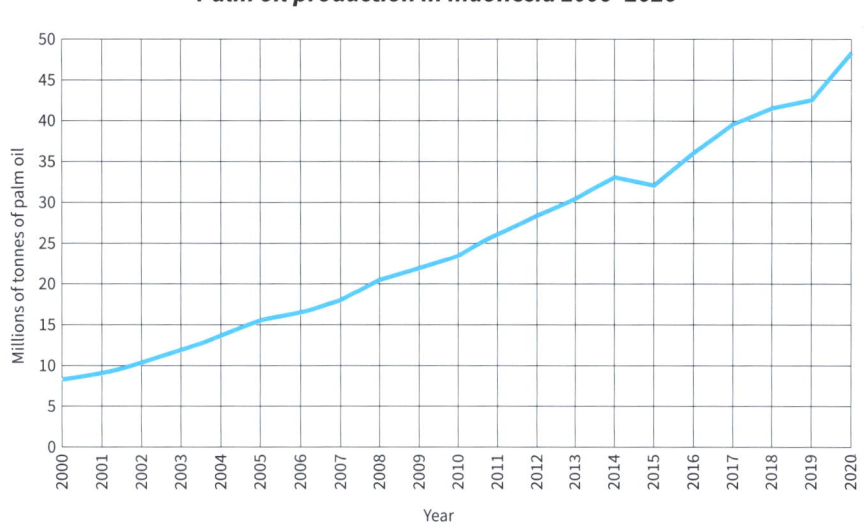

Indonesia's tropical rainforests are being cleared to create palm oil plantations. The area of palm oil plantations in Indonesia increased from 7.8 million hectares in 2011 to 13 million hectares in 2020.

There is high demand for oil palm from NEEs in Asia, especially India. About 75% of the oil palm plantations are on the islands of Sumatra and Borneo (Kalimantan). About 50% of the plantations are small family-run farms. In total, over 2 million people are employed in the Indonesian palm oil industry. In 2020, palm oil made up 9% of Indonesia's exports, valued at $18 billion. Palm oil is used to make biodiesel (a replacement for diesel made from crude oil), shampoo and lipstick. It can only be grown in tropical areas like Indonesia. Worldwide demand for palm oil has lifted incomes, especially in rural areas.

Why did demand for palm oil increase?
- Palm oil has replaced less healthy, more expensive cooking fats in the West.
- Producers have pushed to keep its price low.
- As Asian countries have grown richer, they have begun to consume more fat, much of it in the form of palm oil.

The EU adopted the Renewable Energy Directive (RED), which included a 10% target for the share of transport fuels coming from biofuels (the most common ingredient being palm oil) by 2020. EU palm oil imports shot up 15% the year after RED, an all-time high, and 19% the year after that, as biofuel use tripled in the EU between 2011 and 2014. World Bank policies in the 1970s encouraged the Indonesian government to expand palm oil production among small farmers.

Mark schemes for the exam papers can be found at **www.oxfordsecondary.com/geog-aqa-answers**.

Paper 3 Geographical applications

Figure 3 continued

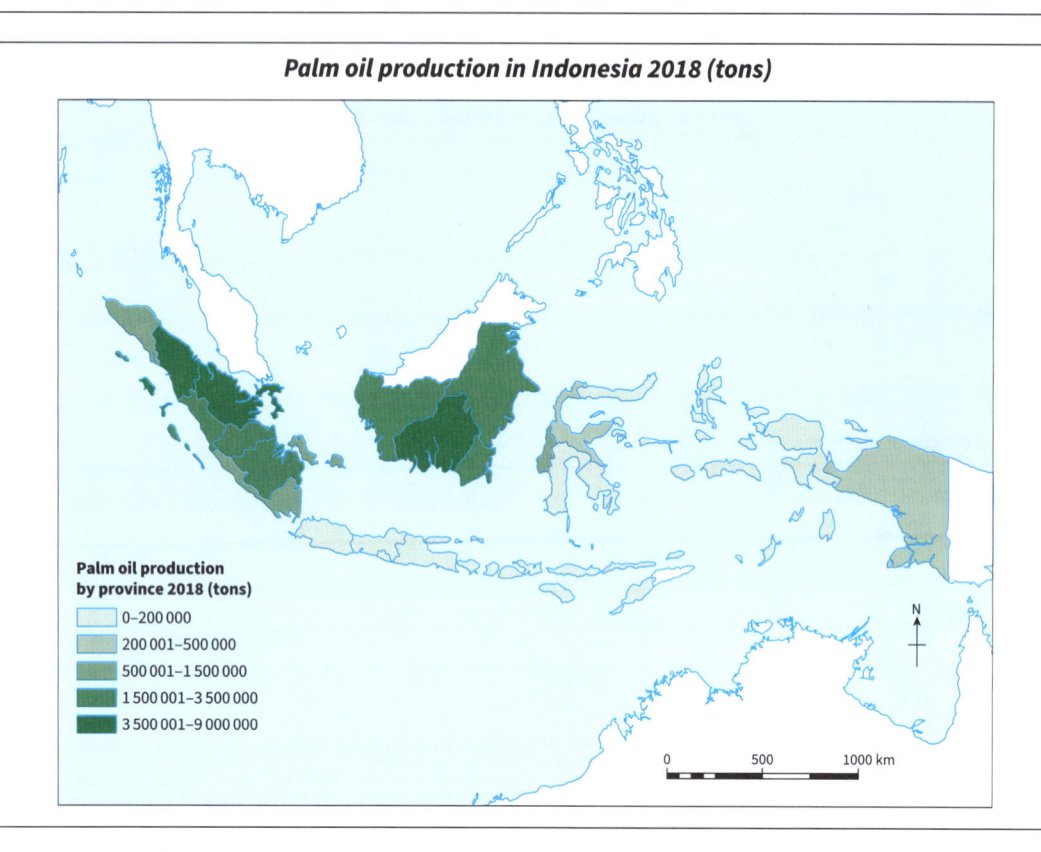

Palm oil production in Indonesia 2018 (tons)

Palm oil production by province 2018 (tons)
- 0–200 000
- 200 001–500 000
- 500 001–1 500 000
- 1 500 001–3 500 000
- 3 500 001–9 000 000

0   500   1000 km

Contrasting views about palm oil development in Indonesia

Organisation	View
WWF is an environmental pressure group and NGO.	'Large areas of tropical forests have been cleared to make room for vast oil palm plantations – destroying habitats for many endangered species, including rhinos, elephants and tigers. In some cases, the expansion of plantations has led to the eviction of forest-dwelling people.' – *From the WWF article 'Environmental and Social Impacts of Palm Oil Production' at wwf.panda.org*
World Growth is a pressure group that promotes globalisation.	'Palm oil provides developing nations and the poor with a path out of poverty. Expanding sustainable agriculture such as oil palm plantations provides plantation owners and their workers with a means to improve their standard of living.' – *From the World Growth report 'The Economic Benefit of Palm Oil to Indonesia', Feb 2011*
Cargill is a TNC based in the USA that grows, processes and sells palm oil.	'Millions of people around the world depend on palm oil. We believe that palm oil should be produced sustainably. We have made a commitment that the palm oil products we supply will be certified as coming from sustainable forests by 2020.' – *Adapted from various Cargill policies on palm oil at www.cargill.com*

Mark schemes for the exam papers can be found at **www.oxfordsecondary.com/geog-aqa-answers**.

Answer guidance

Pages 6–13

Activity 1

Your own answer.

Activity 2

Your own answer.

Activity 3

(a) Paper 1, AO2 = 11
Paper 3, AO1 = 0
Paper 3, AO3 = 18
Overall, AO4 = 25

(b) Paper 3 is more about knowledge and understanding (analysing and interpreting data, AO3).

Activity 4

Use of photo?
✗ No direct reference is made to the photo.

More than one landform?
✓ The student writes about the waterfall and plunge pool.

Understanding of the sequence of landform formation?
✓ There is a clear sequence in the formation of the waterfall.

Activity 5

Your own answer.

Activity 6

(a) and (c)

(b) Peaks: March 127 000; October 134 000
Trough: July 70 900

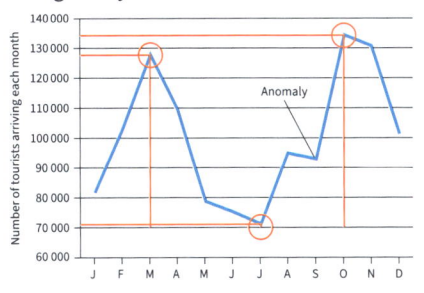

Activity 7

(a) • Foreground of photo
• Background of photo

(b) In the foreground there are vegetable gardens on the rooftop. In the distance there appear to be trees following the roads. There are also clusters of trees in open spaces between buildings.

Activity 8

Figure 5 shows the location of megacities in the world in 2030. Megacities are located all over the world. They are concentrated particularly in Asia, for example in India and China. There are lots of megacities in China. There are few megacities in Africa – only three. Elsewhere, there are some megacities in Europe and in North and South America. A lot of megacities are located on the coast. This is because they are ports and have developed as trading centres. So, as the map shows, there are lots of megacities all over the world.

Activity 9

- 'about 7%' should be 'about 14%' – the student misread the axis.
- 'secondary and primary sectors' should be 'secondary and tertiary sectors'.
- '64%' should be '43%' – the student looked at Brazil by mistake.

Pages 14–15

Activity 1

Social: Blocked roads would have made it difficult for people to receive aid in the form of water, food and medicines. This would have affected their health as well as their ability to travel.

Economic: Blocked roads and landslides would have made it difficult to transport goods. This would have affected local businesses.

Environmental: Flooding would have inundated normally dry environments. Habitats may have been damaged and animals killed or forced to migrate.

Activity 2

(a) Possible annotations include:

Social:
- A low density of buildings in a green environment makes this a pleasant place to work with low levels of stress.
- Opportunities (grass, trees, paths) for recreation and fitness.
- Nearby housing provides accommodation for workers.

Economic:
- Good road access (edge of Cambridge) for the transport of goods and services – minimum congestion.
- Land on the edge of the city is probably cheaper than land in the centre of Cambridge.

Environmental:
- Lots of green areas (trees, grass) provide habitats and encourage wildlife (birds, bees, etc.) for workers to enjoy.
- Modern, newly constructed buildings emit less carbon than older buildings.

(b) Local or national government policy decisions regarding land purchase, incentives for high-tech industry, etc.

Now try this!

- Economic advantages could include references to nearby roads, facilitating transportation of workers, goods and services; several companies on the same site can benefit economically from each other (cost sharing, etc.); relatively cheap land on the edge of the city.
- Environmental advantages could include an attractive site (trees and grassy areas) for people to work; retention (and creation?) of diverse natural habitats (grass, trees, etc.) promoting species diversity; a low environmental impact (air pollution) with the lack of heavy industrial processes (no chimneys).
- You must refer to evidence from Figure 1 and draw upon your own understanding, for example by making connections between evidenced factors and why they are advantageous.

Pages 16–17

Activity

Short term

Local: Land used for hunting may be reduced in size or damaged (D)

National: Road construction will provide jobs (A)

Regional: Destruction of habitats, which may affect ecosystems in the rainforest (D)

Global: Rainforest destruction (especially burning) may increase carbon emissions, contributing to climate change (D)

Answer guidance 167

Answer guidance

Long term

Local: People may benefit from improved education or healthcare (A)

National: Development project may attract foreign investment (A)

Regional: Increased tourism may increase awareness of the importance of the rainforest, leading to better stewardship (A)

Global: Road development may lead to further deforestation, reducing atmospheric moisture (D)

Now try this!

- To achieve a Level 3 mark, you need to refer to evidence in the photo (e.g. damage to electricity lines and houses, ship stranded on land, etc.). You should show a clear understanding of the implications of the destruction shown in the photo, particularly for the long term.
- Write a balanced answer referring to at least two immediate responses (e.g. search and rescue) and two long-term responses (e.g. reconstruction of housing and businesses).
- Use appropriate geographical terminology.

Pages 18–19

Activity 1

(a) Possible labels might include:
- Extensive green area for food production, carbon absorption, recreation, etc.
- Wind turbines and windmill for renewable wind energy.
- Planting of trees (absorption of carbon dioxide, giving shade, protection of habitats, etc.).
- Water body to moderate the climate, provide water storage to prevent flooding, possible water supply, recreation.

(b) Additional features might include:
- solar panels on roofs to generate electricity
- recycling areas
- public transport (buses).

Now try this!

- You need to write about **more than one** strategy. For example, with water you could consider water conservation, groundwater management, recycling and 'grey' water. Two or three strategies are sufficient.
- You should briefly outline each strategy, focusing particularly on why it helps to make supplies sustainable (long-lasting with minimal damage to the environment).
- Use examples if you can to strengthen your answer.
- Use geographical terminology (e.g. 'sustainable', 'security').

Pages 20–21

Activity 1

Investment: China has invested billions of dollars in Africa, helping to build new roads, bridges and sports stadiums; the headquarters of the African Union were paid for by China; China has paid for a power plant in Zimbabwe and hydroelectric power in Madagascar.

Industrial development and tourism: Industrial development and tourism bring employment opportunities and increase incomes; money generated can be spent on transport, health and education.

Aid: Local aid projects provide health centres and improvements to services, such as water; Goat Aid provides goats in Malawi, improving diets and source of income (milk, cheese, etc.); the UK provides aid to Pakistan, Ethiopia and Bangladesh.

Using intermediate technology: Small-scale projects can benefit local communities; small dam and reservoir irrigating land at Adis Nifas, Ethiopia.

Fair trade: Provides fair incomes to farmers; money is invested in community projects to improve people's lives.

Debt relief: Enables countries to invest money and improve people's quality of life; in Uganda money has been spent to provide safe water to over 2 million people.

Microfinance loans: Small bank loans help people establish businesses; Grameen Bank in Bangladesh helps women to buy mobile phones to support their businesses.

Activity 2

(a–d) See the graph below.

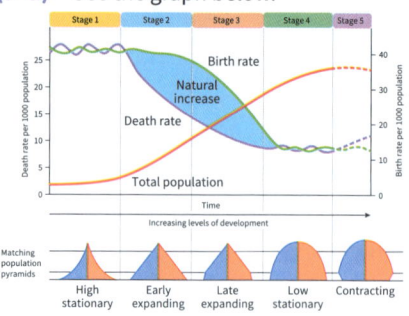

(e) LICs tend to be in stage 2 of the Demographic Transition Model, having high birth rates, falling death rates and high population growth rates. NEEs, which tend to be in stage 3, are witnessing falls in birth rates and a slowing down of population growth rates. HICs are in stage 4 or even stage 5, with low birth rates and death rates and broadly stable populations.

Pages 22–23

Activity 1

Your own answer.

Activity 2

Other factors might include pests, diseases, trade, poverty, tropical cyclones, colonialism and debt.

Activity 3

(a)
- **Land use:** using land for cash crops and industrial plantations rather than for growing food crops can lead to undernutrition.
- **Climate change:** climate change can lead to rainfall variability, which may affect crop yields and contribute towards desertification, leading to undernutrition.

(b) 'Natural systems' could include tectonic activity, such as volcanic eruptions. It also includes weather and climate, such as El Niño events. Ecosystems (land and ocean), carbon and water cycles are also natural systems that can affect human and ecological wellbeing.

168 Answer guidance

Answer guidance

Pages 24–26

Activity 1

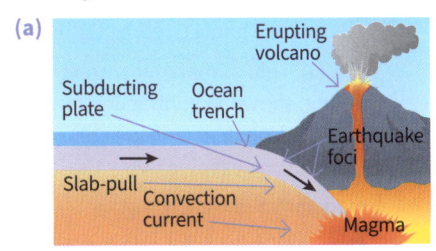

(a) [Diagram showing: Erupting volcano, Subducting plate, Ocean trench, Earthquake foci, Slab-pull, Convection current, Magma]

(b) The oceanic plate descends at a gentle angle beneath the continental plate. Earthquakes are triggered along this boundary zone and consequently are spread over a wide zone.

Activity 2

(a–b) See the diagram below.

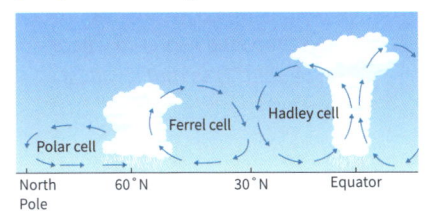

[Diagram showing: Polar cell, Ferrel cell, Hadley cell; North Pole, 60°N, 30°N, Equator]

(c) Rainforest is at the Equator; desert is at 30°N

Now try this!

To achieve a Level 2 you must explain clearly how alternative energy production can reduce the rate of climate change. You should refer to the enhanced greenhouse effect.

As Figure 6 shows, fossil fuels used in industry and power stations result in the emission of greenhouse gases such as carbon dioxide. These gases enhance the greenhouse effect, increasing global temperatures and speeding up climate change. Alternative energy production involves using renewable energy such as wind and solar, rather than fossil fuels such as coal and gas. Renewable energy does not emit greenhouse gases, which is why the increased use of alternative energy can reduce the rate of climate change.

Page 27

Activity

(a) With fire (burning).

(b) The land is blackened, with the remains of tree stumps. Grass is the only vegetation.

(c) Labels might include the following:
- Reduction in variety of plants/trees, destroying habitats and reducing biodiversity.
- Grasses dominate the ground, restricting biodiversity.
- Fire may kill some animals or drive them away from the area, reducing biodiversity.

Now try this!

Use specific examples and make sure that interdependence is stressed.

Hot desert:
- Plant roots hold the soil together and, by providing shade, help to retain moisture and reduce soil erosion (interdependence between plants, sun, precipitation and soils).
- Some people are dependent on camels (pack animals and transport), which are well adapted to the environment (interdependence between people and animals).

Cold environment:
- In summer, insects are abundant, providing food for birds. Birds can fall prey to foxes (interdependence between insects, birds and animals).
- Low-growing bushes in tundra regions can provide shelter for small animals from strong winds (interdependence between plants and animals).

Pages 28–29

Activity 1

Coastal landscapes: Mass movement: sliding = C; Mass movement: slumping = F; Mass movement: rock falls = D; Hydraulic power = E; Abrasion = F; Attrition = B; Longshore drift = A

River landscapes: Hydraulic action = F; Abrasion = C; Attrition = G; Solution = A; Traction = D; Saltation = E; Suspension = B

Glacial landscapes: Freeze-thaw weathering = B; Abrasion = E; Plucking = A; Rotational slip = C; Bulldozing = D

Activity 2

(a) 1: Erosion processes, such as hydraulic power and abrasion, erode a weakness in the cliff to form a cave.

2: The cave is eroded from either side of the headland until it eventually breaks through to form an arch.

3: Costal erosion widens the base of the arch and eventually the roof collapses under its own weight to form a stack.

(b) From left to right: 2, 4, 1, 3

Now try this!

Your answer must consider at least two landforms created by erosion. You should refer to the correct sequence of events and the processes of erosion. Consider using simple annotated diagrams to support your answer.

- Focus on two or three landforms – no more – such as cliffs, wave cut platforms and stacks (coasts); interlocking spurs, waterfalls and gorges (rivers); corries, aretes and pyramidal peaks (glacial).
- Refer to and define the processes responsible, such as hydraulic power (coasts and rivers), abrasion (coasts, rivers and glacial) and plucking (glacial).

Pages 30–31

Activity

(a) Dot map

(b) There are several possible locations for circles to be drawn. Be careful to use the key correctly to identify city clusters.

Now try this!

1.1 Plot the value for 2030 accurately at 17.6 m and join it with a dotted line to the value for 2020.

1.2 Slow and steady growth between 1950 and 1990, from 1 m to 3.1 m (2.1 m in 40 years). Rapid growth since 1990 (3.1 m) to 17.6 m in 2030 (14.5 m in 40 years). The graph suggests a slight reduction in growth from 2020 to 2030.

1.3 The global and national rankings suggest that Guangzhou's growth is outstripping other cities. Globally, Guangzhou is ranked 71st in 1950 and 16th in 2030. Nationally, Guangzhou rises from 7th to 4th in the same time period.

Pages 32–33

Activity

Correct order: E, A, C, B, D

Now try this!

To achieve Level 2, you must make clear links between deindustrialisation and economic decline.

- Deindustrialisation is the decline of a country's traditional industry.

Answer guidance 169

Answer guidance

- Closure of traditional industries creates unemployment. This reduces spending power resulting in closure of shops and other services. Supply industries may also close down, increasing unemployment. Less money going to the government as taxes. Government has to spend money on unemployment benefit.
- Consider referring to a spiral of decline and the multiplier effect in reverse.

Pages 34–35

Activity 1

(a) See the map below.

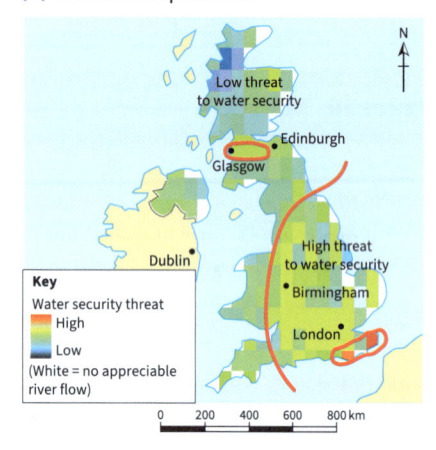

(b) Essentially there is a South East/North West split, with high levels of threat in the South East and low levels of threat in the North West. The highest levels of threat are in the South East (Kent/Sussex). The lowest levels of threat are in the Scottish Highlands. There are one or two anomalies, e.g. a relatively high level of threat in the Central Lowlands of Scotland.

Activity 2

Food: Economic wellbeing: Rising food prices can seriously impact the poorest people in LICs. If they have to spend more money on food, less money is available to spend on education and home improvements. **Social wellbeing:** In LICs, poor diets can affect people's health and ability to work. About 2 billion people are undernourished, which has a significant effect on quality of life.

Water: Economic wellbeing: Construction of dams and reservoirs is very expensive, as are water transfer schemes. **Social wellbeing:** Water shortages affect people's quality of life (washing, cooking, drinking), trapping them in a cycle of poverty.

Energy: Economic wellbeing: Demand for domestic energy is rising as populations grow and get wealthier. As countries industrialise (LICs and NEEs), energy demand increases. **Social wellbeing:** Some energy developments are controversial, such as fracking and the construction of nuclear power stations and wind farms.

Pages 36–37

Now try this!

1. B
2. D
3. C

Pages 38–41

Now try this!

1.1 Example answers include:
- Geographical places, e.g. starts in the Philippines, tracks towards Laos, turns to track towards China. 1 mark for each place and change.
- Direction, e.g. moves WNW from the Philippines, then NNE from Laos to China. 1 mark for each direction and change.
- Strength, e.g. greatest strength 5 over the Philippines, reduces to 2 over Laos and weakens to 1 over China. 1 mark for comparative strength, 1 mark for use of hurricane categories.

1.2 252 kmh or higher (must mention 'or higher' for the mark)

1.3 Derives heat energy from the sea/ source of heat energy lost over land.

2.1 1 mark for reason with extra mark for developed explanation, e.g.:
- Life expectancy gives an idea of the level of health care (1) because if it's high it means fewer people die of diseases (1) /die prematurely (1)/die in childbirth (1)/die in infancy (1).

2.2 73.35 (1), with working to show that median occurs between 5th (74.9) and 6th (71.8) ranked values; total 146.7 divided by 2 (1).

2.3 1 mark for any of: variable levels of health care between countries/high number of deaths in infancy/during childbirth/diseases such as ebola/any other reason on merit.

3
- Quality of drawing does not gain any marks but 3 marks for recognisable labelled features (e.g. a plunge pool at the foot of the waterfall.)
- 1 mark for features including any of lip (1), resistant rock (1), undercutting (1), less resistant rock (1), plunge pool (1), gorge (1)

4.1 176% (1) – plus 1 mark for correct working, shown as subtracting lower value (38) from higher value (105), divided by lower value (38) × 100.

4.2 1 mark for valid reason, e.g.:
- More food miles will be added (1); avocados might have to come from further away (1); there'll be greater pollution from shipping

4.3 1 mark for description with extra mark for a developed point, e.g.:
- It means fewer food miles (1) and therefore less vehicle pollution in transport. (1)
- Food is produced nearer to where it will be sold (1) so that it will be cheaper. (1)

Pages 42–50

Activity 1

(a)
- Buildings may be poorly built
- People have little money so may have little chance to recover

(b)
- Photo: houses have collapsed
- Own understanding: GDP is low

(c)
- Photo: building materials look weak and poor quality.
- Own understanding: Low GDP means there are few recovery or rescue services.

Activity 2

Refer to the annotations in the Worked example on page 45.

Activity 3

This answer gets 2 marks. 'Wooden shacks like the one in the photo …' (1), and 'so that they would fall down' (1). Second part is not relevant.

Activity 4

Evidence: One strength and one weakness required

Command word: 'Explain' means give reasons for the strength and weakness

Focus: The question is about one indicator of development shown in Figure 1, not all three

What you have to write: One strength and one weakness of chosen indicator of development and a reason for each

170 Answer guidance

Answer guidance

Activity 5

(a) • HDI has advantages
• HDI has disadvantages

(b) • Advantage: HDI includes data about a country's literacy and life expectancy.
• Disadvantage: Some people may be much healthier and better educated than this.

(c) • An advantage of HDI is that it gives a good idea of the social development of a country.
• A disadvantage of HDI is that it is a blanket figure for the whole country and different parts of the country may vary.

Activity 6

You should write: 1) an advantage of your chosen indicator; 2) what your chosen indicator measures; 3) why this is an advantage. Repeat for a disadvantage, e.g.:

• Death rate – an advantage is that it is a good measure of a country's health services; a disadvantage is that some places in that country might be much worse or much better than that.

• Percentage of population with access to safe water – this is a good measure because water and how clean it is can determine a nation's health. A disadvantage is that it's a general figure, and rural areas are often worse than cities for safe water supply.

Activity 7

Compare your answer with the guidance given.

Activity 8

This answer gets to the top of Level 2 (4 marks) because the candidate has:

• stated clearly what is meant by HDI and how it is measured
• explained its advantage in combining three measures of development in a single figure
• explained two advantages of HDI – how it is calculated, and why it does not work in countries such as Saudi Arabia
• quoted evidence from the table of data to explain the points.

Activity 9

• Briefly explain the link between health and death rate.

• Explain one disadvantage of death rate, e.g. that it might not tell you about health improvements such as vaccinations.

Now try this!

Your answer should include:

• Use of Figure 1 – showing the relationship between named headlands and areas of hard rock type (limestone/chalk); the relationship between named bays and areas of softer rock type (clays and sands)
• Your understanding – explaining how softer rocks would be eroded more than harder rocks.

Pages 51–53

Activity 1

(a) The four boxes, when read out in order, should form a sequence, e.g.: **Box 1:** *If a large groyne is built, sand builds up behind it because of longshore drift* … **Box 2:** *… which increases beach size and protects the local cliffs* … **Box 3:** *… but that means less sand will be transported further along the coast* **Box 4:** *… and therefore cliff erosion rates will increase there as waves will erode the cliffs more easily.*

(b) Examples could include:

Level 2

1: Names a method of hard engineering and explains what it is intended to do.
2: Explains the sequence of processes that lead to problems elsewhere.

Level 1

1: Names a method of hard engineering but may not explain what it is intended to do.
2: Explains some processes but these are not sequenced or linked to problems elsewhere.

Activity 2

This answer is Level 2. It shows a clear understanding of coastal groynes and their purpose in preventing longshore drift. It applies the situation well by explaining a sequence of the processes leading to problems further along the coast. It is worth 4 marks.

Activity 3

Your answer should include:

• a single change of land use, e.g. from forest to farmland or from farmland to housing or urban development

• how this leads to a change of surface, e.g. from permeable soil to impermeable concrete
• how this affects the hydrological cycle, e.g. removing the interception zone or altering infiltration rates, such as water passing quickly through drains
• explain the effects on rivers and how this leads to flooding.

Activity 4

(a) Examples could include:

Level 2:

1: Names a change of land use and can explain its effects on the hydrological cycle
2: Explains the sequence of processes that lead to greater flood risk along a river

Level 1:

1: Names a change of land use but its effects on the hydrological cycle are not clear
2: Explains some processes but these are not sequenced or linked to how flood risk is increased.

(b) Your own answer.

Pages 54–57

Now try this!

1. Your answer should include:

• references to both derelict land and deprived areas of Glasgow
• reasons for derelict land, e.g. closed industries/de-industrialisation
• reasons for the deprivation found in the same areas, e.g. loss of jobs when industries closed.

You must refer to at least one piece of evidence on the figure.

2. Your answer should include:

• one impact of urban growth, e.g. increased rural–urban migration, or rapid increase in the urban population
• an explanation of how this has affected quality of life, e.g. insufficient housing
• an extension of the explanation, e.g. people may set up cheap slum housing close to the railway line where it is unsafe
• reference to at least one feature of the photograph in Figure 2.

Answer guidance 171

Answer guidance

Pages 56–60

Activity 1

(a) • A spit is formed from deposition and from river flow.
   • A sand bar/tombolo also results from deposition.

(b) • Photo: there is a spit in the photo.
   • Own understanding: explanation of longshore drift.

(c) • Photo: how drift towards the photo has led to the development of a spit, also shaped into a hook by the river.
   • Own understanding: explanation of swash and backwash and net gain of material over time forming the spit.

(d) • Photo: both the river and the sea have been important.
   • Own understanding: a sand bar is created where there is only deposition from the sea – there is no river to affect the shape; mud flats build up in the still water behind the spit.

Activity 2

Refer to the annotations in the Worked example on page 59.

Activity 3

Strengths are:

Point: two landforms are named accurately.

Evidence: landform formation is described in some detail (longshore drift).

Explanation: longshore drift is explained as a sequence of events.

Link: explains the difference between a spit and a bar/tombolo.

To reach Level 3, the candidate would need to:

• use the photo more
• write more to explain the second landform so that the two are treated equally.

By explaining landform processes (top Level 2), but with little mention of the photo (Level 1), the answer is low Level 2, worth 3 marks.

Pages 61–64

Activity 1

Evidence: Impacts – one that you know about, and one that you see in the photo.

Command word: 'Suggest' means give impacts which look reasonable based on the photo.

Focus: Rainforest clearance –suggest two impacts based on what you see in the photo and that you know about.

What you have to write: Either two well-developed or three developed impacts for 6 marks.

Activity 2

(a) • Photo: deforestation has destroyed the tree cover.
   • Own understanding: rainforest soils are very infertile without the forest cover.

(b) • Photo: The soil is now exposed to heavy rain.
   • Own understanding: there is ash on the surface from where the forest has been burned.

(c) • Photo: The exposed soil would erode quickly without any protection.
   • Own understanding: the ash would be fertile but it would not last long if rains eroded it.

(d) • Photo: The impacts on soil erosion would be great.
   • Own understanding: there would be no fertility left in the soil.

Activity 3

Your answer should include:

• one impact of rainforest clearance that you know about, e.g. low soil fertility, soil erosion in rainforest areas
• one impact of rainforest clearance from the photo, e.g. exposed soil, burning of all the vegetation
• explanations of the impacts of each, e.g. rapid soil erosion, lower soil fertility, minimal biodiversity
• reference to at least one feature of the photograph in Figure 1.

Activity 4

Your own comments.

Activity 5

Sample Answer 1

The strengths of this answer are:

Point: shows understanding of some impacts of rainforest clearance

Evidence: refers directly to the photo

Explanation: shows what rainforest clearance can lead to.

However, there are no **links** back to the question. To reach Level 3, the candidate would need to:

• use their own understanding as well as what is in the photo
• use geographical terminology (e.g. 'soil erosion' instead of 'washed away')
• make direct reference to the question, and focus on the word 'impacts'.

By partly meeting the criteria for Level 2, the answer earns 3 marks.

Sample Answer 2

The strengths of this answer are:

Point: shows understanding of some impacts of rainforest clearance

Evidence: refers directly to the photo and to own understanding, e.g. soil erosion, the effects of tree roots on farming, the fertility of the ash compared to the infertile soils

Explanation: clearly suggests what might happen and explains why these impacts are likely.

Links: links back to and answers the question.

The candidate fully meets Level 3 criteria, so earns 6 marks.

Pages 65–68

Activity 1

Evidence: 2–3 impacts from a major UK city you have studied – at least one from your own understanding, and at least one from the map.

Command word: 'Discuss' means give a range of examples (for 6 marks, that means 2–3), which can be seen on the map and from your own understanding.

Focus: International migration in a major UK city you have studied –suggest at least one impact based on the map and at least one that you know about.

What you have to write: 2–3 impacts for 6 marks, and a developed reason for each. You must name the city.

Activity 2

(a) • Map: Asian-British people are concentrated in certain areas.
   • Own understanding: Different migrant communities live in different areas of cities.

(b) • Map: This includes areas like Southall or Hounslow.

Answer guidance

- Own understanding: Most cities have areas where there are mosques or ethnic shops.
(c) - Map: This is probably where there is work available.
- Own understanding: This is for the community to buy particular foods or follow their religions.
(d) - Map: It gives support to people if they live close together.
- Own understanding: Ethnic areas like these make big impacts on changing the look of cities.

Activity 3

Your answer should include:
- 1–2 impacts of international migration that you know about, e.g. the ways in which ethnic communities change the appearance of cities
- 1–2 impacts of international migration from the map, e.g. named areas where Asian-British people live in London
- explanations of these impacts on a named major city
- reference to at least one feature of the map in Figure 1.

Activity 4

Your own comments.

Activity 5

Sample Answer 1

The candidate:

Point: understands that immigration has made a big impact on Bristol; states that migrants have had a big impact on the city

Evidence: names a specific country for immigrants, with data; names an example of the kind of cultural events that have resulted from immigration. It does not matter that these examples are chosen from different cities

Explanation: mentions both the reasons for growth and the changing character of Bristol

Link: gives a concluding sentence at the end of the answer.

The candidate's interpretation of the map about the impacts of international migration is brief and less strong. The answer meets the first Level 3 descriptor fully, but the second one only partly. It gets 5 marks.

Sample Answer 2

This answer only gets a Level 1 mark, because the candidate:

Point: states that immigration has been important for Bristol

Evidence: names cultural events and restaurants resulting from immigration

Explanation: mentions both the reasons for growth and the changing character of Bristol.

However, the candidate does not: name any specific source countries for immigrants; refer to any parts of the map; state anything about the characteristics of cities with large numbers of migrants; link back to the question at the end.

Pages 69–73

Now try this!

1. Your answer should include:
   - two paragraphs, each of which explains strategies used to reduce the impact of hazards or to improve coping
   - named examples of strategies to manage the impact. Use named places, years or periods when a strategy was used
   - evidence which supports your case – explain how your example had reduced the impact of the hazard.

2. Your answer should include:
   - two paragraphs, each of which explains how the impacts of tropical storms might change, e.g. stronger winds, more rainfall, therefore greater damage
   - named examples of past tropical storms and their impacts. Use named storms or countries to illustrate how future storms could be even greater
   - evidence which supports your case – explain how climate change might worsen the hazard, e.g. with raised temperatures, great evaporation and therefore greater moisture content in storms.

3. Your answer should include:
   - two paragraphs, one of which discusses the advantages brought by TNCs, and one which discusses disadvantages. Because the command word is 'discuss', you should make a brief judgement about whether you think there are more advantages or disadvantages
   - named example of advantages and disadvantages – with named companies, countries or examples of incidents
   - evidence which supports your case – explanations to show the extent to which advantages outweigh the disadvantages, or vice-versa.

4. Your answer should include:
   - references to transport (e.g. close to motorways) plus a reason, e.g. access for skilled workforce and customers. For top marks, at least one motorway or main road or the airport should be named
   - reference to the university plus a reason (e.g. using its expertise to develop ideas and new products)
   - its situation – close to Southampton city centre and motorway access to London, Bournemouth and Portsmouth. You must refer to at least one piece of evidence on the figure
   - other factors, e.g. land costs likely to be cheaper on the edge of Southampton.

5. Your answer should include:
   - two paragraphs, which are about the evidence to suggest why people might disagree with the statement. The paragraphs should be different, e.g. one might be about social concerns such as poor housing, while another might deal with health issues
   - named examples of urban problems from specific cities (e.g. Rio) or named communities (e.g. Rocinha)
   - evidence which supports your case with explanations of how particular problems have developed, e.g. why housing is so poor.

Pages 74–79

Activity 1

(a) - There is overwhelming evidence that global climate is changing.
   - There is considerable evidence of rising temperatures.
   - Evidence also comes from land-based glaciers.

(b) - Everywhere in Figure 1 is warmer in 2100 than in 1960.
   - Sea levels have risen by 20 cm in 100 years.
   - On land, melting glaciers and ice sheets are widespread.

(c) - Emission of greenhouse gases have increased, leading to warmer global temperatures.

Answer guidance

- Sea levels have risen because of melting ice.
- Ice is melting because of warmer temperatures.

(d)
- This evidence is global and is therefore reliable – all sources say the same thing.
- Coastal flooding has increased globally, so the evidence is solid.
- Evidence for glacier retreat has been widespread for over a century so it must be reliable.

Activity 2
This answer receives 9 marks. Refer to the annotations in the Worked example on page 78.

Activity 3
This answer is low Level 2, worth 4 marks. This candidate has learnt facts and figures but there is no evaluation. The candidate needs to ask themselves – *'what's the evidence that glaciers are melting, and is it reliable? How do I know it's reliable?'*

Point: There is no real argument here – just facts and figures.

Evidence: Very good knowledge about climate change and warming. There is brief reference to Figure 1.

Explanation: Weak because they rarely refer to warming climate (e.g. flooding in Bangladesh is explained because it is low lying, not because of sea level change).

Link: There is no link back to the question, and no evaluation.

Pages 80–85

Activity 1
Command word: 'Do you agree …?' means you must make a judgement about how far you agree with the statement

Evidence: You need three lots of evidence, each about different things, e.g. jobs, schooling and housing.

Focus: The question is about those who live in the poorest areas of cities in one of the world's LICs or NEEs, so you need to use evidence to judge whether or not you agree with the statement.

What you have to write: Three lots of evidence (three paragraphs) for 9 marks, and a discussion about each one.

Activity 2
(a)
- Employment is better in cities.
- Children can get better education in cities.
- But housing is poorer in cities.

(b)
- People get paid more and there is a lot of work.
- There are more schools across all age groups in cities.
- Many people have to live in favelas or sub-standard cheap housing.

(c)
- There are more jobs in factories in cities.
- Job prospects for school leavers are better if they have a full education.
- Housing is often expensive and low wages mean that people can't afford rent or to buy.

(d)
- Employment offers more changes.
- More opportunities for education than in rural areas.
- Housing is a problem with many living in unhealthy conditions without water.

Activity 3
Your answer should include:
- three paragraphs, each outlining how and why you agree or do not agree with the statement. Each paragraph should focus on a different factor as evidence, e.g. employment, or education, or water or housing, etc. Explain how far you agree with the statement in relation to, for example, jobs or education, etc.
- a one-sentence conclusion to give your overall judgement.

Activity 4
Your own comments.

Activity 5
Sample answer 1
Level 3, 8 marks

Point: Strong points made.

Evidence: Detailed evidence about favelas to support the answer.

Explanation: Good knowledge and understanding of what living in a favela might be like.

Link: Links back to the question clearly to show how they have reached an opinion. Stronger conclusion needed.

SPaG: 3 marks. The answer is in paragraphs, is well spelt, and punctuated accurately.

Sample answer 2
Mid-Level 2, 5 marks.

Point: The student makes three valid points about living in squatter settlements and extends it with some detail.

Evidence: A named city occurs just once in the last sentence. More detail is needed about a specific city. Rio is named twice but there is no detail.

Explanation: The argument is not strong; there are no other named places to compare cities with, and the candidate simply talks about rural areas.

Link: The conclusion needs to be stronger than just a brief statement.

SPaG: 1 mark. The answer is written in one paragraph and there is a lack of punctuation.

Pages 86–89

Activity 1
Command word: 'Assess' means judge the extent to which the development of your chosen LIC or NEE is as a result of its location.

Evidence: Three paragraphs, each of which is about a different factor, e.g. one factor might be about trade and be closely linked to your country's location (e.g. India and its trade with South-East Asia or Europe).

Focus: An LIC or NEE that you have studied; detailed knowledge about its development and the relationship of its development to its location.

What you have to write: Three factors for 9 marks, and a developed reason for each factor. Name the country and write in detail about its development.

Activity 2
Answers should include:
- details about a named LIC or NEE, its geographical location and its development
- details about its development and any links to its location, e.g. whether its trading partners are geographically close or not
- explanations about how far geographical location has influenced the country's development.

Activity 3
Your own comments.

Activity 4
Level 3, 9 marks

Point: Makes strong arguments to show how significant India's location has been.

Answer guidance

Evidence: The candidate knows a lot about India's location and other factors such as language and current political tensions. There is detailed evidence and clear geographical knowledge.

Explanation: Clear reasons explain why the evidence is important in India's development.

Link: Links back to the question to show how they have reached an opinion – a clear conclusion.

SPaG: 3 marks – the answer is well written, with accurate punctuation.

Pages 90–91

Now try this!

1. Your answer should include:
   - three paragraphs, two of which show that your named urban regeneration project has been effective, and one showing that it has been less effective, e.g. it may have been economically/environmentally effective but poor for social factors
   - a named example of a city that you have studied in an LIC or NEE
   - evidence which supports your case, for example, income levels, or housing quality, or points about water supply and sanitation, or education
   - a conclusion to briefly show how far you agree with the statement.

2. Your answer should include:
   - three paragraphs, which are written about the impacts of a severe weather event in order of their severity
   - a named example of severe weather in the UK and of places which were affected, with examples of ways in which they were affected
   - evidence which supports your case with explanations of how severely the places you have mentioned were affected
   - a conclusion to briefly show an overall judgement on the severity of the event as a whole.

3. **Option 1**
   Your answer should include:
   - three paragraphs, two of which show ways in which, to some degree, desertification has physical causes, and one showing an alternative argument about human causes.

   Alternatively, you may argue that human causes are the main factor
   - named examples of physical causes of desertification, e.g. El Niño in Australia or variable low rainfall in the Sahel. Similarly, named human (or other) examples should be used, e.g. overgrazing by cattle, or population pressures on land holdings
   - explanations to show the extent to which your evidence shows support for either physical or human causes
   - a concluding sentence referring back to the title with your judgement.

   Option 2
   Your answer should include:
   - three paragraphs, two of which weigh up one factor, and one which weighs up the other. The two paragraphs should be the answer that you support
   - named examples of locations, countries or regions to which these attempts have been applied
   - explanations to show the extent to which your evidence shows that either economic development or conservation has been more effective
   - a concluding sentence referring back to the title with your judgement about the effectiveness of each.

Pages 92–98

Activity 1
Possible labels include:
- no tropical storms south of 30° south; no tropical storms in the South Atlantic and eastern South Pacific; few tropical storms north of 30° north; no tropical storms at the Equator

Activity 2
Possible annotations include:
- **Social:** widespread destruction will have damaged schools, health centres and services.
- **Economic:** huge cost of clear up and rebuilding; businesses such as shops will have been affected, reducing incomes.
- **Environmental:** complete destruction of trees, affecting natural habitats and wildlife; contamination of land from waste.

Activity 3
'Scientists cannot say whether climate change is increasing the number of hurricanes, but the ones that do happen are likely to be more powerful and more destructive because of our warming climate,' says BBC Weather's Tomasz Schafernaker. Here's why:
- An increase in sea surface temperatures strengthens the wind speeds within storms and also raises the amount of precipitation from a hurricane
- Sea levels are expected to rise by 30 cm to 120 cm over the next century, with the potential of far worse damage from sea surges and coastal flooding during storms.

Now try this!

1.1 915 hurricanes

1.2
  - Tropical storms form over the oceans to provide the moisture needed to fuel the storms.
  - Tropical storms form over low (tropical) latitudes where there are warm surface temperatures (26.5°C).
  - A zone of relative atmospheric instability causes rising air and storm formation.

1.3 Appropriate method for displaying discrete data/easy to read and see trends/actual values can be read using the vertical scale

2. To achieve Level 3, you need to focus on the accuracy of the forecast for Hurricane Dorian. Your answer needs to involve a judgement. Figure 2 should be used to provide evidence.
   - The hurricane track (30 August 2019) suggests Hurricane Dorian was heading towards the Bahamas and then into central Florida.
   - This was accurate in the short term for the Bahamas, where it caused widespread devastation – 50 deaths and damage over $7 billion.
   - It was less accurate in the longer term and the hurricane did not pass into central Florida.
   - So the forecast of 30 August proved to be partly accurate – good for the short term, but less accurate for the longer term.

Answer guidance

Activity 4

(a) **Social: Advantages:** There will be less out-migration from the area. **Disadvantages:** Communities might be split by physical barriers.
Economic: Advantages: Less money will need to be spent on repairing damage. **Disadvantages:** For many years the area will still be vulnerable to storm surges. **Environmental: Advantages:** Natural ecosystems might be restored, such as oyster beds. **Disadvantages:** Impacts on ecosystems and shoreline processes are unknown.

(b) Your own answer.

(c) **Local: Advantages:** Natural ecosystems might be restored. **Disadvantages:** Communities might be split by physical barriers.
National: Advantages: Protecting New York, USA's financial capital, brings huge national benefits. **Disadvantages:** Very expensive – money may be diverted away from other national schemes.
Global: Advantages: Positive impacts on fish stocks and ecosystems. **Disadvantages:** Unknown impacts on ecosystems, such as fish stocks, could negatively impact other countries.
Short-term: Advantages: Construction could lead to the multiplier effect. **Disadvantages:** For many years, the area will still be vulnerable to storm surges.
Long-term: Advantages: While costly, it could prove cheaper than coping with widespread damage from future hurricanes. **Disadvantages:** The scheme will take decades to construct.

Now try this!

3. You should:
   - weigh up the pros and cons
   - identify the factors that you think are most important
   - make thorough use of a variety of evidence drawn from the whole resources booklet
   - demonstrate your 'own understanding' of the wider specification
   - consider higher-level concepts such as development, sustainability and scale – both local (estuary ecosystem) and global (sea level rise and climate change)
   - include a strong conclusion focusing on the most important factor(s).

Pages 99–102

Now try this!

1.1 Accurate bar drawn to 24 people (1) shaded according to the key (1)

1.2 Adaptations might include increasing the number of people surveyed, carrying out the survey at different times, on different days and in different weather conditions, considering using a stratified sampling technique, etc.

Activity

Your own answer.

Now try this!

2. Your own answer.